P9-CEG-675

RELENTLESS
SPIRIT

RELENTLESS
SPIRIT

The Unconventional Raising
of a Champion

MISSY FRANKLIN
and D.A. and DICK FRANKLIN

with DANIEL PAISNER

DUTTON

DUTTON

An imprint of Penguin Random House LLC
375 Hudson Street
New York, New York 10014

LIBRARY OF CONGRESS CATALOGING-IN-PUBLICATION DATA
has been applied for.

ISBN 978-1-101-98492-5 (hardcover)   ISBN 978-1-101-98493-2 (ebook)

Printed in the United States of America
1   3   5   7   9   10   8   6   4   2

Set in Kepler

While the authors have made every effort to provide accurate telephone numbers, Internet
addresses, and other contact information at the time of publication, neither the publisher
nor the authors assume any responsibility for errors or for changes that occur after publication. Further, the publisher does not have any control over and does not assume any
responsibility for author or third-party websites or their content.

Penguin is committed to publishing works of quality and integrity.
In that spirit, we are proud to offer this book to our readers;
however, the story, the experiences, and the words
are the authors' alone.

For my one True Father,
To be your daughter is a privilege. In every word I speak,
every action I carry out, and each intention that lies in my heart,
may it all direct the world back to you.

To my earthly mother and father,
My greatest fear in life is that I will never be able to be the kind of
parent you were to me. There is no greater joy in my life than
knowing that no matter where life takes us and what it may bring,
nothing could ever separate me from your love.
Thank you.

CONTENTS

CONTENTS

RELENTLESS
SPIRIT

R*elentless* . . .
    Steady and persistent. Constant. Unyielding. Showing
no signs of letup, no drop-off in intensity, severity,
strength . . .

There's something very *Beyoncé* about the word, don't you think? It's empowering—so much so that I've taken to writing it on my wrist before I compete. It's engraved on a silver ring I like to wear. I've even got it printed on the band of my favorite pair of goggles.

Relentless . . .

It reminds me to keep on, moving ever forward, hard. But I don't need the reminder, really. It's how I swim, how I live my life, who I am. Seeing that word, writing it down . . . it just reinforces what's already there. It tells me to reach deep down for my very best, even when it feels like there's nothing left. Even when every muscle in my body is telling me I'm done.

When I'm in a hard place, I write it down.

When I'm facing a challenge, I write it down.

When I get to that place where I could not have practiced any harder, smarter, longer, I write it down and move on to my dryland workout, my evening swim, whatever's next on my schedule.

Relentless . . .

There are a lot of quotes on the Internet that talk about what it means to never give up, but those words don't do it for me. If that's what works for you, that's great. But I hear a phrase like "Don't quit!" and it gets me no closer to where I need to be. It tells me I can push ahead but stay on autopilot. It tells me I can get by on minimal effort. It tells me that good enough is good enough. But that's not me. A line like that, it might be fine if the goal is just to see things through, but that's never been *my* goal. My goal is to swim with every ounce of heart, every ounce of spirit I can muster. At all times. No matter what.

Relentless . . . I wear the word on my wrist, strap it to my head, keep it at my fingertips, at the ever-ready.

So I write it down. And just to make sure I'm paying attention, I put it on the cover of my book—the book you now hold in your hands.

Relentless spirit . . . because there is no letup, no drop-off, no quit in me until I touch the wall.

My Teddy Bear Moment

Dear God: Please help me and Team USA do the best that we can do this weekend. Watch over us, help us, calm us. Wish me luck.

—journal entry, written just before my first-ever
national-team appearance

I was fourteen years old. I'd traveled to Canada and Europe with the junior national team, but this was my first time swimming overseas for the national team. As big deals go, this was all the way up there. I was incredibly excited, but also nervous. Not incredibly nervous, I don't think, but a little worried how things would go. I had no idea what to expect.

Think about where you were in your life at fourteen—think about what you were doing—and then put yourself in a situation where you're doing your thing alongside the very best in the world. Where you're caught in a great swirl of attention and excitement bigger than you could have ever imagined. Where you're way, way, way from your comfort zone. It wasn't like me to feel intimidated, but how can you not be intimidated by something like that? How can you keep your stomach from doing backflips? I mean, I was just a kid—a confident, world-class swimmer, but still just a kid.

The jumble of nerves that found me on this rookie trip had nothing to do with swimming—it felt to me like I had that part down. I loved swimming! That was the easy part. This wasn't me being arrogant or cocky. This was just me being me—being honest with myself. I knew my times in the 100-meter freestyle were good enough to put me in the same pool as all those great swimmers. It was what was going on away from the pool that had me on edge. We were in Manchester, England, for the Duel in the Pool—a fun event that has as much to do with building team morale and encouraging a kind of camaraderie with swimmers from other countries as it does with competition. It's set up like the high school dual meets I loved to swim back home, but with an international us-versus-them twist to the competition—the us being the United States team, and the them being a combined group from the British, German, and Italian national teams. (By the way, there were a lot of national-team swimmers who were not participating in this event, so it really was an honor for me to be there with this group.) We'd never lost one of these meets, I learned once I got over to England, but it's not like it was a crazy-intense event. Still, there was a ton of pressure on me to do well, on top of the pressure I put on myself. Mostly, it was a team-building, team-bonding event, and a chance for us to see where we stood on the world stage without a whole lot on the line. A chance for me to see where I stood. And an incredible opportunity to race alongside swimmers I'd been admiring since I was a little girl.

You have to realize, until I started swimming for the national team, I didn't pay a whole lot of attention to what the rest of the world was doing. USA Swimming was the bee's knees, as far as I was concerned, so my focus was on the swimmers who would now be my teammates: Dana Vollmer, Natalie Coughlin, Rebecca Soni . . . these women were like rock stars to me.

The pool was short course, meters. Over the years, I've come to love the long-course events, which really play to my strengths as a swimmer, but I was still getting used to these international distances. When I look back, I can see that this short-course event was the perfect way for me to get my feet wet with the national-team members, but when I was in the middle of it I couldn't help but feel like I was in over my head. Like it was all a little too much, a little too soon. I was ready, but I wasn't quite there yet, if that makes any sense. Again, it wasn't the swimming part that had me worried; it was the everything-else part. It was not knowing if or how I'd fit in. It was moving about with all these giants of the sport, trying to convince myself that I belonged with this group. This last piece had me worried most of all. I'd met Michael Phelps the year before, and I also knew Dagny Knutson, who'd been an amazing high school swimmer, mostly freestyle, but other than that I didn't know anybody on the team. By reputation? . . . yeah, I knew them all. But to say hello? . . . no way. Remember, these were the athletes I'd been watching race on television since I was five years old. To most of them, I was probably just some gangly girl who'd taken a spot on the team that was meant for one of their former teammates—because, let's face it, that's just who I was.

Up until I was thirteen, when I made the junior national team, my parents often accompanied me to meets. (They still do!) However, when I swam for the national team I had to actually travel with the team. This would take some getting used to—and here I was, getting used to it. We had our own flight, our own hotel, our own schedule. My mother and father were there to cheer me on, but for the most part I was on my own. I even had my own roommate—for this trip, it was Rebecca Soni, who'd won a gold and two silvers at the 2008 Olympics in Beijing. Rebecca's gold medal swim in the 200-meter breaststroke set a world record, so I was over the moon. She was one of my idols. I had her picture up in my room at home, and here I was, half a world away, sharing a room with her. (OMG, right?) It would be a cliché to say it was surreal, but I can't think of a better way to describe it, so let's just go with surreal. At times it felt like I could separate myself from the scene and watch it unfold in a slow-motion way, almost like it was happening to someone else. Other times I wanted to get on the phone with one of my girlfriends back home and say, "You'll never believe who I'm rooming with on this trip!" But there's no way I could have made the phone call—I had to play it cool here, folks.

So there I was, smooshed into what had to be the smallest hotel room in all of England—not much bigger than a broom closet—with Rebecca Soni, who couldn't have been sweeter or more welcoming. Really, she was incredible. It was such a great kindness, the way she took me in and made a place for me on this trip. It was December, just a week or so before Christmas—my absolutely favorite time of the year. Everywhere we looked, there were reminders of the season, so I was back and forth between being excited, in a little-kid way, and being anxious, also in a little-kid way. Like I said, I was straddling that line between being ready and being not ready. Between feeling like I belonged and wondering what in the world I was doing there.

Rebecca Soni was more than eight years older than me, which basically meant she could have been my babysitter, but we had so much fun. Our beds were about six inches apart, and the room was so teeny-tiny it felt like we had to take turns standing up and getting dressed, but I remember we laughed and laughed. I can't imagine I was her first choice for a roommate, but she never let me feel like she'd rather be with someone her own age, someone she'd known all along. To Rebecca, I'm sure, this was just another night on the road on a long string of many, another challenge to get past as she trained to defend her gold medal and maybe break her own world record. To me, it was more like a slumber party, a big adventure—one pinch-me moment after another. But Rebecca was great, even though the whole time we were in the hotel it was all I could do to make sure I didn't come across as some starstruck kid.

I tried to play it cool, but I didn't do such a good job of it. (Just to be clear, playing it cool wasn't exactly one of my strengths—and if you must know, I don't think I've gotten any better at it over the years.) Almost as soon as we got settled in, the organizers of the meet brought us out for the opening ceremonies. I'd known this was about to happen, but only in theory. Once it was all laid out for me, once we were good to go and there was a script I was meant to follow, it started to freak me out. The way they had it set up was we were given these special robes to wear, and then each of us was given a little teddy bear. We were supposed to sign our teddy bear and then, at the appropriate moment, toss it back up to the crowd—where I guess some other starstruck kid was meant to catch it and take it home. It was all very adorable—just good, harmless fun. But as they were giving me all these instructions I kept thinking somebody had made a terrible mistake. I was genuinely concerned about throwing this teddy bear—like, really, really concerned. I actually sought out my mom to talk to her about it.

She said, "What are you so worried about, Missy?"

I said, "Are you kidding me? What if some little girl catches my teddy bear and she's got no idea who I am?"

I honestly thought some little girl would grab that bear, look at my signature, crinkle up her face in confusion or disappoint-ment, and throw it back—that's how unsure of myself I was in that setting. I felt like an impostor. It was mortifying, terrifying. I thought for sure I was going to be getting a teddy bear to the face. And then I realized that just a year or so before, I could have been one of those little girls, lining up to meet all these great swimmers, muscling out everyone else in the crowd to grab a teddy bear of my own. It was overwhelming.

Thankfully, my mom was able to calm me down. I might have earned my way onto the Duel in the Pool squad with all these national-team swimmers, but I still needed my mommy. (This also never changed.) She said, "Aw, honey. You're just being silly. Nobody's gonna throw back your teddy bear. They'll be glad to have it, and they'll keep it forever."

She was right, it turned out—at least about the not-throwing-it-back part. I never actually saw who wound up catching my teddy bear, but I waited a couple of beats to make sure it didn't come flying back out of the crowd, and when it didn't I let out a sigh of relief that could have probably been heard all across the United Kingdom.

At this dual meet, each team entered three swimmers in each event. Every heat was a finals heat, meaning there were no preliminary swims. Every time you got in the pool you had a chance to score points for your team. Points were awarded to the top three finishers in the individual events—five points for first, three points for second, and one point for third. Head-to-head relays were winner-take-all, good for seven points. And, because of this finals-only format, the event only ran for two days, which was a whole lot different than a traditional meet, which might run for three days or more and include preliminary and (sometimes) semifinal heats.

The entire team was wonderful to me. It was like I was everybody's little sister. But it's not like I could just smile and be cute and soak in the experience. I had a job to do. I had to put points on the board for my team—that's why I was there. More than that, I had to show everyone that I belonged, that my times weren't a fluke. For a couple of agonizing moments, I thought I'd be found out and exposed. A part of me thought I'd be sent home—one and done with my national-team career. My entire focus was on swimming my one event and trying to show everyone that I belonged in that pool with all these great swimmers, but something came up. Jack Bauerle, the coach for our Duel in the Pool team, took me aside and told me he wanted me to swim the 4x100-meter freestyle relay.

I'd already competed in the 100-meter freestyle, my one event at that meet, and I was mostly happy with my swim. I finished fourth, so I didn't score any points for our team, but I did finish ahead of one of my American teammates, so it made sense that Coach Bauerle was looking at me for the relay. Dana Vollmer had set a US record in the 100-meter freestyle, which was good for only second place behind Francesca Halsall of Great Britain, who'd made it to the finals in the 100-meter free at the last Olympics, in Beijing.

This kind of call, it's a game-day decision. The coach looks at his or her swimmers and figures who's swimming well, who's fresh, who gives the team the best chance to win at just that moment. It was about the last thing I was expecting, to get selected for this race. At first I thought maybe Coach Bauerle was making a mistake. When he took me aside to tell me, I think I even said, "Me? Are you sure?"

It wasn't that I didn't want the honor or the responsibility—just that I didn't think I'd heard right.

He said, "I'm sure. Thinking we might lead you off."

Um . . . what?

This was a whole new level of expectation for me. Once I'd gotten my head around the fact that I'd be swimming that relay, maybe an hour or so before the race, my first thought was that I'd swim in second or third position. That's usually where a coach puts his solid, core swimmers who might have a little less sprinting speed, a little less finishing speed. For swimmers who are a part of Team USA, relays are the most important thing to us, and what we take the most pride in is being a team. I don't know if that's an American thing, but here I was, my first time out as a national-team swimmer, and it was clear to me that this was a big deal. I got that. Each spot in the lineup is important. Every coach has his or her own strategy when it comes to relays, but usually you put your fastest swimmer in the anchor leg. Next, you put your second-fastest swimmer in the leadoff spot, and fill in the middle spots in whatever way makes sense. But it can vary. Some coaches like to go from slow to fast, and others like to start out with their two fastest swimmers and build a real cushion for those final two legs. There's no right way to set your lineup, but in my little-kid head, just then, the idea that my coach wanted me to lead off this relay in such a talented field was plainly terrifying, intimidating.

Coach Bauerle could see I was thrown. I guess I must've stammered something in response, or maybe all the color went out of my face. He said, "Unless you don't think you're up to it." Not really asking, but sort of.

I heard it like some kind of test, and I answered without letting myself think about it. I said, "No, if you think I can do it, then I can do it. Absolutely."

Absolutely. It's like the word was coming from someone else's lips. I was psyching myself up, talking myself into it, the whole time trying not to let on how overmatched I was feeling about all of this. Almost like I was still expecting that teddy bear to come flying back out of the stands. On the one hand, I knew my times were good enough to justify my swimming in the leadoff spot— but then, on the other hand, I couldn't help but see myself as a little kid, going up against all these grown women, who'd been competing for their national teams for years.

It turned out I didn't have a lot of time to worry about any of this because the next thing I knew, we were lining up for the race. I was going to lead off for the US team, followed by Christine Magnuson and Amanda Weir, and Dana Vollmer in the anchor spot. The European team was led by Francesca Halsall, followed by Daniela Schreiber and Daniela Samulski of Germany, and Lizzie Simmonds of Great Britain in the anchor spot. The good news here was that I didn't have a whole lot of time to worry about my opponents. But, even then, I knew that worrying about my opponents would only hurt my racing: I almost never worried about my opponents. To this day, I swim my own race and let everything else fall from there. Even as a kid, I approached each event with a set of blinders on. It didn't matter who was swimming in the lane next to me, I always told myself. I could control only what I could control, so I kept my focus on my own lane. Over the years, I've come to know most of the top swimmers in the field. Many of them have become good friends. I've learned their tendencies, their tactics. I still try to tune them out when I step to the starting blocks, but at least I know this stuff, on some level. It registers. But back then I didn't even know my own teammates, and I certainly didn't know the names or reputations of these top European swimmers—they just weren't on my radar, not yet. It wasn't any kind of strategy. It was just that I didn't know any better. All I could do was get in the pool and swim my little heart out.

So that's what I did. But to me, it felt like I was struggling. And I guess I was, only not in the ways I thought at the time. Remember, this was a head-to-head relay, so there was just me and this one other girl—a girl who just happened to be one of the best freestyle swimmers in the world. I didn't know this, of course. All

I knew was that I had an obligation to my team, to the other three swimmers in the relay. All I knew was I had to do my part. I'd always cherished these relay swims. There's this tremendous sense of responsibility you feel to one another, so I didn't want to let anybody down. But there I was, well off the pace my opponent was setting. When there's just two of you in the pool, it's hard not to keep an eye on the girl in the next lane, and when I got to the 75-meter mark I was ready to start crying. As I went into my third turn and pushed off the wall, I could see that I was about a body length behind. That's a big gap for my teammates to have to make up, so naturally I was devastated. Really, Francesca was just crushing me. I kept telling myself, "Just get your hand to the wall, Missy. Just get your hand to the wall." Like I was willing myself over those final meters. It felt to me like I'd never finish— my "career" was just getting started, and already I'd counted myself out.

Oh my, I felt horrible. Beaten. Thrashed. I touched the wall more than a second behind the European team—and it might as well have been ten seconds. I'd let my team down. I'd buried us. And so I hung my head and tried to disappear. But do you know what? Christine found a way to make up half that body length. Then Amanda held on until Dana could rescue us at the end with one of the most amazing anchor legs I've ever seen. We ended up winning by a full second. Still, I felt just awful, and I was near tears when I got back to the team area. Everyone was hugging each other and jumping up and down, but underneath those congratulations I felt sure that everyone was looking at me, judging me, resenting that they'd had to pick up my slack. Of course, that's not at all what they were thinking, and a part of me knew that wasn't what they were thinking, but I couldn't shake the thought.

After a couple of beats, Coach Bauerle came up to me. He could see I was down, fighting back tears. He said, "Missy, what's wrong?"

So I told him.

He said, "You're kidding, right?" Like he couldn't believe what he was hearing.

I shook my head. I said, "I totally messed up. She got so far ahead of me. I'm so, so sorry."

He said, "You know who you were swimming against, don't you?"

At the time, I only knew Francesca Halsall by name—actually, everybody around the pool called her Fran. I didn't know her résumé. I didn't know about her showing at the last Olympics. But Coach Bauerle filled me in. He said, "She's literally the fastest 100-meter freestyler in the world right now."

Well, that made me feel a little better—but only a little.

And then he said, "Your time? The time you 'totally messed up'? That was one of the fastest American times, ever."

Okay, so that helped, too—but again, only a little. Even at fourteen, I was so competitive, so hard on myself, I couldn't stand getting beat, especially as the rookie swimmer on a relay where I was representing my country. It didn't matter who it was doing the beating. It only mattered that there was all that room for improvement—a full body length, in this case.

So how was I struggling, exactly? Well, it wasn't in my performance, apparently. It was in how I'd framed that performance in my head. It was in the way I'd let the moment get too big for me, when really it was just like any other swim, against any other swimmer, in any other pool. All I could do was all I could do, and it didn't matter what was going on in the lane next to me. It didn't matter that I was going up against the best in the world. It only mattered what I was putting out there. And so the great lesson for me, coming out of that Duel in the Pool meet, was to trust in my ability, to believe in myself, to know that I belonged on this level. It's a lesson I carry with me to this day, but there was something transformative about it as it took shape in my head. Something uplifting—reassuring, too. I had to let myself think that the little girl on the receiving end of that teddy bear with my signature on it would be just as thrilled to find a place of honor for that teddy bear in her bedroom as I had been to find a place on my bedroom wall for that picture of Rebecca Soni.

I might have been only fourteen years old, but I'd earned my spot on that team, same as everyone else. I belonged, same as everyone else. And I could only swim my little heart out, same as everyone else.

ONE

HOW WE GOT HERE

Ohmygoodness . . . that first Duel in the Pool meet was crazy, but it's important to understand that I didn't step to the starting blocks in Manchester, England, as a fully formed national-team swimmer ready to compete on the world stage. That's not how you get to be in such a big spot—at least, that's not how *I* got to be in such a big spot. No way. In my case, I was only able to take my place on that unbelievable relay team because I had the love, attention, and support of my own unbelievable team at home—my mom and dad.

My parents have always been there for me. That's a line you hear all the time from athletes, from young people giving thanks or showing respect, but with me it's more than just a line. It's the essence of who I am—as a daughter, a swimmer, a student, a friend, a caring human being. My parents are at the heart of everything I do, everything I am, everything I might become. Whatever I've accomplished, I will always be their work in progress! Really, I wouldn't be half the person I am today were it not for the extra efforts of Richard and D.A. Franklin. Without my father, I wouldn't be nearly as tall (appreciate ya, Big Rich!), and without my mother I wouldn't be nearly as focused or determined. But my parents' impact goes beyond swimming. It goes to the heart of *who* we are and *how* we are as a family, and I've come to believe it's something to celebrate. That's why I'm writing this book—to invite readers into our lives in such a way that they can see how things happen (and how they *don't* happen!) in our house, in case they might relate.

Actually, I should say that's why *we* are writing this book, because my parents are right here by my side, the same way they are in everything I do. It's a team effort. The words are mostly mine, but the memories, the stories, the lessons learned along the way, are all shared, all connected. The life we've made, the values we've come to share, the goals we've set and met as a family. It's been a true collaboration. We're all in this together, and since my swimming career is what's put our family in a kind of spotlight, we figured it made sense for me to be the one to take the microphone (so to speak!) and share some of our experiences.

So here goes. . . .

I'll start by stating the obvious: there's no blueprint for raising an Olympic champion. There's no blueprint for raising a child, period. The Olympics are not a realistic goal. It's more like a pipe dream, a pot of gold at the end of a rainbow. A happy by-product of a healthy, well-rounded approach to life. So many things have to break in just the right way, at just the right times for a young athlete to even have a shot to represent his or her country on the world stage. Let's be clear: I didn't set out to win an Olympic gold medal. That wasn't even a small sliver of a fraction of a part of my thinking, back when I started out. And my parents certainly weren't thinking in this way—they just wanted to see me happy, and they could see early on that swimming made me happy, so they went with it.

That's all it was, at first. And, in many ways, that's all it remains. Swimming makes me happy. And so I keep swimming.

Now, I'll be the first to admit I've been incredibly lucky and incredibly blessed. But I've also been taught to believe that we make our own luck and build our own blessings, so what *is* realistic is for parents to create an environment where their kids can thrive at whatever it is they choose to pursue. It doesn't have to be sports. It can be art or music, math or science, engineering or computers. It can be doing well in school or becoming a good person. My thing just happened to be sports, although I was also big into *doing well in school* and *becoming a good person*, which in the long run is way more important and everlasting, but since most people know me as an athlete, let's just stick to sports for the moment.

I was an active kid, which is probably the understatement of my lifetime. I was always running, jumping, playing. I was competitive, too. I think I got that from my dad—not because he pushed me or challenged me but because he was a good athlete and I wanted to be just like him. But at the same time, I was the kind of competitive athlete who didn't want to beat her opponent into the ground. I think I got that from my mom—not because she was all touchy-feely but because she was a great collector of friendships and experiences, and I wanted to be just like her, too. I mean, where's the fun in competing if it's just one endless grudge match, if you're chasing down one opponent, enemy, victim, after another? The idea, for me, was to go at it hard with my friends, to push one another, to push myself, an idea that came in equal measure from both my parents, without either one of them ever having to say as much. If one of my friends touched the wall ahead of me, I was happy for her, really and truly. If I'd given my all, and put in my best effort, I was happy for *me*, also, really and truly. And my parents were happy in the same way, for the same reasons.

Looking back, I'd have to say this was all a part of my parents' "game plan" with me: to *show* rather than *tell*. They lit a path and set an example and I could only follow. Except with them it wasn't even a game plan, just an extension of who they were and how they'd chosen to live their lives. See, my parents were a little bit older when they finally got around to having me. A little bit older than *what* or *whom*? Well, a little bit older than my friends' parents, certainly. A little bit older than the parents I would see in movies and on television. And a little bit older than they might have imagined themselves to be, if they'd ever closed their eyes and imagined themselves as parents. My father was forty-nine when I was born, and my mother was forty-five, and I didn't exactly come into this world in a conventional way, as I will explain soon enough. By the time I came along, as my father likes to say when reporters ask about our family, my parents had six postgraduate degrees between them, almost a hundred years of life experience, and enough ups and downs to start a roller coaster conglomerate. They were financially comfortable, professionally comfortable, domestically comfortable. They had a great marriage. Dad had been a Fortune 500 executive, and Mom was a doctor. They'd traveled all over the world and had put whatever egos and insecurities they'd had as young adults to bed. They were on solid, solid ground, good and ready to be parents, if that's what God had in mind for them, so that when this little child came into their world they stood to welcome her with the will and the confidence of two accomplished, seasoned people.

Let me tell you, that kind of preparedness can make all the difference. Although to hear my parents tell it, it's not like they were *preparing* for any one thing in particular. They were just living their lives, building a shared future, and it just worked out that there was finally room in there, room for *me*!

Now, I don't want to get ahead of the story—*their* story, *my* story, *our* story—so let's keep it in the pool for just a little while longer. For as far back as I can remember, these stories were centered around the water. When I close my eyes and picture my childhood, I can almost smell the chlorine. I'm laughing, jumping, splashing. I think what I loved so much about swimming was how calming it was, how therapeutic, how safe and warm I felt in the water. From the very beginning, I knew that's where I belonged. Want proof? There's a great photo taken on one of our Franklin family vacations: We were at the ocean and there we were, just getting pummeled by the waves. I was about three months old, in my dad's arms, and my cousin Zach was about nine months old, in my uncle Harry's arms. Of course, the waves weren't very big at all, so the pummeling was relative, but to us little kids the waves must have seemed giant-size. Or at least they were to Zach, who looks in the picture like he's crying hysterically. We were all together to celebrate my christening. My uncle Harry and my aunt Deb are my godparents. Zach never became a swimmer, but he did become an awesome football player. Kicking seemed to run in the family. His older sister, Kiley, was a great keeper for her soccer team.

Every time I see this picture (and believe me, my mom takes it out and shows it to me all the time!), I'm reminded of how much I loved the water, even as a baby. I was just three months old, and I had this giant, splash-eating grin. It was a freeze-frame moment, captured by my mom or my aunt Deb, but you could see that I was made for the water, even then. You could see I was cut in a different way.

By two or three years old, one of my very favorite things was to stay in the water for so long I'd shrivel up and get prune-hands. You know that sensation? Oh, there was nothing better than getting out of the pool after being in the water all day and just lying back on my towel and feeling all those weird little wrinkles on my fingertips. They were like badges of honor, the swimmer's version of calluses, and I wore them proudly.

My mom always tells people she was a terrible swimmer, and I'm here to report that she's telling the truth. She's *still* a terrible swimmer. (Sorry, Mom!) In fact, she avoids the water, if at all possible. That's one of the reasons she encouraged me to swim, she says. She didn't want me to be afraid of the water. She wanted me to feel comfortable at the beach and at the pool, so that was her focus early on. It never occurred to her that I'd take to it in such a way that I'd beg her to sign me up for our summer club team, the Heritage Green Gators, or that I'd start swimming in races and breaking age-group records and pushing myself to new heights. And I'm pretty sure she never felt that adrenaline shot of pure joy that used to hit me when I'd marvel at my prune-fingers.

It wasn't about any of that back then. It was just about getting me comfortable in and around the water, setting me up so that I could confidently add swimming to my list of activities and move about the planet with one less thing to worry about.

Again, this wasn't a game plan or strategy. There was no parenting book my mother consulted to help her figure out this kind of stuff. No, she and my father went by their gut; that's all. They kind of made it up as they went along, just as so many first-time parents do. They took what they remembered from their own childhoods—the good and the bad—and attached it all to what they wanted for me and my childhood. And it's not like they sat down and talked about any of this with me. They simply let me do my own thing in such a way that every imaginable *thing* was on the table.

Here's an example. My parents like to talk about the difference between *motivating* and *enabling*, but it's not like it was any kind of ongoing conversation in our house when I was growing up. As I became more and more involved in swimming, the differences became more and more apparent, but those differences were never pointed out to me at the time. It was up to me to kind of figure it out for myself.

My father's actually given a couple of talks on this (it's one of his favorite topics!), so I'll let him explain:

> **DAD:** I don't really believe in motivating a child. Enabling, that's a different story. Motivation has to come from within. What do I mean by that? Well, if you've got a truly motivated person, he or she will come to a thing on their own. They'll take it on themselves and

do what needs doing. They don't have to be coaxed or prodded. Having been a CEO, having worked with a lot of young people over the years, I've seen the kind of success that happens when you have that wonderful combination of intellectual capability and emotional and passionate desire. I don't care where you are in a corporate setting, whether you're a marketing person or a warehouse person or a general manager, whenever I've seen those traits come together I would see the best of class. So that was my mind-set when Missy started swimming. We'd talk to other parents at meets, and listen to how they'd have to chase their kids to make it to practice, and D.A. and I would flash each other these looks. It's like they were talking a whole other language. You've got to picture it. Colorado, first week of January. It's 4:00 A.M. There's six inches of fresh snow. Missy's got practice. So what's our role? To get her up and out of bed? To motivate her? Not exactly. Oh, sure, we'd be up and at it. D.A. would be downstairs in the kitchen, getting started on a full, nutritional, carb-loaded breakfast. After practice, there'd be another big meal, filled with protein. And me, before Missy got her license, I'd be up walking our dog Ruger, scraping the snow from the windshield, warming up the car. It'd be pitch-black outside, and we had to head out to some high school or rec center twenty miles away in the snow, in the cold. So we'd be up, we'd be getting ready, but we wouldn't be getting

Missy ready. No, that was on her. Always, it was on her. Once she got out of bed, we were there to feed her, to drive her, to enable her. And did she ever once miss a practice? Was she ever even late for a practice? Do you really need me to answer?

They were pretty smart, my parents. Really, they're the smartest people I know. But a big reason for their smarts in this one area was the fact that they'd come to parenthood after they'd been together a good long while, after they'd each built and nurtured successful careers, after they'd surrounded themselves with successful, striving colleagues who each had their own experiences and approaches. I'm repeating myself, I know, but it's an all-important point. My parents had been through a lot by the time they'd had me, so they could take on their new roles as mom and dad as adults. They knew how the world worked. They knew what it took to be successful. And, just as important, they knew what it was to be disappointed, to set a goal and rise to meet it, to set off on a shared journey and maybe double back a time or two before they finally got where they were going.

Instinctively, they knew the way to get me out of bed each morning was to leave it to me to get out of bed each morning. And I did.

Years later, I heard a great line from my trainer Loren Landow that reminded me of my parents' approach. We were talking about another athlete who couldn't seem to get it together to get out of bed each morning and make it to practice, so Loren said, "I guess he likes the feel of his pillow more than he likes the feeling of success."

Loren's got this great way of putting things, and here he really hit home—in more ways than he knew.

⁓

How many of us know the full story of what our parents' lives were like before we were born? What *their* parents' lives were like? We know what has been handed down to us, what we've gathered from scrapbooks and old photo albums, but that's where it ends for a lot of us.

Me, I took in as much as I could, and this is what I've pieced together over countless dinners and car rides and late-night chats over cookies and milk. When you're an only child, you spend a lot of one-on-one time with your parents—or, in our house, one-on-*two* time. Really, it sometimes felt like I was being double-teamed! That's how present and in-my-face and wholeheartedly available my parents were, and in a good way! I was too young to realize that our family moved to a different rhythm than most other families in our neighborhood. I only knew what I knew, right? But as I got older, as I set off and made all these new friends through swimming, through high school, I began to see that we were cut a little differently.

I guess the best way to share how things were growing up with my parents is to introduce you to them, to let you see how *they* grew up, because it was through these formative influences that they came together to raise me. Let's start with my mother— she had what they used to call a hard-knock life, like in the song from *Annie*. She was born in Halifax, Nova Scotia. Her father was an alcoholic, going back to his time as a radio operator in the Royal Canadian Air Force. He'd lied about his age in order to enlist—he was just seventeen! And to hear my mother tell it, he started to drink in order to keep pace with the older, wilder men in his unit. Plus, it was a pressure-packed assignment, so drinking was a kind of shared release. Only he didn't handle it all that well. While the other guys found a way to set their drinking aside and get their jobs done, my grandfather became more and more dependent on alcohol. It was like fuel to him, my mother always said. It kept him going, and by the time he met and married my grandmother it was a part of his routine. He'd started out in school—he was studying to be a doctor—but the drinking got in the way. He ended up driving a taxi.

Here, I'll let my mother tell the rest of *her* story herself, because I only know these bits and pieces in this once-removed way.

MOM: My parents fought constantly. I found out much later that my father was abusive. He never hit me or my younger sister, Cathy, but my mother had a hard time. We lived with my grandparents. My grandfather was an old country doctor in the Depression, so he never got rich. We had no money. His patients used to give him a chicken in exchange for his services, or a bucket of eggs. This was in Halifax, Nova Scotia, and this was just how things were. My grandmother was a wonderful woman, but she had a drinking problem, too. I didn't know this until I was much older, but she used to do a lot of drinking with my father, and the two of them would just go off. They were always having these wonderful parties at the house. My grandmother used to play the piano and sing, and what struck me as

27

a child as a harmless bunch of parties was probably a series of wild nights with my father and grandmother a little out of control. Eventually, my mother did something about it. She was tired of the abuse. She was scared. My father was always getting rough with her, hitting her. She turned to her boss and confided in him. They ended up having an affair, and in those days you didn't commit adultery. In Halifax, in the 1950s, it was somehow considered worse than my father's drinking and abusive behavior. It was actually grounds for divorce, and the way things worked out, they were both found to be unfit parents. I was just six years old, way too young to understand what was going on, but it ended up that my grandparents got custody of me and Cathy. We never really saw my mother after that. My father still lived with us. He continued to drink. He'd be sober for a while, but then he'd just go off. It was no way for us kids to live, but it was the only way we knew.

I knew only parts of my mother's story before I sat down to write this book, because she never really talked about her childhood. She was the kind of person who focused on the present and planned for the future. The past was the past and there was nothing she could do to change it—and besides, she always said that her life didn't truly start until she met my father. That happened when my mother was a senior in high school and my father was a senior in college, but I'll get to that later.

My eyes fill with tears now when I hear my mother talk about her childhood or read what she's written about it. It's difficult to think of what my life was like at that age, compared to how she grew up. It's so incredibly sad—my heart breaks for the little girl my mother used to be. But then it also fills, because if she hadn't been strengthened by such a difficult childhood I don't know that she would have grown to become such a strong, accomplished woman. And, in turn, that she would have had the tools to raise a strong, accomplished daughter.

After her parents divorced, Mom didn't really see her mother. She died when my mother was just sixteen. Mom told me she went by herself to the funeral home, to see her mother one last time, to say good-bye, to forgive her and to let her know she was okay. I can't imagine what that must have been like, but out of that difficult childhood my mom found a precious gift—a life-long relationship with her sister, Cathy, my auntie C.J. We're all super close, and a big reason for that is the relationship they shared as kids. Their grandmother died when my mother was thirteen years old, so Mom became the woman of the house. Her sister was nine. Mom remembers that it was just before Christmas when her grandmother died, and she had to pull a cookbook off one of the kitchen shelves and figure out how to make Christmas dinner for the family.

By the way, my mother's real name is Dorothie Ann—everybody just calls her D.A. That started when she was about a year and a half old, when somebody pointed out that the family now had another D.A., because she had a great-uncle named David Andrew. So from that moment on, his nickname became hers, and she always joked that if she ever heard her full name when she was a kid she knew she was in trouble—kind of the way I always felt when I heard one of my parents call me Melissa.

Mom did the wash, did the dishes, looked after her sister. She even tried to teach my aunt Cathy the facts of life, but that didn't go so well. Mom ended up taking her to see a family friend, who happened to be a gynecologist. That turned out to be an eventful doctor visit—but I'll get to that later, too. First I want to tell how my parents met, because I'm a die-hard romantic and could listen to or tell love stories all day long if I had to. They were on a double date with other people. Mom's date was the captain of the soccer team at Saint Mary's University, an all-male Jesuit school in Halifax where my dad played football. Dad's date was his girlfriend at the time, but they weren't really a good match, at least, according to Mom. To hear her tell it, this girl just wanted to dance all night, and while she was out there on the dance floor my parents got to talking, and when Mom went home that night she told her sister she was in love.

The conversation went something like this:

"I met this fantastic guy."
"What do you mean? You have a great boyfriend."
"But I'm not in love with him."
"Well, that's okay. Maybe that will come later."
"No, I think I'm meant to be with somebody else."
"Somebody you've already met?"
"I think so. It's his friend. We were on a double date. I
   know we've just met, but I think I'm really falling
   for him."
"Wait, what?"

Aunt Cathy must've been confused (who wouldn't have been?!), but there's one thing you need to know about my mother—when she sets her mind on a thing it's as good as done, and here she'd set her mind on my father. Trouble was, he was in his senior year, and he was heading off to Toronto that week to try out for the Argonauts of the Canadian Football League. She'd known him only a couple of hours, and she really, really wanted things to go well for him, but she knew if he made the team she might never see him again. She was torn.

This is probably a good spot to introduce my father, who, in a lot of ways, had his own hard-knock childhood. He came from a big family in southern Ontario, in a little town called Saint Catharines, which was a company town back then. Everyone in Saint Catharines worked for General Motors, to hear my father tell it. "It was all baseball caps and pickup trucks," he says, of the way he grew up. His father was an electrician, and for a while he had his own firm, but he ended up going bankrupt and bouncing from job to job. The family moved around a lot—more and more, as my father got older. Dad went to four different high schools, which, as a football player, was especially difficult. It's tough enough being a high school athlete, trying to win a spot on the varsity team, and you're not just out for a *spot* on the team but a meaningful role. To have to do this four years in a row is hard to imagine. But my father always says you have to play the cards you're dealt, and this was the hand he was playing. First in Ontario, then up to Quebec City, then over to Montreal, and back again to Ontario for his senior year. And then, of course, he went to college and had to fight his way onto yet another team.

He was the oldest of four children and the second oldest of

twenty-three grandchildren. His uncles were all welders, plumbers, electricians. They were blue-collar tradesmen, up and down the line, but Dad was determined to go to college—and he did, the first in his generation to do so. And yet for all his accomplishments as an athlete, my father never really had any support in this area. His father never went to any of his games, and when he did offer up a football-related comment or bit of insight it came in the form of criticism.

"He was a hard guy," Dad always said of my paternal grandfather. "He never really took an interest in *my* interests, other than sports, because my brothers and sister were so much younger. With them, he would sometimes make an effort. With me it was always, 'Dick, get to work.'"

There was abuse in my father's childhood as well, most of it verbal, most of it visited on my father. Apparently, my grandfather softened as he and his kids got older, and Dad got the worst of it. His father was always after him to stand up for himself, to settle disputes with his fists—something my father could never do. He might have been a football player, but he's a gentle soul. Still, his father rode him. Once, two of Dad's friends buzzed by his father's truck so fast, so close, they nearly forced my grandfather off the road, so he went back to the house, grabbed my father, and drove him to the house where the two friends had driven. Then my grandfather turned to Dad and said, "You're not getting back into this truck until you kick the heck out of those boys."

Dad had no intention of kicking the heck out of anybody, least of all his friends, so he caught heck for it instead.

Money was tight. When he was old enough to realize what

was going on, it felt to Dad like his family was living day to day, paycheck to paycheck. My grandfather put him to work as soon as he could get him a decent job. At thirteen, Dad worked construction. In high school, he worked on the Saint Lawrence Seaway canal system, earning $2.50 an hour tying up ocean freighters.

All along, the money Dad earned was meant to help his family pay the bills, and when he graduated his father told him he would have to start paying for his room and board. I suppose my father was expecting this, but it must have been a shock to hear it in such plain terms. By this time, Dad had squirreled away about $200, which he figured would be just enough to get him through his first semester of college. He'd been talking with the Saint Mary's coach, but there are no football scholarships at Canadian universities, so he had to scramble to get a $400 student loan to help cover the rest of his tuition. Of course, he still had to find a way to cover his room and board, but his plan was to just get himself to school and worry about the rest of it once he got there.

⌒

This part of my father's story always spoke to me, because it says a lot about the kind of young man he was, the kind of husband and father he'd become. The takeaway for me was that things always have a way of working out. In my short time on this planet, I've found that this is a helpful approach. It's a way of looking at the world I've come to admire. What's the point in stressing about a situation as you lead up to it? All you can do is all you can do, right? The lesson here is to put yourself in a position where opportunities *might* find you, where good things *might* come your way—because, hey, a lot of times they will. On the other hand, if you avoid those tentative moments, if you shrink from situations where you can't be certain of the outcome, if you take yourself out of the game before the game is truly over, you'll always come away empty-handed. It's like that famous Wayne Gretzky line, about missing 100 percent of the shots you *don't* take. So why not take the shot? If you don't, you'll never be in just the right spot at just the right time, which *might* just be where you were meant to be all along.

Somehow, Dad got it in his head that all he needed to do was *get* to campus, fight his way onto the football team, find a way to pay for his first semester's tuition, and everything else would work out. And, somehow, it did. Food turned out not to be an issue during football season, because the team took care of that, and Dad made sure his pockets were big enough to take home an extra roll or a banana or whatever else he thought he'd need to help him make it to the next meal. So that took care of his board costs. The room was a whole other story—and it's probably best to let him tell it:

> **DAD:** I ended up staying with a buddy in a basement apartment. It was one room with a coal stove and one double bed. There was just a thin wall separating our place from the other basement apartment, which was rented to a sketchy woman. There was one shared bathroom, down the hall, but I wasn't about to use it. Whenever I had to go to the bathroom, I'd walk three blocks up the street to the Lord Nelson Hotel and use the facilities there. Oh, we'd use the bathroom down

the hall if we could go standing up, but we wouldn't sit down. That was where we drew the line. We were both football players, both over two hundred pounds, but we found a way to make it work, even with that one bed. It got a little tricky, though, when football season ended and we weren't getting food from the college. This meant a lot of Kraft macaroni and cheese, which in those days we could get for about thirty-nine cents for two boxes. We'd buy a month's worth, and then add ketchup or whatever we could find to help change the flavor. My roommate, Garrie, and I, we fell into this nice routine, for the most part. Once, though, we got our signals crossed in a way that led to one of Missy's favorite stories. I love telling it, because it makes her cringe. As setup, I should tell you that we used to use this stuff called Tuf-Skin before our games and practices. Basically, it was this sticky glue we applied to the skin so that we could tape our ankles and keep the tape in place. Naturally, before you put the Tuf-Skin on, you had to shave, and this wasn't the most appealing chore in the bathroom down the hall, which we shared with our sketchy neighbor and her revolving door of clients, so a lot of times we'd just pull out a pot and do it in our kitchen. So this one time, I was shaving in the kitchen, rinsing off the razor and the shaving cream in the pot of hot water, going about my business. And then, being a single guy, being an idiot, I just left the pot to soak in the sink when I was finished. I didn't think to tell Garrie, and for his part, him being an idiot single guy, too, he didn't think to look too carefully when he came home the next day and decided to make some macaroni and cheese. He just dumped out the water I'd left to soak and boiled a new pot, and a couple minutes later I saw him gagging on his first spoonful, like a cat spitting out a hairball. That's when I realized what had happened. He said, "What's all this hair doing in here?" And I said, "Oh, I was shaving my ankles." And then he let fly with a string of curse words I won't repeat here, but you get the idea.

Are you cringing right now? Because that one gets me every time. *So* gross. But underneath this disgusting story there is also a glimpse into my father's personality. Whatever situation he was facing, he'd make the best of it. With a smile on his face, if at all possible. He's got the best sense of humor, my father. We tease each other constantly. If I have a bad start in an important race, he'll say something like, "You weren't exactly in a hurry there, huh?" Not to needle me, but to defuse the situation. To let me know that he knows I messed up, and that *I* know that *he* knows . . . and that it's no big deal. The idea, I guess, is to learn to shrug off a disappointment or a setback. It doesn't matter if it *is* a big deal, like falling short in a meaningful race, or if it's just a small thing, like finding some leg hairs in a pot of macaroni and cheese. It can't touch you or hurt you or change you. Unless you allow it to touch you or hurt you or change you.

It's all a matter of perspective, and to listen to my father, there was never a problem we couldn't get past. My parents are a lot alike in this way. They both had a hard time of it as kids, and when it came time for them to be parents they knew *exactly* what kind of environment they wanted to create for their child, not because they wanted to model their own parents and childhood but because they wanted to *avoid* repeating the mistakes that had been visited on them. For the longest time, in fact, Dad wasn't even sure they wanted to have children. Like I said, his father could be abusive. Again, mostly verbal abuse, but if you press my father on it he'll admit that his father sometimes hit him and his younger brother Doug. Mom's father never hit her, but he was an abusive, unreliable drunk. He'd hit Mom's grandfather a bunch of times. And, once, when Mom was about six, he hit her grandmother so hard she fell backward and broke her back against a cast-iron radiator. She was in the hospital for six months! Mom remembers that she was so upset by the sight of her grandmother, lying unconscious on the floor, she didn't know what to do, so she ran to the kitchen to fetch a glass of milk from the fridge. In her little-girl head, this was a way to help.

Clearly, neither one of my parents had the kind of positive, nurturing childhood that leaves young couples thinking they might want to have children of their own. They'd each grown up feeling different, *less than*. They looked at their friends' families and wondered why they couldn't feel the same kind of love, the same sense of security. What this meant was that without really realizing it, without really talking about it, my parents had come to their own conclusions about how and when and whether they'd step into the role. All of this happened before they ever even met, on the night of that mismatched double date. In their own minds, they already knew. They would not have children until they could be the kinds of parents that their parents weren't. They would not have children until they could provide a comfortable lifestyle. They would not have children until they could be present and wholeheartedly available. If you would have asked him as a young man, my father would have told you he was all but certain he didn't want to have a child. And if you would have asked my mother . . . well, she'd been told early on that she couldn't even have children, so in her mind it wasn't an issue. She learned this devastating piece of news on that trip to the gynecologist when she was just a child herself, when she took her sister to see their family friend for a little help with the birds and the bees.

You see, the facts of life that found my mother on that trip to the doctor were not at all what she was expecting. Read on and I'll explain.

My Daddy's-Little-Girl Moment

WINTER PARK RESORT—WINTER PARK, COLORADO

This is a story that's been told and retold so many times in my family, it's like a game of telephone. You know the game, right? You whisper a phrase to the person next to you, and then she shares it with the person next to her, and it moves around the circle until it reaches the last person, and at this point it's unrecognizable. The name Michael Phelps might come out sounding like Mark Spitz after it's been whispered and misheard a few times. You get the idea.

My father's got his version of this story, told and retold from his own perspective.

My mother's got her version of this story, told and retold in a once-removed way, because she wasn't there at the time.

And I've got my version: I was five or six years old. Or seven or eight, depending on the storyteller. We were skiing at Winter

Park, which was one of our absolute favorite things to do. Mom was waiting for us back at our lake house. She wasn't much of a skier, but my father and I used to spend these great, great days on the mountain. It was our special time together. He'd always been a strong athlete, and a big-time skier, and he said he looked forward to the day when I could maybe keep up with him. He taught me to ski, and as my ski instructor he took the do-as-I-do approach. That was just fine with me. I was supposed to follow along, and for the most part, I did. There was a problem with this approach, however. You see, skiing has a lot to do with physics. Even I knew that at four or five (or six or seven). If one person's skis are longer than another person's skis, those longer skis will go faster and farther. If one person's heavier, the heavier person will go faster and farther. It doesn't matter who's a better skier. All things being equal, it will come down to physics.

Now, a lot of dads, they'll hang back when they're teaching their kids to ski. And to my father's credit, he did just that, but only in the beginning. He wanted to be uphill from me, in case I needed his help. He wanted to keep an eye on me, so he could give me pointers. Once he could see that I was able to make my way on my own, he went on ahead and waited for me at the next fork in the trail, or at the bottom. We had this whole routine whenever we skied together. His idea was I would either keep up with him or not, but it would be on me. Plus, he wanted to ski, same way he'd always skied before he had me, and since that way was all-out, he would sometimes just go for it. He didn't do this on every run, mind you, but when the conditions were right and he was feeling it, off he'd go, and if the trail didn't splinter off in some other direction he'd just keep on going.

Early on, I couldn't exactly stay with him, but I could usually keep him in my sights. He'd never let himself get too, too far ahead of me, though. He'd always make sure we could see each other. But on this day there was fresh snow and the sun was shining and the slopes were relatively empty, so he was really cruising. To hear him tell the story, he was just charging down the mountain, as hard and fast as he could go, and it never once occurred to him that I was keeping pace. In his head, he knew I was fine, and he assumed I was trailing far behind and would take a while to catch up. The trail didn't break off in different directions, so he just kept on going, knowing I couldn't make any wrong turns. He was a hard-charger, like I said, and here he was, hard-charging his way down the mountain, really feeling it, expecting to have to wait for me at the bottom. But I actually kept up with him the whole way. I was right behind, doing some hard-charging of my own, staying right at his heels.

It was the most exhilarating thing, to be chasing my father down the mountain in this way. To me, it was a race, and I turned on the jets the way I'd learn to do when I was swimming and trying to catch the girl in the lane next to me if she jumped out to an early lead. To him, he was just gunning the engine, having fun. He wasn't racing—at least, he wasn't racing me. I knew it would be a big surprise, once he saw me at the very end, so I was careful not to get too close. I skied off to the side, just out of his view, and when he did his little kick-stop at the end and turned to face back up the mountain to look for me, he couldn't spot me at first.

There I was, right off to the side, giggling.

When we got back to the house, he told Mom the story. He was just bursting with pride. He couldn't believe I'd managed to stay with him the whole way down the mountain. He knew the laws of physics as well as I did. He knew how unlikely it was for a little kid to keep pace with a grown man who knew how to ski.

He said, "Would you just look at her." Like he was somehow seeing me for the first time.

When I tell the story, though, I'm not so surprised. I knew I was matching him turn for turn. I knew he wouldn't beat me down the mountain. The whole way, he was within reach. But what I didn't know was how genuinely delighted he'd be to find me at the bottom. What I didn't know was how he'd look at me, from that day forward, not so much like a little kid as like a relentless little dynamo. And what I didn't know was how I'd now see myself, whenever I'd catch my reflection in the mirror. Like someone who could set her sights on a goal and make it happen. No matter what.

TWO

MORE THAN ONE WAY TO
MAKE A FAMILY

S o here's what came out of my mother's visit to that family-friend doctor all those years ago. Remember, she'd taken her sister and hoped the gynecologist would help with a little biology lesson. While they were there, my mother happened to mention to the gynecologist that she'd never had her period. She didn't really think anything of it, but she was thirteen years old and all her friends had gotten *their* periods and she was becoming concerned. The doctor was not concerned until he did an exam, and what he found might have sent Mom reeling if she'd had a nurturing parent or grandparent at her side to help her absorb and understand the news.

There was a problem with her uterus, which hadn't developed properly. That's why my mother hadn't gotten her period—and according to this doctor, that's why she never would. It was a little unusual for a doctor to be examining a thirteen-year-old without a parent or guardian present, and to be sharing this kind of heavy news with her directly. But like I said, he knew the family, knew there was no one at home to help my mother through this. So he treated Mom like an adult and gave it to her straight. His daughter Jean was Mom's best friend—years later, they were bridesmaids at each other's weddings—so he spoke to her as he might have spoken to his own child.

Mom didn't quite know what to make of this news, but the way she processed it was that this was just another way she was different, *less than*. She understood the doctor when he said she could never have children, but at thirteen she couldn't really grasp what that might mean. It all seemed so far away, she always said, like it was happening to someone else, or off in some distant future, so she just kind of collected her sister and the two of them made their way home. For the longest time, she didn't even think about this doctor's diagnosis. The not-having-children part, at least. As for the not-having-her-period part, she was just relieved to have an explanation. For years, she would lie to her girlfriends about it, because she was embarrassed, didn't want to stand out or stand apart in any way, but she managed to push the not-having-children piece to that place deep, deep down in her consciousness where she didn't have to dwell on it.

This is another one of those stories from my mother's childhood that tears at my heart. Really, to have to deal with something as big as this all on her own. It's unthinkable. But my mother is one of the strongest people I know. Even as a kid, she was resolved. You have to realize, she'd been the "adult" in her family for quite a while by this point. Her mother had been separated from her at a time in her little life when she probably needed her most, and then she lost her grandmother on top of that. Still, she found a way to process this devastating news, and shoulder the weight of it, and set it aside for later. It was always there, she says now when I push her to talk about it, but in a back-of-her-mind sort of way, never front and center. That is, until she found a way to reconnect with my father after that initial double date and knew in a couple of heartbeats that he was the man she'd wind up marrying.

Sorry, I don't mean to get ahead of their story. I suppose I should go back and tell what happened during Dad's tryout with the Toronto Argonauts. Turned out he tore up his knee, effectively ending his football career. This was a disappointment, even if making the team was probably a long shot. So he decided to go back to school to earn his MBA. That's the thing about my father—if one goal is just out of reach, he picks himself up and sets off in pursuit of another. It's amazing to me, really, that my father was wired in this way, coming from such a deep blue-collar background, but he was determined to build a better life for himself, even as a young man. Or maybe he was tired of all that Kraft macaroni and cheese!

Saint Mary's didn't have an MBA program, so he'd enrolled at Dalhousie University, which was where my mother was going to school, and they ran into each other soon enough. In the back of his mind, he knew Mom was at Dalhousie, but he wasn't thinking along these lines. And yet it's one of my favorite parts of the story, the way they reconnected about a year after they'd first met. Dad was applying for a part-time job with campus security. Mom was a nursing student and the vice president of the student union, which happened to oversee the student security force. When Dad came out of his interview, he had the job. Plus, an invitation to

Mom's Nursing Ball. "It wasn't exactly clear to me if the date was a condition of my employment," Dad always jokes.

Three weeks later they were engaged.

Now, unlike me, my father is *not* someone you'd call a hopeless romantic (although he *is* kind of hopeless), so I've always loved this part of their story, because apparently they were sitting around one day and Dad looked over at Mom and said, "You would make a really good wife."

Mom wasn't exactly sure what he meant by this, so she just said, "Um . . . thanks, I guess."

A couple of minutes later, Dad looked over again and said, "So what's your answer?"

At this point, Mom was completely baffled. She'd had no idea my father's comment was meant as a question, and never in a million years would it have occurred to her that it was *the* question. What was she supposed to say? After a while, Dad got his act together and just came out with it and said, "Will you marry me?"

So Mom said, "Oh, is *that* what you were asking me?"

Dad didn't even have a ring. When he tells the story of how he proposed he always justifies this by saying, "I couldn't even afford dinner." (See what I mean? *Hopeless*, right?)

My very favorite part of their whirlwind courtship story came next. Right after Dad proposed, and right after Mom said yes, he scooped her up into a great old bear hug. One thing about my father, he's a world-class hugger, and here all 250 pounds of him lifted all 105 pounds of my mother off her feet and enveloped her in a giant embrace. There was one problem, though. He hugged her so hard, he ended up cracking two of her ribs! Can you imagine?

Mom married him anyway, but she knew she couldn't start a

life with this big bruiser of a football player without telling him what that gynecologist had told her all those years earlier. It all came back to her, now that she'd found someone she wanted to share her life with. However, she didn't think she could tell my father in person because she was worried she'd start crying. All that time, she'd carried her disappointment silently, but now that there was someone to share it with it felt to Mom like it would break her. And the last thing she wanted was for Dad to stay with her because he felt sorry for her. So she put everything down in a three-page letter and left it for him on his desk at the campus police station. They'd never really discussed children, so Mom had no idea how he'd react, but in the letter she'd said she would totally understand if this was not what he wanted. Basically, she gave him an easy out, said he didn't ever have to see her again, if that's what he wanted. Oh, she said she loved him, and that she knew he loved her, but if not being able to have a child was a deal breaker, they could part as friends, no hard feelings.

One story I heard for the first time as we were putting together this book: Dad wasn't sure what to do with Mom's news. He read the letter with a heavy heart. He knew it must have been a difficult letter to write. His gut told him how to respond, but his head told him to think it through. He actually went to one of his professors for guidance.

> **DAD:** There was a fellow I used to talk to, the head of the business department. I guess you'd call him an adviser. And when I got that note from D.A., I felt I needed some advice. So I went to him and said, "Look, I'm not close to my father, I don't really have anyone I can talk

to. I really love this person, but she just told me she can't have children." I gave him the whole story, and he didn't even stop to think about it. He said, "Walk away." I said, "What?" I don't know what I wanted to hear, but I wanted this person to at least give it some thought. He said, "Walk away. This is a lifetime decision. You've been seeing this girl for only a few weeks. You'll regret it someday. Better to just move on now." If you want to know the truth, it was probably the last thing I expected to hear from this man. He was somebody I'd come to admire, and I still admired him, but I could not agree with him. It wasn't the kid piece. Who knew where our lives would take us? Who knew if we even wanted to have kids? No, it was the D.A. piece. It had been only three weeks, and already I loved her to death.

Later that day, Mom came back from a student council meeting to her office in the student union . . . and there was Dad. She had no way of knowing how long he'd been sitting there, and he just stood and held out his arms and collected her in a big hug. (No broken ribs this time!) He said, "It doesn't matter. I love you. We'll get through this."

Basically, he said all the right things. Which, knowing my father, was some kind of miracle.

They were married seven months later. By some other miracle, Mom's father made it to the wedding, very nearly sober. Her bridesmaids had to send their husbands to the psychiatric hospital in Nova Scotia where my grandfather had been admitted, and they managed to clean him up and bring him back to campus for the reception, which was held at the student union. My parents paid for the reception themselves, for a grand total of $600. For their honeymoon, a car dealer Dad used to work for gave them a loaner vehicle so they could drive down to Cape Cod for a few days.

It was September 1971, almost a quarter century before I entered the picture.

Jump ahead ten, fifteen, twenty years, and it was still just the two of them, working hard, traveling the world, living their lives to the fullest. Mom went on to medical school and became a doctor. Dad went to work as an executive at a string of companies, including 7Up, Head, Coors, Reebok, and Telecommunications Inc. They lived in Halifax, Toronto, Kansas City, Atlanta, Saint Louis, Boston, Denver, and Boulder, Colorado, before settling in the Denver area for good. (Have I missed anyplace?) They traveled all over the world, on business and for pleasure. In almost every respect, they had a great life, a great marriage, but my mother felt like something was missing—more and more, as time went on. Every once in a while, the subject of children would come up, usually in an abstract way. She'd catch herself looking at other families and one of them would make a remark, say something about how things might have been, how they might be still. Sometimes, Dad would look over at Mom and catch her staring at little kids, on a plane, at the beach, in a restaurant, wherever.

To hear them talk about this time in their lives now, I get the feeling that Dad would have been perfectly okay never having children. But Mom kept coming back to the idea. Or, I guess, the idea kept coming back to her. When it was something she could put off, until the time was right, she found a way to be okay with it, but as time passed, she kept returning to the idea, more and more. She started clipping articles she'd read about adoption and surrogacy, always looking to keep her options open. She even got Dad to begin the adoption process a couple of times, but they moved around so much in those days they'd have to give up on one application and start on another, because every state had different regulations, different procedures.

Time was running away from them—and yet, they were happy, although I like to think their happiness might have been a little incomplete, missing *one* teeny-tiny detail.

Here's how my mom remembers that time in their lives. . . .

MOM: I'm a doctor, right? So I knew all about surrogacy. I knew all the options. And I knew, deep down, that adoption wasn't really right for Dick. He never said as much, but it was clear. He was open to it, but I think there was a disconnect there. Plus, I don't think his heart was in it to raise someone else's child. He was going along just to go along, just to make me happy, so I guess a part of me set that whole idea of adoption aside. As much as I wanted to be a mother, I didn't want to push Dick anywhere he didn't want to go. And then one afternoon I was flipping through a copy of *People* magazine. There was a cover story on Deidre Hall, the soap opera actress, telling all about the child she'd just had with a surrogate. I've kept the magazine, all this time. It was the September 28, 1992, issue, and it laid it all out, everything she'd been through. I'd known all this stuff, of course, but I guess only in a clinical sense. To see it in the pages of a magazine, with a focus on a real family, holding this beautiful little baby, it made it all seem possible. And it told me that people were becoming so much more accepting of surrogacy. There it was, on the cover of *People* magazine, like it was an everyday thing.

Dad thought this whole surrogacy business sounded weird, but Mom kept after him. And it's not just that it was *weird* or *out there* or *unfamiliar*—it was also worrisome. He thought there were a ton of things that could go wrong. The surrogate could change her mind, midway through the pregnancy. There could be some unforeseen health issue. There were just so many variables. But then, when you think about it, there are just as many variables in a traditional pregnancy, so many things that can go wrong. Mom kept after him to focus on all the things that could go *right* for them instead of stressing over what could go *wrong*. Eventually, he came around to the thinking that if they were ever going to have a child, he'd have to start looking at things from a glass-half-full perspective.

Here's the thing: when the possibility of surrogacy first came up in Mom's mind, she was thinking she could use her own eggs. Her problem was with her uterus, after all. Her eggs were fine. But she'd been circling around the idea of having a child for six or seven years, and by now she was forty-two years old. (Sorry, Mom, but these details are key. We can go back to lying about your age after this book comes out!) Anyway, Dad was not a big fan of the whole adoption thing at first, and now with this surrogacy option there was no guarantee that Mom's eggs would be viable. Since the costs of in vitro fertilization were so high, about $10,000 per attempt (on top of the surrogacy fees), it didn't really make sense to go that route. This meant it made the most sense for them to use the surrogate's eggs—that was the simplest way to go about it in those days. All they had to do was match up with a surrogate and they could finally start trying for a family.

Trouble was, it wasn't so easy to find a match. They worked through an agency, of course, and the first person they found turned out to have some health issues. The second person who came up in their search turned out to have some personal issues that gave my parents some concern. The way it works is, the agency finds a suitable candidate, and the prospective parents work with a psychologist and a doctor and it's a pretty thorough process. It can take months to make sure there's a good fit, including a couple of back-and-forth visits. And then, if it doesn't work out for whatever reason, it can take another few months before the agency identifies another suitable candidate, so the whole thing can drag on. And it's not just the prospective parents who are deciding if the surrogate is a suitable match; the surrogate is checking out the prospective parents, too; there has to be a good fit all around.

My parents had been married more than twenty years by this point, and if you'd have asked my father he would have probably said a baby just wasn't in the cards for them. He loved the life he was living with my mom. But more than that, he loved my mom, so he kept going through these motions to make her happy. He was fine with how things were, but he wasn't fine with the hole my mother was feeling in her life. He knew he had to do whatever it took to help fill that hole, even if his heart wasn't totally in it—at least, not at first. Still, he didn't think this would happen. They'd been around and around so many times on this, first with the stops and starts on the adoption front and then with their surrogacy search, it was starting to feel like they were spinning their wheels.

And then the stars aligned and God smiled.

⌒

Okay, so that's the big drumroll setup to the revelation at the heart of this book. My mother had learned early on that she couldn't carry a child to term, and by the time she and my dad were ready to have a child her eggs may not have been viable and it wasn't clear she would have even been able to get pregnant, so I guess you can say I'm a child of science. Make no mistake, I'm also a child of my parents, through and through, but I was brought into this world with the help of a generous, compassionate surrogate and her family. I don't want to mention her by name in these pages, because I don't want to draw any unwelcome attention to her, or to upend her life in any way. But she knows who she is. *We* know who she is.

This woman was a godsend, really. She came into our lives on the third try—and right away, my parents knew. Already, on paper, they knew. Before they flew to this woman's home to meet with her and her husband, they were sent pictures, a health workup, a general questionnaire. Together, she and her husband decided they wanted to share this gift of family with another couple unable to have children on their own—a beautiful, selfless decision that absolutely floors me every time I think about all the different factors that went into it. I mean, who makes that kind of sacrifice? What kind of wonderful do you have to be to put the wants and needs of strangers ahead of your own? To put your life on pause for nine months, so the life of another family can have a chance to start?

Such a blessing! Such a kindness! Really, my parents were overwhelmed by the warmth and generosity of these good people. Mom remembers that their first visit ran way longer than anyone had planned. Everybody just hit it off. They talked and talked. They seemed to share the same values, want the same things.

I hear these stories now and it feels to me a little bit like people talking about a party I wasn't invited to. But I was there, in a way. I was certainly a topic of conversation—*the* topic of conversation.

As origin stories go, this one's pretty cool, don't you think? I'm no superhero, but I've always loved taking in the backstories of these great characters in comic books and action movies. It's so fun, so thrilling—the way we find out how they got their starts, where they got their superpowers, who helped to shape them. Here I listen to my parents revisit the details of this first meeting with the woman who would be our surrogate and I feel some of the same thrill, so I've come to think of these twists and turns as *my* origin story. This is where it all started for me. How it all started for me. If Mom and Dad had flown out to meet this woman and her family and things had gone differently, then I wouldn't be here. But they did, and they formed this beautiful, meaningful connection, almost immediately, and out of that they all decided to move the process along.

Out of that, they decided to make me!

MOM: These were good, generous people, but of course we covered all the agency fees and the surrogacy charges. Whatever it cost, it cost. For people out there considering this option, you should know that it's expensive, but you should also know that the women who step up and take on this blessing aren't motivated by money. Not at all. You can't put a price on this gift— but, yes, it does come at a price. We were just so happy that we'd found this family and that everybody got along, everything checked out. We were so excited. The first insemination didn't work, but they'd told us it could take a while, so I was prepared. I got it in my head that the second insemination wouldn't work, either, and it just happened that we had a trip planned to Maui, and we were going to come back and do the third try after our vacation. But then, just as we were getting ready to leave, I got a call from the surrogate, and I could hear it in her voice that she had some happy news. She said, "We're pregnant!" And I just about dropped the phone. I decided I'd tell Dick on the plane. By this time, I had the pregnancy test, so I handed it to Dick after we'd taken off. He looked at it and just sort of scanned it. It didn't really register. He was so used to consoling me, since we'd had so many disappointments, I think it became his default mode. He said something like, "We'll try another insemination when we get back. It'll all work out, you'll see." So I said, "No, you don't understand. We're pregnant!" Finally, it sunk in, and for the first time I could see this look of pure joy come over him. He'd been half expecting something to go wrong since we'd started on this road, so I don't think he ever let his heart fill with the possibility, and here it just filled and filled. He was just bursting with the news. We both were.

My parents were so excited. Like, over-the-moon excited. They got to the hotel in Hawaii and there was a bottle of champagne waiting for them that my aunt Deb and my uncle Harry (my godparents-to-be!) had sent. It had this big card that read, "Congratulations on your pregnancy!" Anybody could read it, so I'm sure my parents got these weird looks, taking the bottle up to the room. Maybe the concierge thought my dad would drink it all!

Before I was born, my parents used to send these little notes to each other, make cards for each other. Apparently, this was a thing—there was a kiosk set up at the local drugstore, where you could make these custom greeting cards. Mom saved them all. She saves everything! Mom would sign her cards "L.W." for "Little Wife." Dad would sign his cards "B.H." for "Big Husband." Kind of corny, but hopefully you can guess by now that I'm *all* about being corny.

They were sending cards back and forth to the surrogate, too, and Mom's saved all of those as well.

"We talked quite a bit," Mom says of her relationship with the surrogate.

Mom did the whole nesting thing during the pregnancy. She picked out a crib, some furniture, got the whole nursery ready. Dad went to Africa during this time, and he ended up taking a whole bunch of pictures when he was on safari, and Mom blew them up and used them to decorate my room. I wasn't even born yet, and there was this whole Noah's ark thing going on—two elephants, two hippos, two lions. A lot of people, when they learn about surrogacy, they think the birth mother is doing all the work, and they're not wrong, she is, but there's a lot of heavy lifting going on for the soon-to-be-parents as well.

At first, Mom thought I'd be a boy. No reason, just a hunch. Dad had come from a family of mostly boys, so that was part of her thinking, but when she closed her eyes and imagined our lives going forward she saw herself as the mother of a little boy. Soon, though, she learned I was a girl, and she was thrilled all over again. My parents started calling me J.J., for Jessica Jeannette, but that didn't stick. Eventually, they settled on Melissa, and whenever our wonderful surrogate sent a card or a sonogram picture, she'd sign it from "Melissa," like it was me, reaching out to Mom and Dad. When my parents started referring to me as "Missy," the surrogate started signing my name that way, too.

So I was Missy before I was born.

～～

I finally arrived on May 10, 1995. My parents were there in the delivery room, of course. Dad cut the umbilical cord. Mom was the first person to hold me, and she gave me my first bottle. In fact, Mom and Dad stayed at the hospital and handled almost all my feedings, right from day one. They changed my diapers, bonded, made googly eyes, got me ready to go home to the nursery they'd decked out with all those animal photos from Dad's safari.

Oh, there was some paperwork everybody needed to fill out, birth certificates and adoption papers for my mom, and other legal documents I've never bothered to learn about. But if you set all that stuff aside, I was like any other child, born to any other overjoyed, overwhelmed set of parents in the hospital that day. From the moment I hit that delivery room, kicking and screaming, I was Missy Franklin, Dick and D.A.'s kid. We were a family, at long last, and it didn't matter how we *became* a family, only that we *were* a family. That we *are* a family. And the woman who carried me to term, even though she was my biological mother, immediately became more like a deeply cherished family friend, on the back of this incredible, unfathomable kindness. We're connected, but it doesn't feel to me like a biological connection. It feels more like connection by choice—and we all choose to keep in touch, even though we see each other infrequently. Still, this noble, bighearted woman and her family will always be a part of our family, because they will always be a part of me. But when I think of my immediate family, it's just me and my mom and dad. There's no room in that picture for anyone else. No room in my heart for anyone else.

Now, I realize I've raced over a lot of the details of my birth here, although in fairness to me, it's not like I have any firsthand memories of that time in our lives. (Sorry, guys . . . I wasn't exactly taking notes.) But I'm also keeping this part of our story brief because we don't want this to be a book about surrogacy. It's not who we are as a family. It's not who I am. Surrogacy might have jump-started me, but it doesn't define me. It made my family whole, and it fills me with gratitude and grace, but that's it. The woman who carried me is the woman who carried me. My parents are my parents. End of story. Or, I should say, *beginning of story.*

But I do want to take the time here to reflect on what the circumstances of my birth meant to me when I started high school, when faith started to take on a whole new role in my life. See, my parents had never been overly religious. The church had been a part of each of their lives, growing up, but never in a deep or fundamental way. It was there, more backdrop than anything else. And that's how it was in our house, throughout the early part of my childhood. But everything changed during my teenage years. That's when I started attending Regis Jesuit High School, a Jesuit, Catholic school in the Denver area. I'll write about my decision to attend Regis a little later on in these pages. It was a swimming decision, mostly, but it came to be about so much more, and it brought with it a renewed sense of faith and spirituality. It also left me thinking—for the first time, really—about how I'd come into this world, and how the circumstances of my birth might be viewed by my new classmates and in the eyes of God.

I can remember sitting in one of my classes during one of the first weeks of school. The first few times I walked through the doors at Regis, I had a taste of that feeling of *less than* that my mom had always talked about, of being somehow *other*, on the outside looking in. I didn't tell a lot of people that I'd been born with the help of a surrogate, but it was like an open secret in and around town. The taller I got, the less likely it appeared to all the world that my mother had given birth to me. Really, she's such a tiny thing, so the bigger my successes in the pool, the more eyebrows we started to raise in the larger swim community. Back home, folks had known us forever. They'd seen me grown up, so everybody seemed happy to take it on faith that I simply favored my father over my mother, in terms of stature. In terms of demeanor, a lot of people said I was just like my mom.

But that was all starting to change, as I was meeting all these new people, and now that I was at Regis—making new friends, starting a new chapter—I caught myself taking those second looks and raised eyebrows to mean that others might question whether a "child of science" like me even belonged in those hallowed hallways.

One day we were reading a passage from scripture. It was a passage that talked about how God the Father loves us more fully and abundantly than any kind of love we could comprehend on this earthly plane. I read these words and they were awe-inspiring. Heart-lifting. Mind-blowing. I caught myself thinking, *How can someone love me more than my parents? How can that be?* But with God, of course, all things were possible, as I was learning in this new environment. Still, I realized in this moment that the love of my parents knew no bounds as well. They had always been there for me, would always be there for me. No matter what I did, no matter how badly I messed up, they would always love me. Always, always, always. And I think it was because of the certainty of their love that I was able to make room in my heart for Jesus's love. I *got* what that felt like, because it started with my mother and father. And let me tell you, all the love I knew my parents felt for me . . . to think that Jesus loved me even more than that . . . well, it was pretty incredible.

I thought, *How is that even possible?*

Coming into this world the way I did reinforced for me how loved I truly was. I felt that love every single day of my life. Knowing what my parents had gone through to have me, knowing how long they'd waited for me, what my mom had been through since she was thirteen years old, hearing that desperately sad diagnosis from that doctor in Nova Scotia—it was almost too much to think about. But here I was, thinking about it. *Dwelling* on it. Trying to live up to the gifts that had been bestowed upon me and my family.

What's funny, looking back, is that these realizations found me at a time when I needed them the most. When I started in at Regis, I caught myself thinking a great deal about the will of God. There was a lot of talk in our hallways, in our classrooms, about God's plan, and being so young and naive I lined up all of this talk alongside some of the more hurtful things I'd heard out in the world. About the sanctity of the love between a husband and wife. About how there is only one way to make a family. But then, alongside all of that, I was able to make room in my thinking for the blessings that came with my birth. I lived in the light of my family, no question about it. And here I was, determined now to live in the light of God as well. And I had to believe that there was room on this earthly plane for both beams of light. I had to believe that I was here as part of God's plan. In my own way, in my own time. That plan? To be a blessing to my parents, and to receive their blessings in return.

God put me here for a reason. Of this I am firmly convinced. He brought me into this world exactly how he planned. And I wasn't planning on wasting a single second of this gift of life.

My At-the-Ready Moment

I have to admit, there were times when my swimming development ran ahead of my personal development. Here's a good example: I was twelve years old and I'd just earned a spot as an alternate at my first sectional meet, an open-to-all-qualifiers competition with no age requirements. Most of the kids on the team were way older than me—by quite a bit—so it was a big adjustment. Aside from the swimming part, I was competing against girls who were older than me by half a lifetime. I was rooming with high school juniors and seniors, which right there can provide a bunch of learning experiences when you're in sixth grade. In fact, there was high drama on this first sectionals trip because one of the girls had a boy up in her room, and of course she was breaking the strict rules we all had to follow about this type of stuff, so I was just wide-eyed, taking all of this in. Girls

63

were running down the hallways, whispering to one another about how this one would be sent home or that one would be kicked off her team.

Nobody was talking about her favorite Disney princess, as I recall. (Mine is Belle.)

Up to this point, I had been swimming age-group meets—meaning, only with kids my own age, as opposed to an "open" or sectional meet, where I would be going up against anyone of any age who'd posted a qualifying time. I was used to being one of the top swimmers in my heat. I would usually find a way to make my presence known. The other kids were usually worried about me, instead of the other way around. Here, though, my times weren't fast enough to put me on anyone's radar. Nobody really knew who I was or cared that I was there. I was good enough to make it to the meet, but not quite good enough to get into the finals—not for this 100 free, anyway.

When you're an alternate, the idea is you're supposed to be ready to swim if one of the girls has to drop out. It happens, from time to time—only, it never seemed to happen when I was in this spot. But you still have to prepare like you're going to swim the race, up until the very last minute. You just never know how things will go. This means you have to swim your entire warm-up, which for me was the biggest adjustment of all. Why? Well, the competition pool could get pretty crowded, and everyone would just swim right over you.

Now, it's not like I was small and nobody could see me. By the time I was twelve, I was basically as tall as I am now, which is six feet two. But I had no idea how to handle the situation. I was used to little kids, all doing the same basic warm-up, moving in the same direction, as a team, but here you had athletes at the next level, doing more intense warm-ups. It was every man for himself. If you're stopped in the middle of a lane—guess what? You're going to get flipped on or run over. And then someone would yell at you for getting in the way. I just didn't know how to act in that situation, how to protect myself. Other swimmers would be trampling over me like it was their job and I was in their way. If I so much as touched someone's feet I would have started apologizing profusely and praying that they wouldn't hate me forever. Frankly, I was terrified, and after a while my coach Todd Schmitz could see it was stressing me out, so he taught me my first "life hack" for swimmers at big-time meets, back before anyone was using the term. He taught me to warm up in the warm-down pool—a neat way to sidestep all the madness in the main pool.

Over the years, I learned that this wasn't so unusual. The warm-down pool also gets a lot of traffic before a race, but most swimmers look to do their warm-ups in the competition pool. They like to get a feel for where they'll be swimming, so that's where the most intense action takes place. People get pretty aggressive, and this was the first I was seeing it. Turns out there's a whole warm-up etiquette that you're just supposed to know, but at twelve years old I wasn't aware, so all I knew was that I found the whole thing crazy intimidating. All I knew was that I was very much out of my comfort zone. And then, on top of all that, I wasn't even sure I was supposed to warm up anyway, because I was just an alternate. I was so young and naive and inexperienced. All I knew was that if someone told me to be good and ready for a race, I was determined to be good and ready.

When you're first alternate, that means you're in ninth place or seventeenth place on the depth chart, depending on the number of heats in the meet. If you're in ninth place, and there's a B final, the alternate status doesn't really apply.

(For those readers who don't follow swimming too, too closely, a B final is like a runner-up final heat, where the ninth-through sixteenth-place swimmers compete. Sometimes, in large meets, there's even a C or D final—but you don't need me to explain the math on that, do you?)

When you think about it, there aren't a whole lot of situations that would put you in the pool as first alternate—at most meets there's a scratch deadline, and if you fail to withdraw in a timely fashion there are penalties that come into play moving forward, so the only way you really get in the pool as a first alternate is if some unforeseen event happens, like someone getting sick at the last minute. Therefore, the closer you get to the start time, it becomes less and less likely that you'll be called on to swim. But at twelve years old, at my first big meet, I took my position as first alternate very seriously. I went through my whole warm-up in the other pool. Then I took my place behind the head official, ready to go, in case they called on me. I even had my goggles on, which was like way, way over the top in terms of preparedness. My parents still laugh about it—me, standing a little too close to the official, goggles in place, waiting for my name to be called. Much to my dismay, everyone showed up!

The second time I was in this position came two years later, when I was fourteen. I was in Berlin, at a World Cup, representing the junior national team, and Coach Todd was part of the coaching staff, so I was a little more prepared for my "non-moment." I'd been around the pool deck a few times by this point, so I had a much better idea of what to expect now.

At one point, the race about to start, I noticed there was a swimmer missing in one of the lanes. Some girl who was supposed to be there just wasn't there, for whatever reason. For a moment, I thought I'd be called on to swim, but nobody came looking for me. Nobody said my name. Nobody even moved to fill the spot—the seven remaining swimmers just lined up and waited for the whistle. I started freaking out. I didn't know what to do. Was I supposed to just stand there? Tap the official on the shoulder and introduce myself? Sit back down on the bleachers?

Finally, I decided that the thing to do was take charge. I was there to swim, right? I told myself I'd earned my way into this race. Yeah, I had only the ninth-best qualifying time, but now there looked to be this opening, so I wanted to swim in the A final. That's where I thought I belonged, where I was supposed to be, so I approached the head official. In my head, I like to think I was this confident young swimmer, reaching for what was mine, but in reality I'm sure I came across as tentative, not at all sure what was expected of me in this spot. I said, "Hi, I'm Missy Franklin. I'm the first alternate, and there's no one in that lane."

The official looked at me like I was some little kid—which I guess I was. He said, "That's okay, sweetie. We're all set."

Todd was furious, that I was being strung along in this way, but the meet was being televised and names had already been submitted.

The race went off without me—with just seven swimmers and one empty lane. I was crushed, a little bit. Also, relieved, a little bit. I was ready and I wasn't ready, I guess. I mean, I had my goggles on! But if I was really ready, I wouldn't have been so uncertain. If I was really ready, I would have moved about the warm-up pool like I belonged no place else. I might not have pushed my way into the heat, because a lot of times a race will go off without a full lineup—because it's easier for race officials to keep to a tight schedule and not take the time to call up an alternate. I might have been more comfortable in the warm-down pool, until I learned how to fight my way through a warm-up in the main pool, because it's easier to make adjustments that allow you to avoid a difficulty instead of facing it head-on. But sometimes you just have to jump in the pool and go for it, and it took standing there on the pool deck, waiting anxiously for my name to be called, for me to start realizing this.

I was getting there, but I wasn't there yet. My time would come.

THREE

GROWING UP

M y father probably thought I was going to be a volleyball
player. Or maybe a basketball player. He was all over it.
We'd ski together, shoot hoops, toss around a football.

Mom and I had a different relationship when it came to sports. She'd never played sports as a kid, but she wanted me to participate and have fun. In whatever ways she could, she helped to make that happen. She was the one who researched all the different leagues and clubs in the area, found teams and programs for me to join, met with coaches, got me registered and cleared, and shuttled me around town to buy my equipment.

Swimming was just another activity. At first, it was something we could do as a family. We could all splash around at the beach, in the pool—even Mom! But early on, my parents could tell that I was super comfortable in the water. A lot of kids tense up before they jump into the pool. They worry the water will be too cold, or over their heads, or whatever. But not me. I'd just go for it. My mother signed up for a mommy-and-me swim class when I was six months old, so that became part of our routine, and to hear her tell it, as time went on, I was always the first one in the pool. I was in my element, I guess you could say. Mom, not so much, but she did it for me. Soon my parents started bringing me around to our neighborhood pool. In the summer, we were there almost every day.

I loved every single sport I played as a kid. I loved being with my friends. I loved running around, competing. But swimming was different. I wouldn't say I liked it *better* than soccer or volleyball or basketball. And I wouldn't say I was any *better* at it than I might have been at those other sports. But it felt natural to me, being in the water. Like I belonged no place else. In the beginning, of course, the water was just another place to play, a different environment to master, but as I learned to dive and kick and propel myself along the surface, I began to think about swimming a little differently. It was like I was flying, almost— gliding through the water without a thought in my head other than the fact that I was gliding across the water. It was such a simple, magical feeling, and I loved it. The backstroke was always my favorite stroke. I called it "resting." Any time I got tired I would simply flip over and "rest" and it was the most amazing thing. On my back, I could still feel like I was flying but with my head almost out of the water and my eyes wide-open. And I could breathe all the time! Bonus!

As I got older, I learned to swim fast on my back. I could swim and soar and at the same time see what my friends were up to on the pool deck. It was a way to be alone with my thoughts and keep tabs on whatever else was going on—I didn't want to miss a thing!

After a while, I started to notice the other kids I'd been play-ing with at our neighborhood pool would get cold or distracted. They'd get in and out of the water, move on to something else, then jump back in to cool off. Me, I never wanted to leave the pool. Don't get me wrong, I was happy to towel off and run around with my friends, but there was something reassuring about being in the water. That feeling of flying . . . I never wanted to lose it. That feeling of being in my own little environment . . . I didn't want to lose *that*, either. So while the other kids would eventually look for reasons to get out of the water, I'd be looking for reasons to stay in the water.

When I was four years old, I told my mother I wanted to join our summer-league team, the Heritage Green Gators. Talk about a great reason to stay in the water! I was too young, it turned out, but that didn't keep me from kicking up a little dust. I was really upset, so I threw my version of a temper tantrum. In my defense, it was hardly a tantrum. More like a persuasive argument. I didn't kick or scream or fuss. I just made my case. But I couldn't really argue my way past the age restrictions for summer-league swimming. The rules were clear. There was nothing my parents could do, except to teach me how to be a little more patient (still working on that!) and to help fill my days with other activities. And it turned out I was distracted easily enough. I still went to the pool almost every day during the summer, but I started play-ing soccer and doing a whole bunch of other things. Whenever I could, I'd stop to watch the Green Gator practices, imagining myself into the scene, wishing I could take part. The youngest kids on the team were just five and six and seven, but to me they were the *big* kids in town, and I wanted to be just like them.

The next summer, my mother signed me up right away. I would ride my bicycle to practice. Of course, my mom would follow in the car, to make sure I got there. She tried to be stealthy, but I always knew I was being tailed! The coaches would bring doughnuts after practice, and we'd sit around and laugh and play. There was a ton of laughing, as I recall. Also, a ton of doughnuts. I'm not sure which I enjoyed more! Nobody wanted to leave the pool area. The coaches were really keyed in to us kids, and they had all these games we would play to help us develop our form, our stamina, whatever it was we were working on. My favorite was sharks and minnows, where we'd take turns chasing one another all over the pool.

Every week or so, there'd be a swim meet, and we'd make a day of it. It felt to us kids like one giant party. We didn't want it to end. The parents would set up these green-striped tents, and we'd spread out sleeping bags and towels and set up camp. We'd bring playing cards, Frisbees, music. There were enough snacks and home-baked goodies to stock a concession stand. In fact, at most meets there was a huge concession area staffed by the parents. They'd have drinks, snacks, ice cream, you name it. Even barbecued hamburgers and chicken burgers!

The club had a Big Gator/Little Gator program, so we were each paired with an older kid, who'd bring us Gator goodie bags filled with green bouncy balls, green yo-yos, green hairspray. (Are you sensing a *green* theme here?) We would dye our hair with this green sparkly stuff, or we'd write all over each other with our green Sharpie pens. Cute little trash-talking quotes like "Eat my bubbles!" It was just the best. I can't imagine what all that green hair goop did to the pool, or what our "tattoos" looked like after we'd been in the water awhile, but we were just little kids. We didn't care about any of that stuff.

The coaches were tremendous. A lot of them were high school students from the neighborhood who'd grown up in the program, or college swimmers on summer break, so they knew how to keep things light and fun. It wasn't so long ago that they were little Green Gators themselves. In fact, some of them still competed for the Gators, alongside their coaching duties, since the league was for swimmers between the ages of five and eighteen. The competition part was almost like an afterthought. Your coach would come around to the tent with heat cards telling you your heat and your lane, maybe talk a little bit about your technique, and when the time came you'd go and swim your race and then hurry back to your card game, or the Frisbee catch you were having. It's not like the races didn't matter, but the coaches found the right balance between fun and development. There was no pressure. You didn't have to be a great swimmer. There were no tryouts. There was a race for everyone, no matter your level.

My parents still remember those races. . . .

MOM: We all looked forward to those meets. They were so much fun. They were neighborhood against neighborhood, so it worked out that everybody knew one another. It was a friendly, community-building-type event, but even then we could see that Missy had a little something special, a little something extra. There was this one meet, one of the bigger ones, the

Rocky Mountain Swim League (RMSL), and Missy was swimming the 25-meter backstroke finals. From the very beginning, that was one of her best events, and she won the race and we were all so excited for her. I remember, Dick's mother had come down to visit with us, so she was with me and Dick as we were watching the race, and I don't think my mother-in-law had ever seen Missy swim before. She was just so excited, she practically jumped out of her chair. Dick and I liked to play it down. We never wanted to be those parents in the stands who cheered a little too loudly for their own child. We cheered for everyone. In fact, we tried to dial it down when we were cheering for Missy. But Dick's mother was jumping up and down like a cheerleader. And then, someone made an announcement on the loudspeaker. They said that Missy had just set an RMSL record for six-and-unders. It's a record that still stands, by the way—24.48 seconds. She wound up setting a bunch of RMSL records and eventually more than sixty Colorado State records, and a lot of them have yet to be broken, but this was probably the first, and we were trying to soft-pedal it, you know. But there was my mother-in-law, just over the moon about it. She couldn't believe it. She started tugging at Dick's sleeve, saying, "She's gonna be an Olympian someday, Dick!" Best we can remember, that's the first time anyone in the family ever talked about Missy and the Olympics. It was never about that, for us. If anything, it was a little embarrassing, having Missy's grandmother jumping up and down like that, yelling about the Olympics.

I'm not so sure about pinning that first Olympic thought on my grandmother, although I do have a specific memory of that day. But I also have a specific memory of the Olympics that same summer—the 2000 games, which were held in Sydney, Australia—and wanting to be just like the American swimmers I was watching on television. However, I also wanted to be just like the high school swimmers who worked as coaches in the club. To me, those were my role models, my ideals, so despite the family legend, I don't think it's fair to suggest that this first summer of "competitive" swimming lit any kind of Olympic fire in me. Mom's right—it wasn't about that, not then. But what it *was* about was building friendships and fun, building my confidence. It was a place to put all that bundled-up energy you have when you're five years old, combined with a competitive streak that had yet to really show itself. Deep down, it was there. That would explain the RMSL record, right? But it wasn't something I recognized or knew to tap into. It was in the way I was wired, and during swim season it started to come out in the pool. But then, in winter, it came out on the slopes, or maybe on the basketball court.

It didn't *have* to be about swimming. Not just yet.

⌒

One thing my father never wanted to do was be my coach. He couldn't really coach me in swimming, but he certainly had the tools to coach basketball, volleyball, or soccer. He knew those games well enough to grab a whistle and get a group of little girls into fighting shape. That's how it goes in youth sports, in most communities. A mom or dad with an athletic background steps up and volunteers for the job. But that's not always the best situation for young athletes, especially for the kid whose mom or dad is the one with the whistle. It's not that the parents aren't "qualified" to run the show, but in a lot of cases it can lead to a conflict of interests, and incidents of favoritism, and all kinds of tensions and weirdness that just don't belong in youth sports. Truth is, all it takes is someone who can motivate his or her young charges, someone who is good with kids, someone who understands the game and the concept of teamwork . . . but when that same "someone" has a child on the team, things can sometimes get complicated.

As a former college football player, Dad certainly fit the description, but he wanted no part of it.

Why? I'll let him explain. . . .

DAD: My father was my coach when I was a kid, and it was brutal. He was the sponsor of our softball team. Franklin Electric, that was his company at the time. And this was well beyond the age when parents were doing the coaching. This was a group of high school boys, age fifteen to eighteen. I was twelve, going on thirteen, but he put me on the team, and the other boys all resented it. I was a fumbling idiot, compared to these other boys. I made bad play after bad play, screwed up every which way, and of course my father rode me about it on the way home. And I hated him for putting me in this position. It completely undermined my confidence. With boys my own age, I probably would have done just fine, but in this situation I was a little overmatched, out of my league, and the boys on the team were all bitter about the fact that I was the sponsor's son, the coach's son. I'd probably taken a spot in the lineup that should have gone to one of their friends, and that just wasn't right, so when I became a parent, I made a decision early on that I wouldn't get anywhere near the sidelines when Missy started playing sports. It wasn't even a decision. It was a nonstarter. You see it all the time, dads coaching their kids, and I don't agree with it. You can't put objectivity into it when it's your own flesh and blood. It's not good for the child, and it's not good for the team. Even the most well-meaning parent will have his judgment clouded, so it doesn't make sense to go down that road. And as Missy became more and more involved in swimming, D.A. and I tried to steer clear of her coaches there as well. Our thing was always to let them do their thing, to stay out of the way. The coaches should coach, and the parents should parent. The lines were clear. You can have all sorts of mature discussions with your kid's coaches, try to understand what they're doing, what they're thinking, but you get into trouble as soon as a parent steps over the line and says, "Well, I think you should be doing this...."

Dad stayed out of the way, but Mom was very involved, in a sideline capacity. She would often be the team manager, or the "team mom"—a very different role than a coach, of course, without all the potential for conflict and tension. If you know my mother, she's the kind of person who can't *not* be involved, so she found a way to limit her involvement to the more social or emotional aspects of sports, away from the pool or the field. This was her way to help grow my game—by growing *me*. She'd talk to me about what was going on, make a special point to learn the names of all my teammates and to make friends with their parents, but her "coaching" input never went beyond, "Did you have fun?" or "Did you do your best?"

When summer was over I was busy with soccer, basketball—whatever was in season. That relentless spirit that underlines everything I do in the pool? It all started on those other fields of play. I was a competitive kid. (How's *that* for an understatement?) What I loved about soccer and basketball were the team elements of the game. Club swimming was a lot like that, too. In fact, I've always thought of swimming as a team sport. A lot of people don't see it the same way, but they're not swimmers. If you've ever competed for a youth-league swim team, a club team, a school team, or even for your country, you'll know that everybody's pulling for one another and pushing one another, in and out of the pool. Sure, there were different elements at play. With soccer, there were all those other girls you could lean on, learn from, pass the ball to. I liked that, too, and in a lot of ways it was just like swimming, but it's not like I was comparing one activity to another, trying to choose between them. There was time enough for everything back then.

Our soccer coach, Dallas, gave us all nicknames. Mine was "Boomer," because my very favorite thing to do was kick the ball as far as I could. That was my signature move. I wasn't too worried about linking my passes or controlling the ball. To be honest, I wasn't really even worried about making sure the ball was going in the right direction. I just wanted to kick it clear across town. In basketball, I played alongside one of my best friends, Jessica, and she was just as tall as me, so the other teams started calling us the "Twin Towers." In swimming, my father came up with the nickname "Missy the Missile," and it seemed to stick.

I was one of those kids who was into everything. And my parents were with me the whole way. Every game, every meet, every activity or gathering, one of them would drop whatever they were doing and be there to support me. They wouldn't go to practices, but they were available to help me get ready for practices, to shuttle me back and forth, to ask me how things went. (And, full disclosure, they'd be the first parents at pickup time, usually arriving a couple of minutes early to catch at least the tail end of practice, so they could get some idea of what I was up to, the kinds of things we were working on.) I've had the opportunity to meet a lot of athletes, in a variety of sports, and almost all of them were blessed with parents who were also very much present in this way. The lesson? Make time for your kids. Make their interests your own. This doesn't mean you have to be a helicopter parent and monitor your child's every activity, but if he or she expresses an interest in something, and if there's a way to show your support for that interest, it's probably a good idea to do so. Not because you're out to raise a champion, but because you want your child to be grounded, and well-rounded. Because you want to show love and support. I can't tell you how many times one of my little teammates would look up into the bleachers, searching for a parent or family member who'd come to cheer her on, only to turn away disappointed. Obviously, it's not always possible for parents to be as fully present as my mom and dad were able to be for me. After-school sports tend to happen on weekday afternoons, when a lot of people are stuck at work. Weekend activities can sometimes conflict with a family's busy schedule, especially if there are other children. But in our house, there was just me, and my parents had waited so long to have me, and jumped through so many hoops to have me, they didn't want to miss a thing, so they made it a special point to be there for me. Always.

Again, this wasn't anything my parents talked about with me. It wasn't any kind of strategy. It's just who they were, where their priorities were. They weren't out to help me build a solid foundation for an athletic career, only to build a solid foundation for a lifetime. I'm so grateful they took the time and the trouble. Although, if you'd ask them, they'd tell you that it was no trouble at all. That there was no place they'd rather have been than on those sidelines, cheering me on.

I'd been swimming for two summers with the Heritage Green Gators, and I just couldn't get enough of it, so I went to my mother and said, "Mom, I want to do more."

I wanted to be in the water more, swim more, compete more. So Mom started calling around, looking for a place where I could swim year-round. She'd already spoken to a lot of neighborhood parents around the pool, so she had a place to start, but the first team we found wasn't exactly the best fit. A lot of my older friends had already joined the program, so I was excited to be with them. Trouble was, they had a coach in the group ahead of me who sometimes filled in at our practices. He walked up and down the pool deck with a big stick he used to swat against the side of the pool. It was so intimidating! If you did something he didn't like, or even if he just wanted you to get out of the pool so he could work with you on your stroke, he'd bark at you in this thick accent. He'd yell, for no good reason. He scared the daylights out of me. I loved the coaches assigned to our group, but I knew that once I was moved up to the next level I'd have to work with this strict European coach, so I think I shut down. I started coming up with excuses why I needed to miss practice. I'd say I had a headache, or that my knee hurt, whatever. It was so totally unlike me, to want to bail on practice like that, and my mother could tell straightaway something was up, so she let it go a time or two before finally calling me on it.

She said, "What's going on here, Missy? Usually, I can't keep you away from the pool or from your friends. This isn't like you."

She was right. It wasn't like me, but I was too young to put what I was feeling into words, too young to fully understand what was going on with me, so I just shrugged and said, "I don't really like swimming anymore. I don't think I want to go."

A lot of parents would have let the conversation rest right there, but Mom's antennae must've picked up on something, because she kept after me. "Did something happen with your friends?" she asked.

I shook my head. "No," I said. "I love my friends."

"Did something happen with one of your coaches?" she asked.

I shook my head again. "No," I said. "I love my coaches." And then I waited a long beat and added, *"Now . . ."*

Right away, she knew. She put two and two together and came up with four before either one of us even knew the equation. Okay, so if I liked my coaches *now*, it must've meant I didn't like some of the other coaches I'd been exposed to. Just by pushing me a little bit, by keeping the conversation going, my mother figured out that it was this other coach who was upsetting me, this other coach who loomed in my path, because as I progressed I would be assigned to his group. There was no avoiding it, unless I refused to get any better and stayed exactly where I was, in the lower group. My parents couldn't really advocate for me on this one. This coach was probably a very good coach. He had a lot of students who traveled a long way to swim with him. But he was just so strict, so rigid, so cheerless. I was too afraid of him to even approach him with a simple question. I'd see him walking along the pool deck with that stick of his and want to be anywhere else but in that pool. I know that this coaching "style" might work for some people, but I knew it wasn't the best for me.

At this early, early stage in my swimming "career," it was nothing to switch me to a different team. Swimming was supposed to be a fun after-school activity, that's all. If I wasn't having fun, there were other things I could be doing. This wasn't the time to teach me a lesson, or toughen me up, or encourage me to find a way to make things work with this difficult coach. And it's not like my parents were quick to give me an easy out, or to help me run from my problems. No, *this* wasn't *that*. This was just me, letting it be known in my not-so-subtle way that this man terrified me and that I wanted to steer clear.

So what did my parents do? They found another swim team for me to join, and looking back I think they handled the hiccup in just the right way. Understand, this kind of thing happens all the time in youth sports. A kid can get turned off to an activity because he or she is confronted with an individual the kid just doesn't want to deal with. And at a certain age, at a certain level, the kid shouldn't have to. Who knows what makes a kid shut down, or turn off to a sport? There can be a personality clash, or a clash of wills, or something as simple as a clash of styles between the way a coach teaches and an athlete learns. But at seven years old, none of that really mattered to my parents. I don't believe they even thought along these lines. All they knew was that I wasn't happy, so they told me they would find another team for me to join.

Just like that, my headaches disappeared. My knee started feeling better. And when the mean coach from the more advanced group subbed in on one of our practices, I no longer dreaded it so much because I knew it was only a temporary thing. I knew he wouldn't be *my* coach going forward.

All was right in my little world.

Second time around, Mom's search pointed us to the Colorado Stars, one of the more popular club teams in our area. This is where serendipity, or fate, or maybe even divine guidance finds its way into my story, because my very first Stars practice was also the very first day for Todd Schmitz, the coach who took me all the way to the Olympics! How crazy is that? Todd had grown up in North Dakota but moved to Colorado to swim at Metropolitan State University and never left. He'd studied to be a certified financial planner, but after graduation he started bartending and coaching while he was figuring out his next move. He was an assistant swimming coach for a high school girls team, and a coach for a summer-league team that actually competed *against* the Heritage Green Gators, and it just worked out that he signed on to coach the youngest group of Stars—the Starfish, our eight-and-under division—around the time my parents were signing me up. His first day was my first day, so we had this special connection right away. Here was this young guy, early twenties, with long hair (that he wore in a ponytail, mind you) and a cool, spirited attitude. He was just so much fun. I've met a lot of coaches in my day, and they've come in all sizes and stripes, in all different demeanors, but none of them are quite like Todd. One of his great strengths as a coach, whether he's coaching at the youth level or at the national-team level, is he knows that if his swimmers have a blast they'll keep coming back. His style was in complete contrast to the style of that strict European coach—the dude with the big thwacking stick.

The difference was immediately apparent. From the very first day, I just loved my Starfish practices. Todd would turn out all the lights in the pool, and blast the music, and we'd swim in the dark. On Halloween, he'd bring a bunch of pumpkins to the pool and incorporate them into our workouts. He'd have us do relay races. You might have to get across the pool without the pumpkin touching the water. Or, you might have to swim the entire way with the pumpkin underwater the whole time. We would really have to work together as a team to find the most efficient way to work within these constraints—we all wanted to win, right? He believed that if we weren't having fun, he wasn't doing his job. He was so creative, coming up with all these different drills for us to do, so our practices never really felt like *practice*;

our work never really felt like *work*. Plus, he had a ton of energy and enthusiasm for the sport, and those kinds of things are infectious. And the better I got as a swimmer, the more he was able to offer. He could watch me swim just a couple of strokes and give me a dozen things to work on to up my game.

I was thrilled to be a part of a team like the Colorado Stars, and my parents were thrilled for me. It was a big commitment for all of us—a big step up from what we'd been doing. Practices were three or four times a week to start, and soon there were morning swims as well. It all depended on when we could get indoor-pool time, so the schedule was always changing on us, but my parents never complained, not once. Mom kept track of it all, which was a job in itself. Remember, this was back before smartphones and tablets, so it took some doing, coordinating all these different activities. I kept up with all those other sports for as long as I could, all the way through middle school, but there weren't enough hours in the week for me to do all the things I wanted to do.

Looking back, it's amazing to me the sacrifices my parents made to get me where I needed to be. Mom was working as a physician at this time, based in Denver, where Dad was working as a business consultant, so they were spread pretty thin. I don't think I recognized how busy they were at the time—in fact, I'm sure I didn't. I mean, I could see that my parents were committed, I could see they were *always* there, but it never occurred to me that they were juggling work and family obligations and time they might have spent doing something else. Mom even signed on to serve as chaperone as I started traveling to meets out of state. One year, I did well enough at states to be selected for the

Colorado All-Star Team. I was just nine years old, and I'd be swimming several individual events and on the under-ten relay teams at a meet in Lawrence, Kansas. It was a very big deal, but I didn't know anybody else who was going. There might have been a few older kids from the Colorado Stars making the trip, but they were *much* older than me, so I was going to be on my own. I was more excited than nervous, because I always liked meeting new people, and I always got along well with the older kids. But Mom was more nervous than excited, because she worried about me being so far from home, essentially on my own. She didn't exactly buy into Dad's playbook on giving children a wide berth when it came to youth sports, at least not when it came to related activities away from the sport itself, not when I was just nine years old. The way the trip was set up, our parents were supposed to drop us off at the University of Denver at four o'clock in the morning for the twelve-hour drive to Kansas, and the thought of sending me off like that, in the middle of the night, headed for the great unknown, must have been a little too much for my mother, so she volunteered to chaperone. I don't think she told me until we got to the University of Denver, but she had her bag packed and was ready to go.

MOM: It was quite a trip! Twelve hours each way, in a noisy bus with nonstop Disney movies! What I didn't know before we left was that the older kids were meant to room by themselves, in groups. The younger kids, the under-tens, they had to have a parent assigned to the room with them, which of course made sense. So I had three kids assigned to my room. Missy and I shared one

86

of the double beds, and the other two girls shared the other bed. We didn't really know these girls, so I made an effort to get to know them. These girls were my responsibility, and of course they wanted to be with the other kids on the trip, so in the evening they wanted to leave the room and join the rest of the group. I didn't like that idea. I felt I should know where they were at all times. I couldn't have them running up and down the stairs in the hotel, so I ran a tight little ship and I thought everything was just fine. But then, Missy pulled me away from the girls and asked to talk to me in private. We went into the bathroom and closed the door and Missy said, "Mom, they're calling you the worst chaperone ever." I said, "Why?" So she told me it was because I wouldn't let them have any fun, and all the other girls were running around the hotel. They felt like they were missing out. So I told Missy I knew just what to do, and we went back out into the room and I told the other girls why I was being so careful. I told them I was only trying to keep them safe, to take care of them the same way I'd want someone to take care of Missy if she was on a trip like this without me. We had a nice little talk, and we had a fun night in the room together, and later that night the cutest thing happened. We'd all gone to bed, and the room was quiet, and I woke up and saw that one of the other little girls had come over to our bed. She was homesick, she said. She couldn't sleep. She said, "Can I get in the bed with you and Missy?" And she crawled right in. It's like we'd known each other for years and years, instead of half a weekend.

I remember that trip. (Mom really *was* the worst chaperone ever—I don't care what kind of spin she wants to give it.) That was one of the first, but before long there was always a trip coming up on the calendar. There were state meets and zone meets and zone camps. One of the big reasons I started paying attention to my times was because that's how you qualified for these trips. It was the greatest motivation, because the trips were so much fun. I started building this network of great swimming friendships— kids I'd meet at zone camps or sectionals. We'd see each other year after year, and after a while, once we were old enough to start e-mailing and IM'ing each other, we were able to keep connected all year long. (Throwback to AOL Instant Messaging!) It got to where we'd know who was going to be on this trip or that trip, so we all had something to look forward to. It made it all so much more exciting. The swimming part was key, and I was pushing myself to swim a personal best each time out, but at this early age the drive to do well had as much to do with making sure I was eligible to go on all these great trips as it did with improving my times.

It was just a couple of years after I'd joined the Stars that I started to notice our family was a little different from the other families we were meeting through swimming. I was still just a little girl, but I could see how a lot of the parents would interact with their kids on the pool deck, in the hotel, wherever. Some of my friends would get these scared looks on their faces before a race, like they were afraid to mess up. Or maybe, after a disappoint-ment, I'd see someone start to cry or panic because they knew they were about to get chewed out by a parent or a coach. My parents were not at all like that, and if Todd had been that kind of coach, I wouldn't have worked with him for very long. The only pressure I felt before any of these meets or camps was the pressure I put on myself—and because we tended to approach swimming in a fun-first way, there was never really all that much pressure. Looking back, I know this mind-set flowed in a meaningful way from my parents. They were chill, so I was chill. They didn't make winning a priority, so I didn't make winning a priority.

The first bit of pressure I felt when it came to swimming had more to do with scheduling and logistics than it did with any-thing going on in the pool. One of the ongoing conversations in our house, going back as far as I can remember, was about taking on more than I could handle. Even at a young age, my parents treated me like a mature person, capable of making my own deci-sions, and taking responsibility for those decisions. By the time I was seven or eight, they wanted me to learn to think things through. So I did, and I took my job seriously. Early on, these con-versations were no more in-depth than a parent telling a child she couldn't have all the ice cream she wanted because she'd get a bellyache, but after a while I understood that I had to pick and choose among the things I loved to do. School came first, of course. It was understood that if I couldn't stay ahead of my homework and keep getting good grades, I couldn't participate in *any* of these activities—forget *all* of them. So that was a given. And they never once came right out and told me I *couldn't* sign up for this or that activity. The one rule my parents did have was that I couldn't drop a sport in the middle of a season, so these conversations always happened *before* they signed me up. They wanted to make sure I understood that I was making a commitment to my teammates, to the coach, to the program, and that I was meant to see it through, and I took that commitment seriously. We all did. Nothing seemed to set my father off like the news that one of my little teammates had up and quit in the middle of a season. It happened—quite often, in fact—and it was one of his pet peeves. And so, in time, it became one of mine as well.

And it wasn't just sports and organized activities I had to learn to prioritize. There were birthday parties and sleepovers I wanted to be a part of, too. The more I started traveling to these different swimming events, the more I was taken away from my friends. They were all active in sports, too, or maybe in dance, or art, or music. Most of my friends were busy, busy, busy. But very quickly, my version of *busy* was different from theirs, because mine took me away from home, so there was this constant tug and pull, between where I might have wanted to be in the moment and where I knew I wanted to be over the long haul.

Here's Mom again, to tell how it looked from where she sat.

MOM: Whenever there was one of these conflicts, Missy would come to me and say, "Mom, I've got a decision to make." She'd never throw up her hands or pout around the house. She was a thoughtful child. "I've got a decision to make." That was always my cue, and I'd usually say, "What's that, sweetie?" And she'd lay it out for me. Let's say her friend Sarah was having a sleepover party on Friday night. Missy would tell me all about it, what they were going to eat, who was coming, what movie they were going to watch. I'd listen and say, "So what's the problem?" I wanted to hear her say it. I thought it was important for her to understand the dilemma. She'd say, "Well, I've got a meet on Saturday, and I really need to get my rest." So we'd talk about it. I'd say, "What do you think we should do?" It wasn't her problem, it was our problem, but I wanted Missy to come up with the solution. Most times, she'd find a compromise. Maybe she'd go for dinner, and stay to watch the movie, and I'd pick her up at ten o'clock. When she got older, she'd stay out a little later. She'd take a nap in the afternoon to make up for it. Whatever time she wanted me or Dick to come get her, we never complained about the hour. We were just happy Missy was getting to enjoy this time with her friends, but it was so hard for her, missing out on so many get-togethers.

Sure, I missed out on a lot. And I knew it, every time. But the trade-off was always worth it. Swimming opened up such a world of possibilities for me. Even at nine or ten years old, I could see that it was becoming so much more than a fun outlet. It was empowering. To invest all that time in such a single-minded, laser-focused way, in the pursuit of a dream . . . it shapes you, becomes a part of your personality, going ever forward. Only, here's the thing: the "dream" kept changing. I might have thought about winning a gold medal when I watched the

Olympics on television, but that wasn't anything more than the dream of a little girl. I might have thought about making the national team, or qualifying for Olympic trials, or posting a national age-group (or NAG) record. With each race, each meet, each opportunity, the dreams kept getting bigger, but the "goals" underneath those dreams were always the same. To have fun. To work hard. To do my best. That's what it came down to, really.

And, so, I kept swimming.

My Letting-Go Moment

There was a lot of pressure on me to try out for worlds in the summer of 2009, although it's tough to say, looking back, where that pressure was coming from. It's tough to even call it pressure. Whatever it was, it wasn't coming from my coach, Todd Schmitz, and it certainly wasn't coming from my parents— putting pressure on me wasn't exactly their thing. It's more like it was in the air and all around. Like it was a natural next step. And I guess in a lot of ways it was. I'd been to Olympic trials the year before, so I was already knocking on those doors, ready to take it to the next level. But at the same time, I was still only fourteen years old and there was a lot for me to learn, a lot I could still accomplish at the junior level.

I was ready and I wasn't ready—the story of my young career, it seemed.

The way these meets fell that year, I could swim at the world championship trials and attempt to make the worlds team or I could go to junior nationals. I couldn't do both. So we talked it through. Me and Todd. Me and my parents. Todd and my parents. All four of us, together. We went at it every which way, trying to see what made the most sense. And the thing of it is, I had been swimming really well. I was starting to make a splash. (Sorry, but I'm never one to pass up a corny pun.) People in and around swimming were taking notice, which was really exciting and really weird. I don't mean weird in a bad way, only in a still-getting-used-to-it way. It was unsettling, to have to swim with all these new sets of eyes on me. *Unfamiliar*—that's probably the best word for it, because I was just trying all this stuff on, seeing how I'd perform under the weight of all these expectations.

I'd been making noise at the local level for a long time, setting a bunch of state records and national age-group records, but now the stakes were starting to change. Now we were hearing from coaches, sponsors, USA Swimming officials, a bunch of people who cared about the sport and started to take an interest. All these folks, they were rooting for me, but they didn't exactly know what was best for me. For that, I could look to only Todd and my parents. Todd for the swimming part, and my parents for the Missy part.

This last was key, because my mother and father were the ones who had my back. They were the ones who'd been there for me since the very beginning, who'd continue to be there for me long after I swam my last race. For them, it wasn't just about swimming. It was about me. That's not always the case with young athletes. A lot of parents, a lot of families, they're in a hurry to get to that big stage. You see it in all sports at the youth level, this tendency to push a young athlete to reach for the stars when really what he or she should be doing is building a solid base. Getting comfortable with his or her body, with his or her ability. So that was the tug and pull here. Do you race through every open door, or just the ones that take you where you want to go? At the world championships, which were in Rome that year, my best shot at making the team would have been the 100-meter freestyle, and maybe a relay. As much as we all might have wanted to go to Rome (what fourteen-year-old kid doesn't want to go to Rome?), it didn't make a lot of sense. We ran a kind of cost-benefit analysis, and in the end the practical benefits of competing at the juniors, where I could swim all my events, outweighed the cost of competing at worlds, where (if I made it!) I would most likely swim only one event.

So it was decided, and I was totally on board. As a bonus it worked out that the U.S. Open (the biggest meet of the year for American swimmers other than the World Championships trials) was the week before juniors, in the same pool, so I was able to swim the last couple of days of the open and then take a day off before juniors kicked in. The more time in the pool, the better; the more time in competition, the better. That was the thinking. I ended up breaking a bunch of national age-group records—in some cases, dropping a full second, maybe a second and a half.

I posted five NAGs, four of which still stand as of this

writing, and since those readers who are also swimmers might appreciate it, I'll share those times here:

50-meter freestyle—25.23
100-meter freestyle—54.03
200-meter backstroke—2:09.16
200-meter individual medley—2:12.73

I was beyond thrilled with my results. Out of this one meet, I got my first *Swimming World* cover, so things were starting to click for me. I was turning heads, opening eyes—all of that. Plus, I was feeling strong, invincible—all of that, too. But then something happened to throw me off my game. Remember, one of the reasons I went to juniors that year was to swim all my events, to grow into my God-given ability, to gain some experience. One of the benefits of competing at juniors was learning how to manage all these different swims, all these different strokes, all these different distances, in a back-to-back kind of way. What a lot of people don't realize is how crazy it can feel, in the middle of one of these five-day or weeklong competitions. If you're swimming in multiple events, you're in and out of the pool. There's no letup. There are preliminary heats and finals. There's the time you need to warm up, the time you need to warm down, the time you need between races for rest and recovery. Sometimes the schedule works in your favor, depending on what events you're swimming, and sometimes it works against you, and some swimmers have a hard time keeping it all together. You can't just dive into the pool and put it all out there and hope for the best each time out. You can maybe get away with that on the youth circuit, in local events, but it doesn't work when you're competing against the best of the best. It doesn't work over time. You need some kind of game plan—a long-game plan. And here I was, still figuring it out, learning what I could ask my body to do, how to take care of myself, how to push myself.

It all came to a head for me in my preliminary heat in the 200-meter freestyle, an event I really wanted to do well in. And it wasn't just me—a lot of people were expecting me to do well. It was a morning swim, and I also had to swim the 100-meter backstroke that same morning, so in my head I was dragging. Physically, I was doing okay, but I'd allowed myself to overthink, to worry. The day hadn't even started yet and already I was stuck—that's the way a frantic competition schedule can mess with you, and here it messed with my head a little bit more than I might have expected because I was the center of so much attention. I was trying to find the right balance between preserving my energy and putting in just enough effort to advance to the finals. In prelims, when you get to a higher level of competition, you hold a little something back, especially if you're swimming multiple events on the same day. I was still learning how to apply this strategy, but I understood it in theory. There's no sense going all out and making finals by several seconds, and then finding you have nothing left with the race on the line, right? Trouble is, it's not so easy to see where you are in a crowded field. It all comes down to your times, but if you happen to catch a slow heat, and you're all the way out in front, you need a certain amount of experience to know your pace, to know your body. It's not always enough just to beat the field—the eight fastest times can come from other heats, so you need to understand your body clock. You need to find that sweet spot between just enough and everything you've got.

Well, you can pretty much guess where I'm going with this—I touched the wall at 2:00.81, exactly two one-hundredths of a second behind the girl who slipped into the eighth spot in the finals and about a full second short of where I'd hoped to be. That sweet spot? I wasn't even close to it. Those great expectations? I wasn't about to meet them—not just yet. I saw the time flash on the board and right away I knew. I wasn't where I needed to be, and in my defense I don't think the way I fell short came from a place of cockiness. I wasn't overconfident or coasting. I wasn't taking my spot in the finals for granted. I just didn't know my body, that's all. I didn't know how to manage a busy race day, and as a result I didn't go after it as much as I should have. It was a lesson I had to learn eventually, but eventually kind of snuck up on me that morning.

So what did I do? Well, it would be nice to write that I sucked it up and pressed on, but that's not exactly how it went down. First I had to walk the length of the pool deck to talk to Todd, with my tail between my legs. I'd never really understood that expression until that moment. (We were dog people. We had a great big Alaskan malamute at home, Ruger, and whenever he'd get into some piece of great big dog trouble he'd shamble around the house with his head hung low, his tail between his legs.) I'd messed up and I had to make this walk of shame, in front of all these people who'd been expecting me to do well. So yeah, my tail was definitely between my legs. That walk took just about forever. My head was hung way down low. I wouldn't let myself cry, though. Not yet. The tears would come, but first I had to stand there and listen to my coach chew me out. Better believe it, he lit into me pretty good. He wasn't yelling, not really, but he was not happy with me. Not at all. He gave it to me straight. He said, "You can't just come out here and be comfortable, Missy. You need to push it."

I could only nod, to let Todd know I was listening. If I tried to speak I would've lost it. If I tried to answer him or justify my swim he would've lit into me even harder—in front of all those people!

He said, "It doesn't matter where the other swimmers are around you. You need to give what you have to give in the morning, and save what you have to save for the afternoon."

Again, I nodded. I knew this, of course, but it took hearing it from Todd again for me to remind myself that I needed to swim in that "sweet spot" I talked about earlier, and keep my focus on what it was that I had to do, and not on what everyone else was doing.

He said, "This is a race and you need to race. Never forget that. We don't just go through the motions. We race."

Oh, man . . . I was about to lose it. Right there in front of my teammates. Right there in front of all those fans, the entire swimming community. Right there in front of my parents. Because he was right. He was 110 percent undoubtedly right. But then, just as I thought I'd melt into a puddle by the side of the pool, Todd switched things up. He was done yelling—or, sort of yelling. He was done telling me how I'd screwed up. He knew that message had been delivered and that now it was up to me to determine how it would be received, so he moved on to what I needed to do next, and what I needed to do next was breathe. And focus. And let it go. He put his arm around me and said, "So now you have two options, Missy. You have the hundred back in twenty minutes. You can warm down and get ready to swim your race, or you can stay upset and let this affect you and have a crappy hundred back. Up to you."

Yes, I realized. It was up to me. Totally up to me. The 100-meter backstroke was one of my strongest events—but more important, it was my next event, and I had to rise to it. I had to lift myself up and over this disappointment and get back to work. So this was an important lesson, a great takeaway. A lesson I'd understood in theory and now had to put into practice. A message I'd received and now had to process. This was the first time I really understood the power of letting go, of setting aside a disappointment or a setback and moving on to the next thing. I still felt horrible, though. You have to realize, this was also the first time I'd competed under the weight of all these expectations, under so many sets of eyes. There were all these people watching me, pulling for me. I wondered what they were going to say. They were calling me "Missy the Missile"—a name my father had come up with, a name he'd been proudly promoting, trying to work it into every conversation, every interview (much to my dismay and embarrassment). And here I was in a big race, in a big spot, and the missile was a dud.

For the first time in my young career, I felt like a disappointment. To my parents, to my coach. To myself, mostly.

I bit my lip, still fighting back tears, and headed for the warm-down pool. I put my goggles on, and that's when I finally let myself cry. Oh my goodness . . . I cried and cried. It's what my teammates and I call croggling, when you cry into your goggles like that. One of the side benefits of swimming when the heart of a little girl has not yet become the heart of a champion. Nobody can see what's going on behind those goggles, especially when you're in the water, so I let it all out. I let myself be upset, and when I'd shed the last of my tears, I had let the moment go and was on to the next thing, just like Todd had said. Yes, it was up to me, totally up to me, and I was determined to power past this low moment. It was time to move on, to move up and out, to get back to work. I told myself I didn't like this feeling and would do everything I could to avoid feeling this way ever, ever, ever again.

And so, right then and there, I decided to give it my all, and it put me on top of the medal stand later that night in the 100-meter backstroke. Not only that, I came back and found a way to post a killer time in the B final of the 200-meter freestyle: I swam a 1:58.67—another NAG, this one good enough to have won the finals. As moments go, this B final in the 200-meter free was bittersweet. I'd set a record but lost the race, but in the end I won something far greater than another medal. I'd won this great lesson, found this new power. I came out of that pool thinking, *Okay, this happened. What can I take away from this experience that will make me a stronger swimmer, a better person?* Yeah, I'd screw up from time to time. No, I'm not always going to be at my best. But the thing to do when that happens is to not let it beat you down. The thing to do is move forward. Don't let these disappointments hinder you; let them help you grow.

Let go.

I've thought about that low, dispiriting moment about a

million times since that morning, and each time, I take myself back to just how I was feeling at fourteen years old. I remind myself how I hated that feeling, how it sometimes happens that the feeling finds you anyway, despite your best efforts. Because swimming is like anything else in life. Sometimes you just don't have it and you're caught short. Even the best swimmers in the world have an off day, but when the moment doesn't go your way you have to set it aside and reach for the next moment. In the end, it's just one moment at a time, and it's on you to string those moments together in a winning way. Some of them will go great, and some of them won't go great. You just never know. All you can do is all you can do, and here I believe Todd would have placed the emphasis on the second "all"—as in, "all you can do is *all* you can do."

And do you want to know a funny thing? I didn't talk about any of this stuff with anyone. Not with Todd, not with my parents, not with my friends on the team. Normally, I talked to my parents about everything, but here there was nothing to say. It was a lesson for me, and only for me, because I knew my parents couldn't learn my lessons for me. My coach couldn't learn my lessons for me. It was on me to power through the agonizing feeling of falling short, of knowing I could have done better, knowing I'd let down a whole bunch of people. To find a way to set it all aside and move on.

It was my lesson, and mine alone. And I've never forgotten it.

FOUR

MAKING A SPLASH

I wish I could pinpoint the moment I started thinking of myself as a swimmer. It's not like I woke up one morning, pulled my goggles over my eyes, and started looking out at the world in this one way. All along, the picture of myself I'd carried in my head was that of a gangly, athletic kid, way, way taller than all of my friends. I was no more a swimmer than I was a volleyball player, a basketball player, a daughter, a cousin, a friend.

But somewhere in there a switch got flipped, and swimming became something else—something *more*. And in this new light I became something else—something much, *much* more.

Early on, there was still the matter of what to make of this new self-image. It's one thing to see yourself as a swimmer, and quite another to attack each race like it mattered more than anything else in the world at just that moment. That *competitive* switch? I think I always had it. There was no need to flip it because it was already on. For as far back as I can remember, it was on. See, I don't think you can teach someone to be supercompetitive. That's something you're born with, or not. I absolutely believe a competitive nature can be nurtured by your environment, but I also believe it's got to at least be a *part* of your nature to start. That said, a lot of the athletes I've met who've gone on to compete at a pretty high level, they come from big families. Usually, there are older siblings in the picture. A lot of times, it's the younger sisters with the rough-and-tumble big brothers who go on to become the superstar athletes, like Mia Hamm. But I didn't have that. I was an only child. There was me and my parents, and the images and influences I took in from paying attention to the world around me. In my case, my competitive switch didn't get flipped by playing tag football in the backyard with my brothers every day after school. It didn't come from jostling for position in the family pecking order, or fighting to make myself heard. It came from my parents instilling in me a sense of pride and purpose in everything I did. I was taught to do my best, to give it my all. To *be* my best, to *be* my all. Whatever I was doing, I was meant to do it well. Once I started showing some talent in the pool, that mind-set became a part of my approach. I kept hearing my parents' voices, whispering in my ear, cheering me on, encouraging me to be the best I could be. They weren't teaching me to win, necessarily, and they weren't telling me to be better than the girl in the lane next to me—just to be the best version of myself in each moment. Because nothing else mattered.

Out of that, completely on my own, I started stacking my best self against all the other best selves in the pool. Because, let's not kid ourselves, the girls I was competing against were building on the positive, nurturing impulses they were getting at home, too.

They had parents who were working to instill some of these same values in them, too. And so I made a game of it in my head. Every time I got up on the blocks, I'd look left, I'd look right, and I'd catch myself thinking, *Okay, this is my best. Let's see your best! Let's see whose "best" is best!*

Right away, it became a fun challenge for me. But what's curious is that I never framed the challenge in terms of *beating* my opponent. It wasn't about winning so much as assessing—just to see where I was alongside everyone else. Does that seem like a thin distinction? Like I'm splitting hairs? I can see where it might, but to me the difference wasn't just semantics. It was everything. It was more about seeing what was out there, what I was capable of. If another swimmer touched the wall ahead of me, I was happy for her. I've said this already, I know, but it bears repeating. And I was happy for me, because it allowed me to see what my opponents' "best" looked like, and to think about what I'd have to do to make my "best" a little better. This, too, was in me, somewhere deep down. I came to it on my own, although I'm sure it flowed in a fundamental way from my parents, even though they never sat me down to talk about competing in just this way. If I'd asked them, they'd have told me that the only opponent who could beat me was me. They were referring to the limitations I might place on myself, of course, but also to the wall I'd hit if I allowed myself to overthink or overanalyze my swimming.

Every time I got out of the pool, it didn't matter if it was a good race or a bad race in terms of the result, I judged my performance based on whatever goals I'd set. As a swimmer, these goals had nearly everything to do with my times. If I met my times, I was happy. If I beat them, I was happier still. If I came up short, I was upset. And if I was upset, my mother would come up to me and talk me through it.

She'd say, "Was there anything more you could have done?"

And I'd think about this—really and truly. Sometimes, there were things I could have done better. Sometimes, there weren't. We'd talk about it, and then she'd send me off to my room to get ready for dinner and say, "Something to work on for next time, honey."

The idea wasn't to make my "best" better than the other girls' but to make it better than it was, every opportunity I could get. To set it up so that I'd have some new target to shoot for, every race I swam.

My best effort—that was the only expectation ever placed on me by my parents. In school, in swimming, in sports in general. It was such a tremendous gift, for them to empower me in this way. And I'm not just saying that because this is *their* book, too, and they're reading over my shoulder! Truth is, I grew up surrounded by other kids with pushy parents who were always on them to go, fight, win! It's like these parents graduated from the Vince Lombardi School of Parenting, where the motto was "Winning isn't everything; it's the only thing." Their children would always get so knotted up inside before a meet or a game, and if things didn't go their way they'd get even more upset than they might have been on their own, because they were made to feel like they'd let their parents down. It was an awful dynamic, but I'd see it all the time, and it would always break my heart to see other kids terrified after a disappointing race because they knew their parents would be unhappy or angry at them. Things were different in our house. It's like my mom and dad graduated from the Marlo Thomas School of Parenting, where the motto was "Free to be . . . you and me."

Make no mistake, I wanted my parents to be proud of me, but the way to do that was to put my best foot forward. That's all.

> **MOM:** That was really the only thing we ever empha-sized in our household, to give it your all. And Missy took that message to heart. Whatever sport she was playing, whatever activity she was pursuing, she gave it her all. Even her friendships were molded in this way. She wouldn't take anyone's feelings for granted, went out of her way to let her friends know how impor-tant they were to her. Even though I was never an ath-lete, I could relate to placing importance on winning and doing your best. Dick played football, of course, so he understood what it meant to compete and to win, but I think we both realized that the message we wanted for our daughter, the environment we wanted for our daughter, was more about effort and the pur-suit of excellence, rather than the excellence itself. It might seem like a fine distinction, but to us it was meaningful. It was the difference between working to become a champion athlete and working to become a champion human being. To us, it only mattered that you put in your best effort, and that you tried to do a little better each time out.

The competition piece, it came from within, and along with it came the drive to be the best swimmer I could be. Early on, I recognized the value in listening to my coaches, working on my strokes, perfecting my turns. When I first met Todd and started swimming for the Colorado Stars, I was still at the level where the kids with the most natural ability tended to do well. But that would change. With Todd's help, I started paying attention to my technique. I learned where I was strong, where I was weak, and what I could do to fill the space in between. I learned, for example, the importance of having a high elbow, which fingers were supposed to enter the water first, the most efficient way to pull and hold water. Of course, there's no one *right* way to swim— every swimmer has a distinctive style, what works best for him or her, so I became a student of the sport, studying everyone in the pool. I got so good at it I could pick someone out just by the way he or she swam, the same way you could recognize some-one's gait when you fell in behind them at a crowded mall. One look and you'd think, *Hey, that's so-and-so,* just by the way they moved.

I didn't start studying film until much, much later, but by the time I did I was mostly looking at ways to improve my own stroke, the things I had to work on. A lot of times, they'd set up these clinics for us and we'd study Michael Phelps's turns, or Natalie Coughlin's underwaters, and try to learn by their exam-ples. That's a great way to learn, really, but I always found the most effective use of this type of technology was to turn it on myself. When I could see what I was doing right, what I was do-ing wrong, what I needed to change, I was able to get back in the water and make those adjustments.

Like every young swimmer, I had to learn a proper racing dive. It's a rite of passage. My father had taught me to dive when

I was little, when I was diving just for fun. He had no idea what he was doing, but his methods were effective enough. The way he taught me was by diving himself. I'd watch and try to copy him, which was pretty much the way I'd go on to study Michael and Natalie on video. I was a good mimic, I guess. A lot of kids, they forget to tuck in their chin, or maybe they're just afraid, and they end up doing a belly flop, but that was never a problem for me. It was actually a blast. Once I got the motion down, I used to practice at every opportunity, usually when my father and I were goofing around in the pool or at the lake. It got to where diving became the most natural thing, the most fun thing. But what my father couldn't teach me was a racing dive—basically, how to start.

> **DAD:** I couldn't really teach Missy how to swim in terms of technique, but I could help her get comfortable in the water. Although if you must know, she didn't really need my help. She was just a natural. I had her in the ocean with me when she was an infant, and she just loved it. She was snorkeling with me by the time she was three. I hadn't meant to take her out with me—she was so young—but we were on a beach in Maui, and we made the mistake of letting Missy put on all that gear, the mask and the snorkel and the fins, just to splash around in the whitewater. We were on the South Shore, and it was a beautiful day; the water was clear. I was on our blanket, reading a novel, and all of a sudden I heard D.A. let out a scream. She'd been watching Missy, and she'd started to wade out to keep

a close eye on her, but D.A. wasn't a very good swimmer, and she was trying to keep up with this little girl with fins who swam like a fish even then. I raced into the water and started swimming with all my might, and I finally caught up to Missy all the way out there, beyond the shore break. She was getting knocked around by the waves, but she didn't care. She was totally fine, totally in her element. She'd been chasing some fish, apparently, and she was fascinated by the way they moved, by all the colors. She kept pointing and laughing and saying, "Did you see that one, Daddy?" and "Look, there's a yellow one!" and "Aren't they beautiful?" Poor D.A. almost had a heart attack, her little girl out there among those big waves, but Missy just had no fear in the water. No fear at all.

And then there's one other story I just have to tell, as long as I have the floor. We were up at our house in Grand Lake, the tail end of winter, and Missy was determined to be the first one in the lake that season. She was about seven years old. I don't know what put that thought into her head, but when Missy got started on a thing, there was just no stopping her. So we went out to the lake, and there was ice and snow all around. The lake was still frozen, but there were holes in the ice where the current was running. It was starting to thaw. She walked in to her knees, screaming with delight, and then she was in up to her waist, still having a blast. I hollered at her to be careful, but she just waved me off and dove in the rest of the way, headfirst, and when she popped back up I took her picture. Her hair was all frozen-wet, but she was smiling.

That's a great story, Dad—but what my father failed to mention was that my parents bet me I couldn't dunk my head in the freezing water, so obviously I *had* to do it!

One of the great benefits to swimming with Todd and the Colorado Stars was that the club didn't really believe in specialization. A lot of times, even at the lower ends of the youth level, you'll see a swimmer start to focus almost exclusively on one stroke, one distance. That's a mistake, I think. If you spend all that time at eight and nine and ten years old doing breaststroke, then you might start to believe you're a breaststroker for life. If you mix it up, you give yourself a chance to grow into an event, and you set it up so you can better help your team, once you start to compete for your club or your school.

Probably the best argument I could make about the importance of practicing every stroke is to point to my own development as a swimmer. My stroke changed as I grew. I developed new areas of strength. In fact, my three Olympic trial cuts in 2008—my first!—didn't include backstroke, which has now become one of my strengths, so you never know how things are going to work out.

We would swim everything, and we'd learn as a group. The coaches wouldn't get into the pool with you—that's really something you only see at the beginner, learn-to-swim level. Our coaches would demonstrate the proper technique by the side of the pool and then we'd have at it. Very quickly, we could see which of our teammates had it down, and those were the ones we tried to copy in the pool. There's a lot of imitation when you're just starting out, which is why it's so important to have an attentive coach, because if you find yourself mimicking the wrong person you can develop some bad habits.

The drills they had us do were very basic. For example, for our freestyle stroke, they would have us do an exaggerated fingertip drag, which was designed to help us keep and maintain a high elbow catch, but when you're a little kid you're not thinking about your form. You're just thinking, *Yay, we get to drag our fingertips in the water!* So there were a lot of fun drills like that, intended to reinforce what we were supposed to be doing. (And if you must know, the fingertrip drill is still my favorite.)

Todd remembers that I didn't like his practices in the very beginning, because I used to like to race so much. I don't remember it quite this way, but I'll have to give him the benefit of the doubt—after all, he was the adult back then (barely!), and I was just a kid. But I do remember how I loved to race. I loved being out in front, swimming in clear water. And I just loved that feeling of getting up on the blocks and knowing there were all these awesome swimmers around me, and that we were all going to push one another to go really, really fast.

It was my very favorite thing.

As I moved up the ladder with the Stars, I started swimming with Nick Frasersmith, the coach who'd eventually take me to my first Olympic trials, in 2008, when I was thirteen years old. Nick played a central role in the two major decisions I had to face as a youth swimmer—decisions we considered as a family but were ultimately left to me. (At least, my parents allowed me to *think* the decisions were mine, but for all I know they might have exercised their veto power if I'd leaned another way.) I'll get to those decisions in a bit, but for now I simply wanted to introduce Nick, because it was while I was swimming with him that I started to make some real noise beyond the state of Colorado. (It's not like I ever stopped working with Todd, but for a while there, as I moved up to the next Stars group, he kept coaching the younger kids while I spent more and more time with some of the other coaches at the club, and it began with Nick.)

One of the first big meets we traveled to when I started swimming with the older Stars group came with one of the first big disappointments of my career, together with one of the first great surprises. We went to Indianapolis, to the Indiana University–Purdue University Indianapolis (IU–PUI) campus. We all knew the meet by the initials IU–PUI, so for years we called it the "Oooey-Pooey," never really knowing what we were saying, or what the initials stood for. It was a big team trip, and a great adventure, and for a lot of us it was the first time swimming at a major meet out of state. We didn't take a lot of our younger swimmers, so at twelve years old I was one of the youngest ones there.

Over the years, I've come to love the IU–PUI pool. For whatever reason, I tend to swim well there, and I get such a great vibe, but on this one trip things didn't exactly go my way—at least, not at first. I remember that we tapered for this meet, which was completely new to me. At twelve years old, there's no real reason to rest. I could swim all day at that age. But Todd and Nick were expecting me to do well in the 200 back, so they wanted me to rest. That was best my event, and I'd been going best time after best time, so it felt to them like the NAG for eleven- to twelve-year-olds was within reach.

Remember, my parents were never the type to put any pressure on me, so they kind of soft-pedaled my coaches' expectations, but I knew what everyone around me was thinking. And they never let me feel like I was *expected* to break a record or go a certain time, but they celebrated like crazy when I did, in this way letting me know that there was a certain value in winning. Adults can be funny. They put it out there in this casual way that you can set this great record, and in the same breath they try to tell you it's no big deal. (Talk about confusing!) I knew my times, and knew what I was capable of, but I tried not to let that get in the way of the adventure. Mostly, I wanted to have a good time with my friends. To fly on a plane together, to camp out at the gate while we were waiting to take off, playing cards, laughing. An NAG was almost the last thing on my mind, but it wouldn't be accurate to suggest I wasn't thinking about it at all. I was thinking about it because my coaches were thinking about it, because my parents were thinking about it.

Once we got to the meet, I still didn't feel any pressure, but something happened. Actually, that's not the best way to put it, because it sounds like something happened beyond my control, which wasn't at all the case. What happened was I was disqualified, so obviously it was on me. I hadn't been DQ'd from a race since I was eight years old, and *that* had been my only time!

Usually, you see it with a swimmer who's overeager—maybe it'll be because of a false start. But here it was because I'd spent too long going into one of my backstroke turns. The way it works, if you spend too much time on your stomach going into a turn, that's a disqualification—they don't call it *back*stroke for nothing, people! It was more of a technicality. I knew all the rules, of course, but I was off by a beat or two. (Hey, I was twelve!) In backstroke, at every level, there's a specific amount of time you're given to make each turn. If you're on your stomach for too long, over too great a distance, that's a DQ. Even as kids, we spent a lot of time working on our turns—it can get tricky. As soon as you flip over, you kind of stop moving. You can still kick with your legs, but you start to lose momentum, so by flipping onto my stomach too early I'd given myself no advantage. In fact, you can make the case that I'd actually given myself a disadvantage by flipping too soon, because I'd sacrificed a lot of forward momentum.

Still, I had no idea I was about to be called out on this. I just swam my race—and I was first to the wall, as hoped. But then I saw this official marching over to my lane, her eyes locked on mine. I didn't know what to think. At first I thought she was coming over to say hi, maybe congratulate me, but then I could see she wasn't smiling, so I had no idea what was up.

She said, "I'm so sorry, Missy, but you were too long on your stomach going into your turn on the third wall. We had to disqualify you."

I remember thinking it was interesting that she'd mentioned the violation came on the third turn. I knew I was way out in front, knew I was swimming well, knew I had a shot at the record; I guess the size of the moment was a little too big for me, just then. I was so worried about my sprint to the finish, I let my mechanics get away from me.

My heart sank. Really, I was devastated. To come into this big meet with all these great expectations, and then to go and do the polar opposite, to get disqualified . . . it was so unnerving, so upsetting. Also embarrassing. Despite being so young, I had a little bit of a leadership position on our team, so a lot of my friends had gathered around the pool to see me swim this race and possibly set that record. To have to take this walk of shame, after everyone could see what had happened, it was a lot to take in.

Let's just say I croggled my little eyes out in the warm-down pool, but then I had to come back the next day and compete in another few events. My teammates were very supportive. They came up to me, hugged me, said all the right things. My parents and coaches, too. What could anyone have said, really? I was still at that stage in my career when I was learning how to deal with mistakes, and disappointments, and having a bad race, but I knew to set my embarrassment aside and focus on my next event. I'd lost points for my team, and I was determined to win them back, so that became my motivation. It was the only thing that mattered, really. Here's where a lot of the lessons I'd learned from my parents kicked back in, about the importance of being a team player. I couldn't mope around for the rest of the meet like some Debbie Downer. My job was to cheer on my teammates and swim my best and try to have fun. Because, even then, I was supposed to be the fun, energetic one. That was my role.

The next day, I had the 200 freestyle, which wasn't my best

event. I hadn't really started to specialize yet, but I was stronger at the 100 free than I was at the 200. I had a good swim in prelims and then came back to set an NAG in the finals, which nobody was expecting. My time of 1:49.84 made me the first girl under the age of thirteen to break 1:50 in the 200 free, short course, which was just so thrilling. And so unexpected. (And just as a side note, I'd go on to become the first woman to break 1:40 seven years later—so that was a fun record to have, especially because of the mark that had come before it.)

And the thing of it is, nobody knew it was an NAG at the time. Nobody, that is, except for my mother.

Here, I'll let her tell it. . . .

MOM: I could see from where I was sitting that Missy and Todd didn't even know it was a record time. They weren't expecting it, so of course they weren't looking for it. Even more than that, I could see from the way the race officials were moving around the deck that nobody had any idea. But when I go to these meets, I have all my little stat sheets, assembled by my sister, Cathy. We sit together and we know all the cut times, all the splits. We're like the official scorers. Missy teases me about it, because she just wants to swim. She tells me I'm a little nuts, and I guess I am, but this is how I follow along. I knew I had to tell them it was an NAG, so I shouted down to Todd from the stands, which is something I never do. We're always incredibly careful to keep quiet at these meets, Dick and I, but here I couldn't help myself. Missy looked up and

I could see she was mortified, to have her mother shouting down to her coach, like I was one of those pushy parents, but when I finally got Todd's attention I yelled, "That was an NAG!" Todd looked puzzled. Usually, he's pretty good about knowing which records were in play, which times Missy was shooting for. He said, "No, D.A., I don't think so." So I waved my sheets in the air and started to climb down to the railing. He came over to meet me, and I kind of tossed my sheets over to him. I said, "Look!" I was so excited. So he looked, and sure enough, it was an NAG, so right away he was just as excited as I was. We both started jumping up and down, and then Missy picked up on it, and she was thrilled. Still mortified by her nutty mother, running down the steps, waving these sheets of paper, but thrilled.

What happens when you set an NAG is that meet officials start to go a little crazy. It's like nobody had ever set a record before. As I remember it, this was the last event of the night, and a lot of people had started to leave, but we had to stay while they certified the course and measured the pool, dotted all the i's and crossed all the t's. I always thought that was so funny, that they didn't certify and measure *before* the start of every major meet. It seemed a little upside-down to me, but there it was. Once all the logistics were in order, they took me out to the 10-meter diving platform and had me pose for a bunch of pictures, and I remember thinking that these records were one of the great things about our sport. Right then and there, in the middle of this cool moment, cameras going off, hugs flying, I stopped to think that I hadn't just won this one race. This NAG meant I'd also beat out everyone my age who'd ever swum in this pool, in this state, in this country. It reminded me that every time I stepped to the starting blocks, I was competing against the history of my sport.

~~

Out of that "Ooooey-Pooey" meet, I started to get a little more attention—and not for my DQ, thank goodness!

A couple of months later, we were in Orlando, which would have been one of my last opportunities to make my trial cuts—the times I needed to post in each event over a defined calendar period in order to qualify for Olympic trials in those events. There'd be other meets before Olympic trials, which were to be held in Omaha that year, but that meet in Orlando was the one Nick and Todd had me tapering for, and that was the one right in front of me, so there was a sense that that would be my last, best opportunity for that Olympic cycle. It was so completely unbelievable that my coaches were even thinking that way when I was just twelve years old, but because it was an Olympic year they said it made sense to hold it out there and see what happened. I'd been posting some strong times, just a little bit off the cuts, but not by a significant amount.

Now, I hadn't done a lot of long-course swimming since the previous summer, and I guess it makes sense here to talk a little bit about the differences between long course and short course—at least, as it applied to me. Even as kid, I was stronger in long course, because my walls have never been my strong suit. Why? Because I've always struggled with my underwaters. If I were to swim a short-course event these days it would be mostly underwater. It can really impact your time if you don't have strong underwaters, because if you're going fifteen meters underwater each time you flip turn off a wall, you don't leave yourself any time to make up the difference. You could have a much faster stroke, but the swimmer who's mastered his or her underwaters has a clear advantage.

Long-course events are a great equalizer. You'll see a lot of swimmers who've excelled at short course really struggle transitioning to long course, because what made them strong at one distance doesn't really translate to the other. In long course, they have to rely on their strokes to a far greater degree, and maybe their strokes just aren't that strong. You can't get to long course and *not* rely on your strokes, because that longer distance will just eat you alive.

I was swimming both lengths at this Orlando meet, which meant I was swimming short course in the morning and long course at night. When I was twelve, I could get away with that type of thing—really, it was no biggie. For the first three days of the meet, I had the 100 and 200 free and the 100 and 200 backstroke, and I was swimming really well. I was going best times in all of my events, but in each race I was falling just short of the trial cut—by a few hundredths of a second, maybe a tenth of a second. I think if you added up *all* the tiny fractions of a second I was off, the total would have still been a fraction of a second, so even though I was swimming great, it wasn't quite the level of *greatness* you need to make it to Olympic trials.

I suppose I could have told myself I was still just twelve years old, and that coming *this close* to the trial cuts was a kind of moral victory, but I'd never used my age as an excuse. That wasn't going to get me anywhere. It didn't matter that I was twelve and everyone else in my heat was sixteen, seventeen, eighteen. I didn't get a head start, or an extra second taken off my time, just because I was five years younger. It didn't matter what it said on our birth certificates. I was good, but not good enough. End of story.

Still, I was happy with how I was swimming. I wanted to go to Olympic trials, but I couldn't really get down on myself, going all those best times. Was I disappointed? Sure. Was I devastated? No, not really. A lot of other swimmers were devastated not to be making their cuts, but they were much older than me, and the four-year Olympic calendar can be cruel. I could come back and qualify at sixteen years old and still be one of the youngest in the pool, so time was on my side. But that wasn't true for everyone.

But that was just the first three days of the meet. On the final day, I had the 200 individual medley (IM) and the 50 free—not exactly my best events. My underwaters weren't strong, so the 50 was always tough for me, basically because you're underwater for a greater percentage of the overall race distance. In a 100 or a 200, you have all that extra distance to cover, so you have a chance to cover up the shortfall. But in the 50, if you're behind in that first fifteen, coming off the start, it creates such a challenge to try to catch up—and let's remember, your underwater on a dive is just as important as your underwater on a turn. There's just so much that can go wrong for me in a 50-meter swim. Hard to believe all these things have to line up in just the right way for me to even have a fighting chance, all in about twenty-four seconds.

Even so, I'd somehow made it to the finals in each of these two events, so as I was getting ready for them I kind of set aside my hope to make Olympic trials and told myself it just wasn't going to happen this time out. And I was good with that. My four strongest events were done, and I'd come up just short, so now the thing to do was leave everything I had in the pool.

By every other measure, I was having a great meet, so I decided to just enjoy it and try to finish strong. The IM came first. I was in the outside lane, and I could see that I was second to the wall on the fly, and I remember being pretty surprised about that. Normally, I was back in the middle of the pack, so either I was swimming really well or the rest of the field was flat. (For the sake of posterity, let's agree that I was swimming really well, okay?)

Next came the backstroke leg, and this was where I usually made up some ground, maybe even started to pull ahead a little bit. The goal was always to build up a bit of a cushion, because my breaststroke was horrible. (No changes there!) But because I'd had such a strong fly, I was able take a nice lead in the back, so when I got to my breaststroke the plan was to do my best and try to hold on. Somehow, I did—with a surprising time. At this point, as I made my turn, I could see Todd running alongside me on the pool deck. Since I was in the outside lane, he was right in my face, going completely psycho.

Now, one thing you need to know about Todd—he makes a lot of noise when his swimmers are competing. Mostly, it's just to make sure we can hear him, but I've heard other swimmers, other coaches, other parents, complain about the way he sometimes whoops it up. When you're swimming for him, you appreciate the encouragement. We all think it's hysterical, when we're watching one of our teammates and he's hollering and whistling and doing his thing. But here he was, just four or five feet away from me, jumping up and down, screaming. It was over the top, even for him, but from his tone and his body language I figured it must have been pretty good.

Every time I pulled my head out of the water, I'd catch a glimpse of Todd, who stayed right with me over that final fifty.

When I touched the wall, before I even turned around, I heard Todd scream—like a caterwauling *yee-hah!* kind of scream. He was super excited, almost obnoxiously so. And in that moment I couldn't think what he was so excited about. I'd gone best times in my 100 and 200 free, in my 100 and 200 back, and he was no-where near as pumped about those results. For a beat I thought maybe he was so excited because I'd done so well in an off-event. It's not like I'd won my heat or anything. I finished second, which was a good showing for me at this meet, but not *this* good.

Keep in mind, I had no idea what the trial cut was for the 200 IM, because nobody thought it was within reach, so the thought that I'd hit that number didn't even enter my mind. (That number: 2:20.49.) I wasn't gunning for it, so I wasn't thinking about it. But I did hit that number (2:19.12!), and Todd knew I'd hit it as soon as he saw my splits coming out of my breaststroke and heading into my free. That's why he was so stoked. But even when he was screaming at me—"That was a trial cut! That was a trial cut!"—it still took a while to sink in.

It was almost surreal, to swim at that level, when you're not even going for it, but before I had a chance to get my head around what had happened, I had to swim my 50 free in twenty minutes. It wasn't until I was warming down, swimming easy, that I was able to process the race and what it meant. That's when it finally registered. When I allowed myself to think, *Oh my gosh, I just got my trial cut. I'm going to Olympic trials!* I started beaming ear to ear, I was just so happy. I wanted to be anywhere else but in that warm-down pool. I wanted to be in the stands, celebrating with my parents and Auntie C.J. I wanted to be on the pool deck, celebrating with Todd and my teammates.

I couldn't even focus on my 50 free, but I'd been through those paces so many times before it was like I was on autopilot. I'd had the mini-disappointment of just missing my times over the first three days, even though my times were better than ever, and then the surprising thrill of qualifying in one of my weakest events, so there was absolutely no pressure headed into this final event.

I just had to swim. And guess what? Without the weight of the expectations I'd brought with me to Orlando, I was able to relax and swim with abandon . . . *and I qualified in the 50 free, too!* With a time of 26.21, just under the Olympic trial time of 26.39! It was like the icing on the cake, and totally unexpected.

Crazy, huh?

Then, just to put an exclamation point on things, I got my trials cut in the 100 free at another meet a few weeks later, so I was headed off to Omaha to swim in three events. I turned thirteen by the time Olympic trials rolled around on the calendar, but I was still the second youngest swimmer there. (The youngest was Grace Carlson, who went on to swim at Stanford, who made it in *her* 50 free just a couple of weeks before trials.)

And I was the happiest little thirteen-year-old ever, ever, ever.

DAD: One of the things I used to marvel at about Missy was the way she handled pressure, and the way she handled it was basically to set it aside. The magnitude of this moment, swimming at Olympic trials, it was felt mostly by her mother and me, not by Missy. And the ways we felt it were not like what we were seeing from the other parents in Omaha. There were more than ten thousand people in the stands in Omaha. But that didn't faze Missy. Nothing fazed her. I thought back to how things were before a big football game in college, the pregame tensions that filled our locker room. We had these 250-pound linemen, dressed in full gear, sweating like pigs, vomiting in the toilet before game time. Even pro athletes will tell you how they get nervous before they take the field. At the youth level, in a sport like swimming, I used to see it all the time. Children used to melt down by the side of the pool before their events. Sometimes, they'd get so nervous before a race that they refused to swim. Here in Omaha it was all ratcheted up, because there were 1,250 swimmers gathered, from all across America, and only fifty or so would walk away with a spot on the Olympic team. And it's not like you can come back the next year and give it another go. You're on a four-year cycle, so for most of these kids, this was their one and only shot. And maybe you'll come up short by a hair, just a fraction of a fraction of a second, and then you think of all those families who've put so much into this moment. We didn't want Missy to feel any of that pressure. To D.A. and me, just then, this was the absolute pinnacle. Just seeing Missy make it here to Olympic trials, we couldn't have been more proud. We had no reason to think she'd go any further than this right here, and that was okay with us. We were thrilled just to be there with our daughter, and watching her swim on this stage, at this level. Whatever happened after that, it would just be a bonus, but we weren't counting on anything, and I think Missy took this in and began to feel the same way. Obviously, she wanted to do well, but she knew this moment wouldn't define her.

⌒

Omaha was memorable for a lot of reasons, but I want to turn my focus away from the pool and back to family. Just to be clear, the swimming part was one *pinch-me* moment after another. I ended up going best times in all three of my events, but I didn't make the semifinals (the top sixteen!) in any of them. And I was completely okay with that. I was just so happy to be there and to be at my absolute best and to be in the company of all these amazing swimmers. Think about *that*! I was thirteen years old and surrounded by some of the best people the sport has ever seen— changing in the same locker room as them, walking in the same hallways as them, getting in the same pool as them, lining up to give autographs to the same fans as them. I wanted to swim well and be at my best, but I knew my main goal at this meet was to learn as much as possible while I was surrounded by such incredible company.

So that part was great, and couldn't have gone any better. Because, let's be real, there was no way I was touching the wall ahead of any of those giants and earning a spot on the Olympic team, and at thirteen years old! This was as good as it was getting for me, just then. It's the best I could have expected. But what stays with me most from that first trip to Omaha was the part I *wasn't* expecting—namely, the way my family rallied around and turned up to support me. I'm not talking about my parents, because they were a constant in my life. In those days, they went to pretty much every meet. And I'm not talking about my auntie C.J., Mom's sister, and uncle Doug, Dad's brother, who'd already established themselves as my biggest non-parent fans and hit the road with us at many of my meets.

No, for this trip, my cousin Darryl arranged a big surprise for me—one of my favorite memories from my swimming career, then and now. He worked the phones and set it up so he and three of my cousins were able to meet us in Omaha and see me swim in what might turn out to be the biggest meet of my life. Like my dad said, we had no idea back then what the future might hold. This might have been as far as I'd ever go in the sport, and my parents and I would have been okay with that. Just making it to those Olympic trials would have been a fine and fitting highlight, something I could always look back on with pride, if that's as far as swimming would take me. So of course it meant the world to me that my cousins would drop whatever they were doing and come to cheer me on.

All of this happened without my knowing. My parents had

rented a two-bedroom loft in Omaha, and I knew Auntie C.J. would be joining them there. What I didn't know was that my cousins Darryl, Chelsea, Sean, and Laura would be there, too. I'd always loved my cousins and cherished the time we spent together. As an only child, I think our big family vacations meant more to me than anyone, because my cousins had siblings to goof around with back home. Me, I just had my seven cousins, so I always looked forward to seeing them. They were *my* siblings. Trouble was, we were spread out all over North America, and now that I was traveling to all these meets and spending all that time in the pool, it was harder and harder for me to get away. Our schedules never seemed to match up. It never even occurred to me that they would come to Omaha, just to see me swim for a grand total of a few minutes. Darryl and Laura were all the way up in Toronto, and Sean and Chelsea were in Racine, Wisconsin, so it made no sense to even think about it.

My uncle Drew volunteered to drive Sean and Chelsea from Racine to Chicago, where they met up with Laura and Darryl, who were driving from Toronto. From there, it was about another five hundred miles to Omaha. Laura and Darryl shared the driving—Chelsea and Sean were just fifteen and sixteen. They got to Omaha in time to make it to prelims on the first morning of competition. When I went out to the hall of the natatorium after my morning swim I stopped to sign some autographs, and there was Chelsea, standing in line with the other fans. I think I looked right through her at first, not putting two and two together, but then I figured it out and screamed with delight.

Oh my gosh! I was over the moon, and from there we fell right into our goofy cousin routines. It was such a special, magical visit, and it came with its own unexpected twist. We all got stuck in an elevator for several hours. Mom was freaking out, worrying that one of us would break a leg from a seven-story drop. While we were waiting for the firefighters to arrive, the five cousins pulled out a deck of cards and started playing euchre on the floor of the elevator. We just figured we might as well make the best of a bad situation. It ended up that we had to crawl through the elevator ceiling and get out on the floor above—not exactly the way a swimmer is meant to get her rest between events when she's in town for Olympic trials, but I didn't care. I was too busy laughing hysterically at my cousin Chelsea flirting with the firefighters! The rescue personnel kept telling us not to look down, because we could see the open elevator shaft going all the way to the subbasement level, and I remember looking back at my poor mother, who was plainly terrified as they guided her to safety. We kids all thought this was a great thrill, but Mom is still a little freaked out by elevators!

Yeah, I might have been trapped in an elevator for a couple of hours, waiting to be rescued by the local fire department, but that was nothing. What mattered was that I was an only child surrounded by my "big" family, in a place I never imagined I'd be, at a time in my life when I never thought I'd be there, competing against some of the best swimmers in the world. It was all good.

⌒

Like a lot of clubs, the Colorado Stars is a not-for-profit, coach-run organization. It was started by Nick Frasersmith a few years before I joined, and quickly became one of the most popular clubs in the area. One of the reasons for that was that Nick hired a bunch of fun, talented coaches to work with different age and ability groups. But there's not a lot of money in club swimming, especially at the smaller local clubs. Todd had another job when he started coaching part-time. And Nick was working two other jobs—as a high school coach and a groundskeeper. Coaches like Nick and Todd did what they did for the love of the sport, not for the money, but they still had to make a living, so at some point I think Nick decided he needed to spend time with his young family. When that happened, Todd became the CEO and head coach of Stars, and the head coach of the senior group, so we were reunited. The club continued to operate as before, with the same focus—only now Todd was the face of the team. And, significantly for me, he was once again my hands-on coach, because I was swimming with the senior group.

Several months later, Nick wanted to come back to Stars. The job he'd taken didn't work out, and he thought he'd made a mistake, leaving the club he'd started, but by this point Todd was doing great and the club was thriving and there was no way to bring Nick back into the fold without pushing Todd away. I was just a kid, not really paying any attention to this stuff, and my parents weren't really focused on it, either. Nick and I never really talked about it, so this is just me, connecting the dots. But then we learned that Nick was starting another club, and a lot of my friends were planning to leave Stars to go swim with him.

I was really broken up about this, because about half my friends were planning to leave Stars to follow Nick. For me, this was a huge blow—but my parents left it to me to figure this one out for myself. This was one of those major decisions I mentioned earlier, and in a lot of ways it was a no-brainer. I was sticking with Todd—he was like a father figure to me, a mentor, and a coach, all rolled into one. I absolutely *loved* training with him, and I had no doubt that beyond my own passion for the sport he was the main reason why I'd been able to swim at such a high level. But staying put on Stars came at a price. It would cost me a ton of friendships that meant the world to me. One of the things I loved best about swimming were the people I got to see every day because of it. I'd been swimming with some of these people since I was seven years old, and it's not like I could just see them in school. We lived all over Colorado. Some families drove an hour or more just to make it to our practices.

Even worse, I started hearing from a lot of my friends, away from the pool, who were calling me up and trying to get me to leave Stars and join this new club. A lot of the parents were talking and scheming, too. It was a confusing time, especially for a naive little girl who just wanted to swim and be with her friends. There was a lot of intrigue, but to Nick's great credit he never came out and asked me to leave Todd and join his club instead. He's an incredible coach, an incredible teacher, an incredible person. He would never have done that. He did, however, let it be known in a more global way that *all* of his old swimmers were welcome, so it became *the* hot topic among my group of friends. It was heartbreaking, really, because so many of my friends were deciding to go swim with Nick. I completely understood their decisions, because Nick was such a wonderful coach, but that didn't change the fact that I was going to miss each and every one of them—so, so much.

Logistically, it was tough as well, because Nick ended up with our pool. That sounds a whole lot worse than it was, because neither club had its own facility. Stars rented space from one of the high schools, and when the club's contract was up, since Nick was probably the one who'd negotiated it in the first place, he was able to get the contract for his new team. Of course, it helped that the pool was at the high school where he coached—the high school I'd eventually choose to attend.

But I'll get to that. . . .

> **MOM:** Do you want to know when Dick and I realized Todd was the right coach for Missy? She was eleven or twelve, and every year Todd would sit down with his swimmers individually and go over their goals. From a very early age, Missy had to present her goals. At seven, maybe it was to remember to bring her swim cap and her goggles to every practice. At eight, maybe it was to pack her swim bag herself, so Mom didn't have to do it. Whatever it was, it was a big goal at the time, and Todd would then incorporate these things into what he was doing. So at twelve, Missy went to Todd and said she wanted to get her Olympic trial times. Just to put this in perspective, Missy had her sectional times by the time she was eleven, so she knew all about this stuff. She'd hear other kids talking about their junior national or national times, and she knew Olympic trial times were even faster, and this was what she wanted. And Todd was great about it. Instead of saying, "What? You must be kidding," he went, "Great! How are you going to do it?" And Missy walked him through it. She'd already thought about it.

She'd work more on her starts, because she was slow off the blocks. She'd work harder on her dry-land workouts. She had a whole list, and together the two of them came up with a plan to make Missy's goals happen, the same way he helped her remember to bring her goggles to practice when she was little. Todd shared that conversation with me, but Missy didn't. It was between her and her coach. And I just thought that was wonderful.

Now, if you've followed my career, you'll know that my relationship with Nick Frasersmith didn't end when he left the Colorado Stars, because he became my high school coach after that, at Regis Jesuit. My decision to go to Regis was the other major decision my parents left to me to make, and even though it came about for mostly swimming reasons it very quickly became one of the most formative, foundational, faith-affirming decisions of my life. Really, it changed everything.

All along, I was on track to go to Arapahoe High School, which was about five minutes from my house. Littleton, Colorado, has a great public school system, so there was no reason for me to look to go anywhere else. That is, there was no reason to go anywhere else until seventh or eighth grade, when I started to come into my own as a swimmer. Remember, by eighth grade I'd already gone to Olympic trials. Clearly, swimming meant a lot to me, and it made sense to find the best high school swimming program in the area, so I could grow as an athlete and compete at the highest level and still get the best possible education. The challenge was finding a school and a program that would accommodate my insane, uncertain travel schedule, now that I was going to all these national and international meets. The swimming program at Arapahoe was very strong. In some years, the school ran out some terrific teams. So I went to Arapahoe and took a tour of the school, met with the principal, spent some time with the swim coach and members of the team. I knew a lot of the girls already, of course, from local club meets, but I really wanted to give the school a long look.

I also looked at one of Arapahoe's rivals, Cherry Creek High School, which was another public school, with a much bigger student body. Their high school team had been state champions twenty-six times in the past thirty-five years—a real swimming powerhouse. But I felt lost in the halls of Cherry Creek. I wanted to be at a school where I could say hi to everybody when I walked down the hall, where I could get to know my teachers, where I could walk from one end of the campus to another without feeling like I was already on a college campus. It just wasn't for me. Plus, if I decided to go there we would have had to move, so it really was a nonstarter.

Then I visited Regis Jesuit, and the moment I walked into the front hall of the school I knew my search was over. I felt God for the first time in my life, and I felt him in that instant. And it's not like religion had been a big part of my life, or that I was even looking for him—really, all I was seeking was a place with a pool and the promise of a good education. But there he was. I'll tell you more about that in a later chapter, I promise.

I was overcome, overwhelmed, overjoyed. And in that moment, I knew. This was where I was meant to go to school. This was where I belonged. I still went and took the tour, met with some teachers and administrators. As a member of the junior national team (and—hopefully!—the national team), my parents and I wanted to be sure my teachers would support me and be flexible with my attendance, assignments, and exams. Academics were very important to me—they still are! And I wasn't asking to be excused from anything. In fact, I welcomed the work and the challenges of high school. It's just that if I wanted to keep swimming at this high level, I needed to be in an environment where I could accomplish *all* my goals, on a slightly adjusted schedule and I was helped enormously in this by John Koslowsky, our athletic director, and Gretzhen Kessler, our principal.

It helped that I already knew Nick Frasersmith and some of the girls on the team, but there were some issues my parents and I needed to consider. On the plus side, there was the fact that I felt 100 percent comfortable there, more like myself than I'd ever felt in the halls of my middle school, or at Arapahoe or Cherry Creek or any of the other schools I was considering. On the minus side, Regis was located about ten miles east of my home, which presented a problem. Also, I'd never thought about going to an all-girls high school, never thought about going to a Catholic high school, never thought about going to a private high school. We'd never been a deeply religious bunch around our house, so I wondered how I'd fit in. And I worried how we'd pay the private tuition.

One by one, we addressed these concerns. It turned out my auntie C.J., who didn't have any children of her own, had started an education fund for me when I was born. It was meant to help pay for college, but my aunt and my parents agreed that the money could be used to cover the Regis tuition, so that became less of an issue. The whole *no-boys* thing was a worry, because boys are fun and stupid and cute and interesting to have around, but the more I talked to the girls I already knew at Regis, the more I saw the benefits of going to an all-girls school. So that was never really an issue. (And anyway, Regis Jesuit was coinstitutional, not coeducational, so there was a boys' school on the other side of campus. If I ever needed my fix of fun and stupid and cute and interesting I could get it each day after lunch.) And the religious aspect was never a negative—it was just new and unfamiliar, but it felt to me like such a blessing to be able to add that whole new dimension to my life, so that wasn't an issue, either.

DAD: She came out of that visit to Regis Jesuit and she felt so at home. They called everybody their "sister." Everyone was so connected. Missy had this instant feeling of belonging, and it wasn't about religion, not at first. And I must say, I have a real passion for the Jesuits, even though I was a lapsed Protestant. The dean of men at Saint Mary's University, Father John Hennessey, was a Jesuit priest. And between him and the football coach, Bob Hayes, those two men really straightened me out when I was at school. And here Father Philip Steele, the then president of Regis, so warmly reminded me of all the virtues of Father Hennessey, all those years ago. Sure, it would have been easier for Missy to get on the bus here and go to Arapahoe. Sure, it would have been more affordable. But it came down to passion, and when your child lights up the way Missy lit up, you better pay attention. And now I look back and think it was the best decision

Missy could have made, and D.A. and I were there in support of that decision. I'll tell you a story. I was in a Starbucks one morning, across the street from one of the public high schools, having coffee with two businessmen. As we talked, we noticed a group of teenage girls, and one of the men I was with made a comment about how they were dressed. He mentioned that he had a teenage daughter who went to Arapahoe, and that he and his wife were so frustrated that she spent so much time worrying about her makeup, her earrings, her blouses. Every morning, it was such a big production, just to get ready for school. The other fellow concurred. He said that he had a daughter, and it wasn't uncommon for her to try on three different tops, two different skirts, try her hair two or three ways. Then it was my turn, but I couldn't share their frustration. I could tell them only that things were different in our house. I said, "It's not like that with Missy. There are no boys at Regis. She gets up in the morning, she swims, she puts on her uniform polo, her tan slacks, puts her hair in a ponytail, no makeup, no lipstick, no earrings, and goes to class. That's it." They looked at me like I was giving them a line, but out of that conversation I came away thinking Missy made the best possible decision she could have ever made.

The only argument against Regis was the commute. This was kind of a big deal—possibly even a deal breaker. We'd used the pool at Regis for years for some of our Colorado Stars practices, so we knew exactly how long it could take, especially in bad Rocky Mountain weather or during the worst part of the Denver rush hour. It could take twenty-five minutes, or it could take an hour and twenty-five minutes.

My parents both worked . . . Mom's clinic was in the complete opposite direction, so even on a good day when the roads were clear, it would take about a half hour to drop me off, and then she'd have to double back and continue on another forty minutes or so. All told, it would be about an hour and a half each morning. That was a lot for me to ask of her—only, I never really had to ask. My parents let it be known that they would do whatever I needed. The driving back and forth fell mostly to my mom, because her schedule was a little more flexible. But she would have taken me six hours out of her way, if the school I felt I was meant to attend was even farther from home. She always said she loved that time in the car with me each day—and so did I! Because of how wall-to-wall my schedule was, even then, our time together in the car was sometimes the only time we had during the day to just be together.

When we broke it down, we realized it wasn't just the back-and-forth to school we now had to consider as a family. There were morning and afternoon high school practices, as well as club-team practices. On Mondays, Wednesdays, and Fridays, we had morning workouts with the Stars, which in some months was at another pool entirely. That usually ran from five o'clock in the morning until seven. School started at eight, so if we were swimming nearby I would just get breakfast with some of my friends, and maybe catch up on some homework I didn't get to finish the night before. And then there'd be afternoon and evening practices as well.

Most days, Mom was ferrying me around town from four thirty in the morning until eight o'clock at night. And do you know what? She never once complained. Dad never once complained. And I never missed an opportunity to thank them for their selflessness, their sacrifice. But, if you'd have asked them, they would have said that it was no sacrifice at all, that it was a blessing to be able to do this for me.

Dad ended up doing most of the weekend driving, and he even found a great silver lining in these carpooling trips, because he used to take our great big malamute with him on these drives and spend an hour or two with Ruger in the park—time he probably would have never found to spend with him otherwise.

To have parents who would upend their lives to make it possible for me to go to the school of my dreams—it meant the world to me. It still does. And like I said, the car rides became a very special part of our days. Although, I've got to admit, I was pretty sleepy on some of those morning commutes. But then Mom or Dad would pick me up and I would tell them about my day, and they would tell me about their days, and we would just talk and talk, and laugh and laugh.

And the time just flew.

My State-Championship Moment

I don't wish to get ahead of the story here, but I believe it's useful to place this next moment in context. I swam all four years in high school. Freshman year, I did the whole shebang—every practice, every dual meet, every team pizza party. But that was my only year at Regis that I was fully present during high school swim season. I knew that after my first year I'd be pulled in all kinds of directions, since I was hoping to make it back to Olympic trials, and from there (if all went well!) to go on to London.

The thing is, in order to be considered a card-carrying member of the team and to be eligible to compete in the state championships, you needed to make it to a certain number of practices and compete in at least two dual meets throughout the season, so I made sure to meet that threshold during my sophomore year because we all felt we had a chance to go far as a team. The previous year, when I was all-in as a freshman, we'd finished second to Cherry Creek High School, which we were all pumped about. For little Regis Jesuit to compete against large schools like Cherry Creek . . . it was a big, big deal, and out of that showing we started to get excited for the following year, my sophomore season. There was a senior class that year in Colorado that was probably the best recruiting class ever, ever, ever to come out of the state: Bonnie Brandon, who swam for Cherry Creek and ended up at Arizona; Jordan Mattern, who also swam for Creek and who'd go on to swim for Georgia; Kelly Naze and Caroline Piehl, who swam for Creek and Smoky Hill and were off to California, Berkeley; and Alex Todd, who swam with me at Regis and was headed to Purdue.

I had my sights set on worlds that year, in Shanghai, so I couldn't devote myself exclusively to the Regis team the way I had as a freshman, but I was there as much as I could be. The way it worked out, the 2011 World Aquatics Championships in Shanghai was like my coming-out party on the international stage. Everything came together for me at that meet—I peaked at just the right time. More than any other single meet to that point in my career, this one put it out there that I was a swimmer to watch. It was my very first international long-course meet, so in a lot of ways it was my very first opportunity to show the swimming world what I could do on the world stage. And—happily, thrillingly—I did just that. I took home five medals in all—three gold, one silver, and one bronze. On a personal level, I was probably most proud of my 200-meter backstroke—my first individual world title, breaking my own national record and swimming the third-fastest time ever. But even then, there was something extra special about our win in the 4x100-meter medley, with a time of 3:52.36, a full three seconds ahead of second-place China and the second-fastest time in history. (Like, *what*?!)

For a lot of swimmers, stepping off of that kind of world stage and competing for a high school team might have been a bit of a letdown, but I never saw it that way. In fact, I was looking forward to getting back in the pool with my Regis friends. In some ways, it's like worlds that year were a kind of tune-up for our state championship back home. That sounds crazy, I know, but this was really how I thought at the time. I set it up in my head so that my high school season was the most important part of my swimming calendar. Whenever I could, I'd race back to swim with my team. Even if I couldn't get to practice in time to swim with the group, I'd try to catch the last few minutes of a session. Nick Frasersmith understood completely and couldn't have been more accommodating, and my friends on the team were super supportive. They knew I'd be with them full-time if it was at all possible. And they knew I'd be all-in and back at it in time for states.

It turned out, I cut it pretty close. I think I had a day to rest before the state meet was under way, which wasn't all that much time, considering how hard I'd been training. But my Regis teammates had been training hard, too. Seriously, these girls were putting in a tremendous effort, all season long, and it was an honor to get to swim with them at states and see if we could finish off our season with a flourish. They'd all worked so hard to make it to this moment, and here it was. Oh my gosh, I was so proud of each and every one of them, just as I knew each and every one of them was proud of me. Does that sound sappy? It does, doesn't it? But we all loved each other so much, and pulled for each other so much, I can't put it any other way! And don't forget how much I love my cheery sappiness!

The way the meet played out, it was down to Regis and Creek. It was like a grudge match left over from the year before, and it had all the makings of a storybook ending to our season, especially for our senior swimmers. Honestly, if you worked up this same scenario in a script for some Disney movie, nobody would've believed it. We were back and forth on the scoreboard; first we were ahead, then Creek was ahead, and then we were back on top. We kept trading the lead with Creek. It was just insane. And the way it worked out was that every position, every swimmer, mattered. We needed points up and down our lineup, all meet long. Second place mattered . . . fifth place mattered . . . eighth place mattered . . . you get the idea. Our marching orders were simple: beat a Creek cap. That's what we kept telling each other. Whatever you do, pick out a Creek cap in the pool and touch the wall ahead of the girl wearing that cap.

If everybody did her job in this way, we'd come out on top.

And do you know what? Our whole team stepped up, and it was such a rousing, thrilling experience, because every Regis swimmer who'd qualified for states was in a position to make a difference, to score points for our team. It didn't matter that I'd been to Olympic trials or that I was training for worlds, or that someone like Alex Todd was swimming at her own high level. Every girl on the team was essential, and for a lot of them this would be the biggest athletic stage they'd ever be on, so to watch all these great friends of mine really thrive in this environment, under this kind of pressure—well, it was something to see. It was so inspiring! These girls worked hard every day, and to have it culminate in a shot at a state title was just magical, so every girl on the team really kicked things up a whole bunch of notches and did what she could to keep those Creek swimmers in our rearview mirror.

At states, relays count twice as much as individual events, which I thought was awesome. It reinforced for me why I'd always thought of swimming as a team sport, and here it came down to the final 4x100 free relay event. The way the math worked out, whichever team came out in front, Regis or Cherry Creek, would be state champs. Neither one of us had to win the relay, necessarily; we just had to beat the other team.

The state meet always had this tremendous energy attached to it. There was a ton of excitement. Each section of the stands was oozing school spirit. People drove clear across the state to be there, got dressed up in their school colors, cheered their lungs out, and really got into it.

Creek's strategy was to lead off with their fastest swimmer, and to put their second-fastest in the anchor spot. And for a while, it looked like the strategy was working, because they were ahead after the second leg. On the third leg, we started to close the gap. I was swimming the anchor for Regis, because Nick Frasersmith had a different strategy. He wanted his fastest swimmer to anchor, so it fell to me to close the gap and find a way to win.

Here's how we lined up, for those of you Colorado high school swimming fans keeping score at home:

For Regis, it was Hillary Thomas, Alex Todd, McKenna De-Bever, and me.

For Creek, it was Bonnie Brandon, McKenna Newsum-Schoenberg, Fiona Kane, and Jordan Mattern.

I'll let you in on a little secret: in this type of spot, I always preferred being the predator—meaning, the one who had to come from behind. When you're the predator, you can see the swimmers in front of you and take their measure. When you're the predator, you know exactly what you have to do before you give chase. When you're the prey, you don't always have a good idea where you are in the water, relative to the swimmers coming up behind you. You know how big a lead you might have had when you dove in, but that's about it. After that, you're kind of flying blind.

When you think about it, it's the same role I played when I chased my father down the mountain that day at Winter Park.

Anyway, this whole predator-prey dynamic is one of my favorite things about our sport, the way you can be trailing when you start your swim and reel in your opponent and turn the relay around. Or the way you can be out in front without having any clear idea who's coming up behind you. I was always so amped up, swimming that last leg, that the danger was potentially overswimming the first twenty-five out of sheer excitement and not leaving myself enough energy to finish the final seventy-five. When you race individually, you all start at the same time, and your race management is entirely different, but when you're coming from behind on a relay, it's a different strategy and mind-set.

Luckily, happily, mercifully, I'd had a lot of experience in this kind of spot, so I didn't tank on my first twenty-five. I just kept building to a big finish, taking a bite out of the lead at each turn. (Sorry, guys, but I'm sticking with that predator metaphor.)

It just so happened that the "prey" in this case was one of my closest friends, Jordan Mattern. We were on the same club team and had been on many relays together over the years, so I knew what she was capable of, and that I needed to be at my best in order to touch the wall ahead of her.

Meanwhile, I could see with every breath that my teammates were going completely wild on the pool deck. I could hear the roar of the crowd, and I could make out our Regis section, getting louder and louder as I got closer and closer.

I did my job, in the end. I picked out that Creek cap in the pool and put it behind me, and we were state champions!

Regis: 3:22.42.
Creek: 3:24.39.

And Jordan Mattern did exactly what she needed to do by swimming the fastest leg for her team, so she put up an amazing fight at the end—but I was able to tap into the relentless spirit that had by now become a part of me, and to answer with an amazing fight of my own.

For the record, our time in the 4x100 free set a state record that still stands, with both times besting the previous record of 3:24.85, set by Creek the year before.

Let me tell you, I don't think I've ever been so emotional at a meet. There were instant tears, all around. It was my first time experiencing a thrill of this magnitude, and even though I'd go on to experience other great thrills—at the Olympic trials, at the NCAAs, at the Olympics—there's nothing like that first adrenaline rush of joy that finds you when your dreams come true in the pool. I was just hysterically sobbing—me and all the other girls on the team. It was overwhelming, really, and one of the reasons we were all so emotional was that Regis had never won a class 5A state title. So that was huge for us. Another reason was that the girls on that team meant so much to me. We all meant so much to each other. (Bring on the sap!) And for a lot of them, this would be the very pinnacle of their swimming careers. So that was something, too.

What an honor it was, to be able to join my friends on that pinnacle, and to help them get there by swimming that anchor leg.

What a blessing it was, to be a part of a team that was able to bring Regis Jesuit its first state title at this level.

And what a challenge it would now be, to find a way to keep that spirit of teamwork alive in my swimming. That was the great takeaway for me, that I was wired for this type of thing. Up until this championship, I hadn't really formulated my plans for swimming in college. Oh, I'd definitely be going to college, but a lot of top swimmers choose to focus on their international swimming careers, where they can compete and train long course all year round.

But not me, I decided—right then and there, by the side of that pool. Swimming was a team sport, after all. I'd never trade this moment, and I'd set myself up to have more moments just like it.

FIVE

LONDON

S o here we are, about halfway through the book, and it feels like the right time to break from format. I've done most of the "talking" to this point—which, if you know me, isn't all that surprising. But as we're gathering our thoughts, and looking at the defining moments of the 2012 Summer Olympics, it feels like a lot of those stories have already been told—at least, a lot of *my* stories have already been told.

As readers might remember, I did a ton of media interviews leading up to the games and during our time in London, and the attention only increased when we got back home. That's what happens, I guess, when you come home with all that hardware: a bronze medal I'd picked up on the first day of competition as part of the 4x100-meter freestyle relay, and four gold medals (in the 100- and 200-meter backstroke, and as a member of the 4x200-meter freestyle and 4x100-meter medley teams). I swam in seven events in all, so it felt to me like I was competing, warming up, warming down, or being interviewed the entire time I was in London, and for another six months after I got back to the States.

It was such a crazy, thrilling time in my life, and in the life of my family, but there are only so many ways I can share and re-share the same stories, so what we've decided to do here is turn the cameras on my parents. Oh, they did a ton of interviews, too, but for the most part reporters wanted them to talk about *me*. Nobody really asked them what the whole Olympic experience was like from *their* perspective, so we figure the thing to do is hand the controls to them over these next pages and let them tell it like it was . . . for them. You'll hear from me a bit later on, with one of my favorite London stories, but for now I'll leave it to Mom and Dad to tell the tale.

Sound like a plan?

DAD: Jeez, Miss . . . I thought you'd never give up the floor! But that's right, our London experiences were a whole lot different than any of the athletes'. And, certainly, a whole lot different than Missy's experiences. I think we all started to realize how our lives were about to change in Omaha, at Olympic trials. What a thrilling moment for our family! We'd been to Omaha before, of course, in 2008, but the stakes were different then. Missy was just so happy to be there. I told people that making it to this level was achievement enough, and I sincerely believed that at the time. I still do. If that's all it ever was for Missy, D.A. and I would have been so enormously proud of her, and it would have

My parents on their wedding day in Halifax, Nova Scotia, September 4, 1971. Dad forgot to wash his hair!

Here's a great shot of Mom and her sister Cathy. Mom is about seven, and Auntie C.J. is about three.

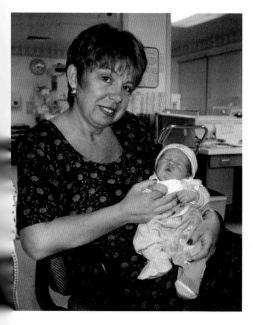

Two days old, heading home from California to Colorado.

All dressed up for my christening, on Dad's fiftieth birthday. My dress was a present from my godparents, Aunt Deb and Uncle Harry.

At fourteen months, at our home in Grand Lake—already rocking the team gear!

Date night with Dad. We were headed off to see *Annie*, which is still one of my favorite shows.

With Mom after a day in the sun. Look at all those freckles!

First day of kindergarten. Check out my color-coordinated outfit—I'm pretty cool.

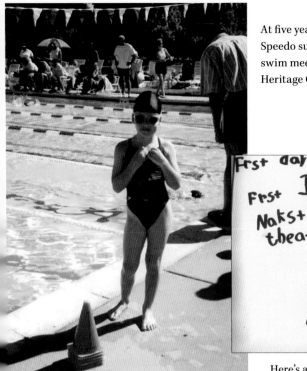

At five years old, in my Speedo suit, for my first swim meet with the Heritage Green Gators.

Frst day OF Swim Pracdis
Frst I DiD Frestil
Nakst I DiDdakshok
theat Wuse A Grat
day Todaoy

Here's a page from the very first book I wrote. It was a little shorter than this one!

At seven, skiing with my father at Winter Park, Colorado. Already loved the trees and moguls!

With the fam in 2002 in Muskoka, Canada.

At twelve, at IU–PUI, waiting for the pool to be measured to verify my National Age Group records.

At twelve, with my coach Todd Schmitz at the Sportswomen of Colorado awards ceremony. How young we both look! I hadn't given Todd any gray hair yet!

So proud to earn my first Team USA uniform before my trip to Vancouver with the junior national team for my first international meet.

At my first Olympic trials. I'd just turned thirteen.

After the London games, my hometown of Centennial presented me with a key to the city. (My cheeks still hurt from smiling!)

With my best friend, Kristen Vredeveld, freshman year. We were painting the Big C—a swim team tradition.

With Kristen, Elizabeth Pelton, Kaylin Bing, and Sophia Batchelor at PAC-12s, freshman year.

There's nothing like old friends. Here I am in December 2014, reunited with my Regis HS crew: Melanie Higgins, Briana Labrie, Kendall Higgins, Jessica Weed, C. C. Cutler, and Abby Cutler.

My support team in Rio, outside the natatorium: Roy, Darryl, Doug, Mom, Linda, Dad, and Auntie C.J. down in front. I didn't get to see them during the run of the games, but it meant the world to me that they were there.

Oh my goodness—the sight of all these handwritten notes on pink hearts decorating our front lawn was such a sweet surprise when we got back from Rio after the 2016 Olympic Games. There were hundreds of them!

Author selfie: just back from Rio for a final writing session with our phenomenal collaborator, Daniel Paisner.

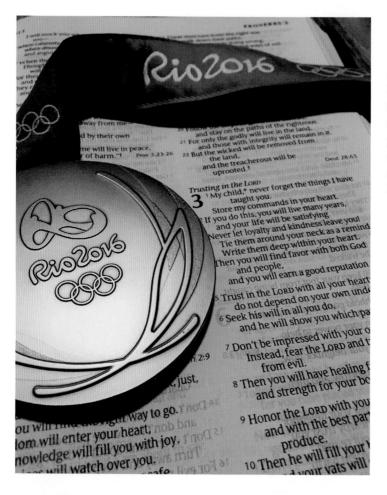

After a disappointing Rio, I found strength in scripture. Here's a social media post I put up to lift my spirits and to remind others to trust in the Lord, no matter what.

been something she could have held on to and looked back on for the rest of her life. I said the same thing this time around, too, in 2012, only now there were certain expectations. Now Missy had pushed her way into the conversation. People were talking about her as one of the best in the world in her events, so even though I was saying all the same things, and believing all the same things, there was a part of me crossing my fingers and holding my breath and hoping Missy could swim her way onto the Olympic team. The meet started on a Monday, and Missy swam a grueling schedule. It's always one of the toughest meets in the world. Eight long days, filled with a roller coaster of emotions. Only the top two finishers in each event make the team, so there was very little margin for error.

Missy had her work cut out for her, but D.A. and I were in a better spot than a lot of the other parents in the stands. Most of them had athletes swimming in just one or two events, so for those families the tension was really high. It worked out that Missy had one of her strongest events on the second day—the 100-meter backstroke. She had her preliminary heat in the morning, and the semifinal that night, and then she came back for the finals the following night, so pretty much right out of the gate we knew she was going to London. We were just so terribly excited for her, so wonderfully excited, and we still had the rest of the meet ahead of us, and Missy could still qualify in the 200 back, in the

100 and 200 free, in the relay events. It was all wide-open, all right there for the taking, but now the pressure was off. And here I don't mean the pressure on Missy so much as I mean the pressure on us! She was great about the pressure, just kind of shrugged it off, but for her mother and me, it was agonizing. I looked in the stands, and all around were these parents whose athlete maybe wasn't scheduled to swim until the end of the week. They were on pins and needles that whole time, waiting to see if they were going to London. Or maybe their one event came early on in the schedule, and they were disappointed on the very first day. And there were quite a few of Missy's friends in Omaha that year who ended up just missing out, and we were friendly with all the parents, we knew all the swimmers, so there was a lot of tension and disappointment. Like I said, it's just a roller coaster of emotions for these families, as it was for us as well, but for us at least the thrill ride worked, in a good way, right away.

Naturally, we tried to keep a lid on our celebrating around the pool, because we knew so many others would leave the meet without a spot on the team. We were able to race up to Missy's hotel room afterward and decorate it with red, white, and blue ribbons, and help Missy celebrate that she was now an Olympian. Whatever happened from here on in, nobody could take that away from her. The third night of trials, and already she was an Olympian, and I remember feeling some of those same emotions when she made it to

trials four years earlier. That this was enough. Something to look back on. Something to cherish. Always. If
this was as far as swimming would take her, this was
enough. This was something. This was everything.

⌁

MOM: What a lot of people don't really think about is
that these games were like a rite of passage for us. Remember, Missy was our only child. She came into our
lives like a little miracle, and here she was, seventeen
years old, getting ready to head off to college in just a
year. It was a bittersweet time. It's like our time with
her was coming to an end, and in a lot of ways the
Olympics were symbolic of that. For me, anyway. One
night, about a month before we left for London, I found
myself feeling a little wistful, a little reflective, and I
sat down and wrote a long e-mail to Karen Crouse of
the *New York Times*. Karen had covered swimming for
years and years, and she'd become a family friend, she
was close with Missy, and I knew if there was anyone
who could understand the tug and pull I was feeling
about these special moments in Missy's life, it was her.

Here's what I wrote:

"My daughter is seventeen, still a minor, a teenager,
and still a child in many ways. My daughter is an
Olympian. . . . No, I don't think it's really hit me yet. I
watch the Comcast Olympic trials replays over and
over again, wondering how I missed so much! I smile,
and tears roll down my cheeks as I hear her called an

Olympian. Yes, my little girl. I think about all those meets. I smile as I think of my OCD routines . . . clean towels, three pairs of goggles in her bag, two caps, and then the snacks and drinks . . . always, too much! As she started qualifying for the 'big' meets, like zones, sectionals, junior nationals, nationals, Olympic trials, my routine changed somewhat. Although she packed her own suitcase, I couldn't let go of that swim bag that she carried onto the plane with her. Now there were always NEW towels and NEW goggles in her bag. Although I made her adjust the goggles so that they were perfect when she needed them, I left the sticker protectors on the eye pieces to protect them and allow her to see which ones were still unmarked and fresh for her.

"Two weeks ago she left on another travel meet, this time to join the Olympic team. I got out the washed new towels, three pairs of her ever-familiar Speedo Women's Vanquisher goggles, pulled them out of their packages and had her try on each pair and cut the straps . . . not too short, as I didn't want them to slip on her. She stopped her reading and patiently performed this task without complaint. She had done it so many times and knew this is what 'I did.' This is how I was 'part' of her swimming. I added the new Speedo nose clips that she has used for the last two years. I also put one out for Coach Todd's bag and put one in my carry-on that I would take to London in three weeks! I smiled thinking about what I would do with this nose clip if I noticed her panic on deck when she dropped hers to the bottom of the pool. Carefully, I arranged them all in her bag, the goggles and nose clips in one Baggie placed on top of the caps in the back pocket. One towel cushioned the bottom of her bag, and on top went her familiar snacks and water bottle. I made sure the Kleenex and Aleve were easily accessible in her side pocket. (She had a little cold.) Then I pulled out her wallet, a special one I found that had two compartments for bills. I put dollars in one and pounds in the other. I felt a little guilt . . . I had forgotten the euros (they were going to France first, for training camp). I put Pascal, her cowboy teddy bear, beside her bag. She would be upset if he didn't make the trip with her.

"I look out the window and see our neighborhood pool right across the street. That's where it all started, not just for her but for all of us. I learned how to be a timer, a runner, a concession helper. I liked signing up for ribbons, which we could do the next day over a glass of wine, away from the kids. [We'd decorate ribbons with the swimmer's name and time, usually for the top eight finishers in an event, along with some "participation" ribbons, which we'd then present to the swimmers at a later date.] How many times did I worry she would miss her event as she was having fun playing in the tent with her friends, her heat card quickly stuffed down her wet suit . . . somewhere? How many times did I remind her to go to the bathroom before her event only to watch her wiggle on the blocks. I move on to the early club days on the Colorado Stars . . . all precious memories. I remembered her excitement when a meet was in Colorado Springs or Fort Collins, both an easy sixty- to ninety-minute commute. We'd make it a 'travel meet,' pack up the car, put our dog in the back, and head to the hotel. She loved getting in our room, unpacking and checking everything out. In the early days she traveled and stayed with us. I think we loved it so much because outside of the pool, we had nothing to do but cuddle together. . . .

"Where have those days gone? My daughter is an Olympian. . . . I can't wait to see my daughter, the Olympian. . . . We won't have seen her for a month. She is a minor, so we will go to the Olympic Village on 8/5 and sign her out, then bring her home to our rental . . . and we will cuddle, just like we'd always do. After all, it is just another travel meet . . ."

And then I signed off with a little smiley-face emoticon—:)—which really didn't show how I was feeling at all. Happy, yes. But also a little sad. What's the emoticon for that?

⌒⌒

DAD: It's true, D.A. was a bit of a wreck after trials. I suppose I was, too, in my own way. And it's not like these moments caught any of us by surprise. We'd been building toward them and building toward them since Missy was a little girl. In a lot of ways, we'd had London on our calendars since Missy's first trip to

Omaha, back in 2008, and now that it was upon us it was almost too big to be believed. Of the three of us, I have to say it was Missy who kept it together best of all. She was focused. She was determined. She knew what she had to do. There wasn't really any time for hugs and tears and nostalgia. If anything, I think she felt bad for some of her friends who didn't make the team, girls she'd been swimming with for years. But that's one of the things that makes her such a great competitor, I think. She's an emotional person, but she's not an emotional athlete. She puts everything into her swims, all of her passion and purpose, but at the same time she takes a very clinical approach. She does what she has to do, and here she might have taken the time to cry a little for a good friend who might have fallen just short in Omaha, to celebrate a little with her mom and dad, but then it was back to work, so when she headed off for training camp and her final preparations before the games, it was very clear in her mind what she had to do. There was what she'd worked for, all along, and now it was close enough to touch.

⌒

MOM: For me—and, I think, for Missy—one of the most emotional moments of that Olympic season came in July, specifically on July 20, just seven days before the start of the games. Missy was with the team at training camp in Vichy, France, when the news broke about a midnight shooting at a movie theater in Aurora, Colorado, not too far from her school, Regis Jesuit. The shooting made headlines here at home and all over the world, but as the story was breaking, before there were even cameras on the scene, Missy heard about it from her friends on social media. This was that horrific shooting at the midnight premiere of *The Dark Knight Rises,* the new Batman movie. Missy had a lot of friends who were planning on going on opening night, so she was frantic. She called home right away. She didn't know what to do.

We'd already gone to bed, so we hadn't heard anything about it, but it was early morning in France, so Missy was all over it. She was sobbing when she called, and it took a while for me to figure out what she was saying. I woke up Dick and told him to turn on the television so he'd know what we were talking about and so we could both see what was going on. I couldn't believe what I was seeing on the screen, what Missy was telling me. Oh my, it was awful. And for Missy, half a world away, it was especially devastating because she had no way of knowing if her friends were okay. Obviously, a midnight showing of a big new movie, the place was probably filled with high school kids. We had a good long cry together, and said a prayer for the victims, a prayer for her friends, and then after a while Missy had to go to a team event—a practice, or a press conference, or something. But when she hung up the phone I couldn't stop thinking about my not-so-little girl, all the way over in France, worrying that her world had been shattered back home. I wanted to reach across those phone lines, reach across the ocean, and collect her in a great big hug, tell her everything was going to be all right. But, of course, I couldn't, so I did what I thought was the next best thing. I called Teri McKeever, the head women's coach. This was something I'd never done, gone behind Missy's back to talk to one of her coaches. That's just not our style. But here I felt so far away from Missy I wanted to do whatever I could to comfort her. It wasn't about swimming. It was about her heart. Teri hadn't heard about the shooting, so she was a little confused at first about why I was calling, but after I was able to explain the situation she understood right away how upsetting this was for Missy. She immediately went to Missy's room to check on her.

There was a Team USA press conference scheduled for that morning, and we both knew Missy would be asked about the shooting, so we wanted to prepare her for that. Teri reached out to Karen Linhart, the terrific publicist for USA Swimming (and who now works as Missy's publicist as well). Karen talked to Missy beforehand and helped her gather her thoughts, and when I watched that press conference it just broke my heart. The pain in Missy's eyes, the concern and sadness in her voice. It's a wonder she got through it, but she did get through it. As the details came through, and Missy's friends checked in on Facebook and

Twitter, she learned that her friends were okay, but there were twelve people dead and seventy injured. Missy announced that she was dedicating her Olympic swims to the victims and their families, and to all of her friends back home in Colorado, who had just endured a devastating series of wildfires that had displaced thousands of families across our state, and now this tragedy. It was one of those times as a mother you just want to whisk your child away and hold her close and tell her everything's going to be okay, but she was five thousand miles away, preparing to swim the biggest meet of her life.

⌒

DAD: Just getting to London, and getting to all these events, was a whole other ordeal. You don't have a lot of time after trials to make all the arrangements without paying through the nose, so you have to get out ahead of it. The tickets to the events were the least of our worries. The United States Olympic Committee (USOC) provides each athlete with two seats to each of his or her events, so D.A. and I were covered. Of course, those seats were all the way up in the rafters, real nosebleeders. For one of her swims, we were literally five rows from the roof. We didn't think to bring binoculars, but we certainly could've used them. We'd spent all that money, traveling to London, and then we spent the whole time trying to pick our daughter out in the pool. It was kind of absurd, really. And then of course we had our family scattered all around the arena. They had to scramble for their own seats, and sometimes they had a better view than we did, but we were just so happy to be there, so happy everybody could be there.

～

MOM: It took a lot of planning, getting everybody to London, making all the arrangements. Of course, we didn't even know if Missy would make the team, but we had to get on it. We couldn't wait until a few weeks before the Olympics, after trials. There had to be a certain amount of wishful thinking. Flights and hotel rooms sold out quickly, and tickets to the events were hard to come by. And so, thinking positively, I went to work on this in September 2011, almost a full year before the Olympics. My godson and nephew Darryl, Missy's cousin, was my partner in crime, and we were careful to keep Missy out of the loop. She didn't want to take anything for granted about London. She didn't want to jinx it, or lose her focus, and I respected that, of course. But I also didn't want to be caught short, so I started researching the area, the transportation system, hotels, restaurants.

I didn't know a whole lot about London, so there was a lot to process. I knew we had a lot of family members who would want to join us, so I looked for a big place and finally settled on a beautiful three-bedroom apartment in the Canary Wharf area, with an amazing waterfront view. Darryl and his father, Doug, Dick's brother, just loved it, and so did Dick, so I wired a £600 deposit to the owner and let everyone in the family know. Everyone except for Missy, that is. She had no idea who was coming, or when. She had no idea about any of this, really. She would have been so upset, to learn about all these plans, which of course had to be set in motion before Missy'd even earned her spot on the team at trials. She would have thought I was jinxing her, but I wanted to be prepared. Next thing I knew, I started reading all these articles about incidents of fraud in the London rental market, specifically related to the Olympics, so I went back on the rental site to make sure we were okay, and wouldn't you know it, "our" apartment had disappeared from the site. I scrambled to get in touch with the building manager, who informed me that the unit was not for rent, had never been for rent, and that the pictures I'd forwarded from the listing had been lifted from an old sales site.

We'd been scammed! And around the time I started putting two and two together, I read that there had been more than one hundred arrests in a widespread rental scam in and around London. I made an appointment with the Arapahoe sheriff's office and gave them all my information, and they then notified the British police. Then I notified USA Swimming, so they could let other families know to be on the lookout. I felt so totally duped, and embarrassed, and of course we were out all that money, which in those days was about $1,000. The good news was that I was able to find a much bigger seven-bedroom home, just a mile and one tube stop from the Aquatics Centre, with room enough to accommodate our large group. And they were even flexible enough to let us stay on for another week after Missy was done with all her events and decided she wanted to stay in London for the closing ceremonies.

It turned out we were indeed a large group. There was Missy's uncle Doug; his wife, Asako; and Doug's two kids, Darryl and Laura; and Laura's boyfriend, Wei. Dick's other brother, Missy's uncle Drew; his wife, Angela; and two of their three kids, Chelsea and Derek, would join us for a stretch. (Sean couldn't make it—you were missed!) My sister, Cathy—Missy's auntie C.J.—was there as well, but she was in London in an official capacity, as the doctor for the Canadian women's soccer team, and her partner, Linda, was back home in Canada, so we were a little underrepresented on my side of the family. Aunt Deb, Uncle Harry, Kiley, and Zach were back home as well, but they would be glued to the television coverage the entire time. Oh, and we were also joined by our great Colorado pals Rob and Molly Cohen, who'd come to trials with us as well. In all, I'd say Missy had a pretty sizable cheering contingent, but there was quite a lot of planning and negotiating that went into it, and all of that had to be done without Missy's knowing. She absolutely refused to talk about London until she made the team—she was adamant about it—and the only way I could respect that was to go behind her back.

(Sorry, Miss!)

⌢

DAD: D.A. really did a fabulous job, setting everything up. But my brothers and their families were on their own when it came to tickets. And then we got there, sitting way, way up in the rafters, and there were all these empty seats down below. It was one of the biggest controversies of the London games, the way all those corporate seats had been set aside and left unused. It wasn't just at the Aquatics Centre but at all the venues. And we probably had the worst seats of anyone in the family. On the one hand, it didn't much matter. We were just so overjoyed to be there. But on the other hand, all those empty seats down below, it was a little upsetting, a little frustrating. We'd come all this way to see Missy, we'd put so much into these moments as a family, and then to be so far removed from the action . . . sure, it was frustrating. We'd been to almost every single one of Missy's meets to this point, and we had our little routines. Missy knew where to look for us in the stands. D.A. was in the habit of arriving early and staking out a spot a couple of rows up, so Missy would seek us out before and after her swim. Here, she had no idea where to look. Frankly, from all that distance, way, way up in the sky, we couldn't even be sure what we were seeing down below. We had to watch the monitors that weren't blocked out by the rafters. Believe me, we had one heck of a time craning our necks to see the live video feed on the big natatorium screen!

It was almost funny, how bad our seats were. At one point, NBC News sent up a young cameraman to film us. He lugged a forty-pound camera on his shoulders all the way up those stairs. The poor guy was sweating and out of breath. Clearly, this wasn't the best assignment! Then he looked at his notes, and over to us in our seats, and he had this really puzzled expression. Finally, he looked at us and said, "You wouldn't happen to be the Franklins, would you?" I was feeling a little frustrated myself, so I thought I'd have some fun with him. I said, "No." I was completely deadpan. I was just busting his chops, and I left him hanging for a few seconds before admitting who we were. I don't think he thought it was so funny, after carrying all that equipment all that way, but he appreciated that I'd finally come clean.

Another time, we got a call from someone in Stan Kroenke's office. His son had seen where we were sitting on television and told his father about it, and now Mr. Kroenke wanted to invite us down to join him and his group poolside. For those of you who don't know, Stan Kroenke is the owner of the Denver Nuggets, the Colorado Avalanche, the Colorado Rapids—just a big, big figure in the professional sports scene back home.

He knew who Missy was and he didn't think it was right, her parents sitting all the way up in the nosebleed section. I must say, I had to agree with him. There were no electronic tickets, so we had to pick up the tickets ourselves. Where? We had to go to Mr. Kroenke's yacht, so D.A. and I took a taxi to Canary Wharf one morning, which was a little bit out of our way, but it was all so very exciting. We didn't mind the detour, not one bit. And then, to be called in from out of the cold like that, and brought down to where the action was, we were so incredibly grateful for his kindness. And the seats were just terrific. As I recall, the royal family was seated one section over, to our right, so we were really in good company.

Unfortunately, Missy didn't medal that night. It was the night of the 200-meter freestyle finals, and she finished in fourth place, one one-hundredth of a second off the podium. (She'll tell you about that race in the pages ahead!) It was so frustrating, to see her miss out like that, by such a small margin, but at the same time we were so incredibly proud of her, so overjoyed to be with her, up close, in just that moment. For the first time that week we really got to feel what it was like to be in the middle of all that Olympic excitement, and even though Missy didn't win a medal, I look back on that race as one of the most thrilling moments of the games for us as a family, because it was then that I understood what it meant to be the father of an Olympic athlete. When we were up in the rafters, in the nosebleed seats, it felt a little bit like these Olympic Games were a dream. But to be so close to the action, so close to the royal family . . . we were swept up in the moment.

∼

MOM: Missy's first gold medal came in the 100-meter backstroke. Her walls were not exactly her strong suit, so the 200 back was really a better race for her, because she had all that extra time over that longer distance to overcome those turns, but we were all hoping she'd do well. I wouldn't say our expectations were high, because that was never our mind-set. We just wanted her to swim her best. Her main competition was Emily Seebohm from Australia. The two of them were always neck and neck. Emily had won prelims, with a time of 58.23 to Missy's 59.37. In the semifinals, she came out ahead, too, with a time of 58.39 to Missy's 59.12. After the semis, we walked by Emily's mother as she was being interviewed by a television reporter about the finals, to be held the next night. Obviously, she was so excited, and proud of her daughter, and optimistic, and I remember thinking how poised she was, handling the reporter's questions, when inside she must have been just bursting.

On finals night, we were up in the second-highest row in the natatorium. By this point, we'd invested in a pair of binoculars, so we could at least have an idea what Missy was up to down there on the pool deck. We arrived early and made our usual trek through security and up twenty flights of stairs to our section. There were no elevators! And, no concessions or bathrooms! So we had to make sure we had everything we needed and took care of all our business before settling into our seats. I was so excited, but also feeling a little numb, a little like I was in a dream. My fingers were tingling, and at one point I worried I was hyperventilating, or maybe even not breathing at all. A few people stopped us to chat, or to wish us well, as we made our way to our seats, and I can honestly say that I have no recollection of what they said, or what I might have said in response. Gosh, I hope I was nice!

It felt like forever before the race finally started. They paraded out all the finalists. Emily, as the top seed, was in lane four. Missy was in lane five. They both got off to strong starts. Emily popped up ahead of Missy, which was not unusual with these two. At fifty meters, Emily was ahead, 28.57 to 28.82. To the naked eye, all the way up there on the roof, it was oh so close. After the turn, we could see that Emily still had the lead. I reached out and grabbed Dick's arm, like I was holding on for dear life. Missy started to catch up a little. All around us, Team USA family and friends were on their feet, screaming. Dick jumped up and threw his arms in the air and started shouting, "Go! Go! Go!" Meanwhile, I just stood there, silent, my hands over my mouth. I was in shock—didn't know what to think, what to cheer, what to do. When the girls touched the wall, it was difficult to tell who had won. It was so close. Finally, the timing board lit up with the results: Missy Franklin, 58.33. Emily Seebohm, 58.68.

It took a moment for the times to register, but then when it sunk in I was absolutely overcome, overjoyed, overwhelmed. It was just too, too much to be believed. Too, too incredible. Dick and I were jumping up and down like crazy people, and there were hugs and congratulations and high fives all around. Our family was spread out over the natatorium, but we had a chance to hug and celebrate later that night. We heard from our goddaughter Kiley back in the States that her father, Missy's uncle Harry, cried watching the race on television. It was just such a tremendous, joyful moment. Oh my, I tear up just thinking about it, writing about it. (Trust me, I'm a mess!) And then, after what seemed like the longest time, we started to make our way out of the Aquatics Centre. For some reason, the moment felt incomplete. Wonderful, but incomplete. Something was missing, and that something was Missy. This was really the first meet we'd been to where there was such a disconnect. She was so far away, so busy with Team USA and media commitments, it's like we weren't even in the same city. And I don't think it really registered that there was this missing piece; it's only in retrospect that I noticed it, and only after what happened next.

What happened next was this: as we were leaving the Olympic Park, after the very last medal ceremony,

Mike Unger from USA Swimming called and told me to stay where we were. Someone came to collect us and ushered us through a gate—and there was Missy, running toward us! We all hugged and cried. The first thing she said to me? "Mom, I love your new top!" And right then, with that little tossed-off comment about the outfit I'd picked out, the missing piece was in place. In the middle of this swirl of unbelievable excitement, we could be a family again. The next thing she said was, "Do you want to see my gold medal?" Of course we wanted to see her gold medal! She'd stuffed it into the unzipped pocket of her warm-up jacket. I could've strangled her! And there it was, this beautiful, heavy, glorious gold medal. The mother in me wanted to take it and store it safely away, but this was Missy's moment, Missy's medal, and I held my tongue as she tucked it back into her pocket, where it could have easily fallen out. What could I have said? My daughter, the Olympic gold medalist, handling the prize of all prizes as casually as some of her friends handled their iPhones . . . What's a mother to do, right?

⌒

DAD: I always tell people that D.A. and I had some serious separation anxiety during our time in London. You don't often hear that phrase, about a parent referring to a child, but that's really how we felt, because there was like this great wall separating our experiences from Missy's experiences. We were used to being at a small aquatic facility, with maybe two or three thousand spectators at most, and there was always an opportunity to see Missy, before or after. We could make eye contact, or signal her from the stands, let her know we were there for her. It felt at least like we were at the same event, in the same building. But here at the Olympics there were close to twenty thousand people in the Aquatics Centre. Here at the Olympics, she was being pulled every which way, especially after she won her first gold medal. There were interviews and team meetings . . . every conceivable distraction, and some inconceivable ones, too.

We went to the opening ceremonies, but Missy and the team couldn't participate because their events started the next day, and that was just how it was the whole time we were there. And she swam so many events, it's like we never left the pool. When we got home, people asked us about our trip. They wanted to know how we enjoyed London, if we took in any sights, if we saw any other events. I always felt a little sheepish, telling them the truth, which was that we'd traveled five thousand miles just to go back and forth from the hotel to the pool, climbing up all those flights of stairs, sitting and waiting for Missy's heat in the prelims in the mornings and then hopefully her semifinal swim in the evening and the finals the next night. Every day, it was the same drill. Imagine going to the Super Bowl in the morning, and traveling to the stadium, and going through security, and finding your seats, and then doing it all over again in the evening. And then again the next day, and the day after that. It's almost unfair to say it was exhausting, given how hard Missy worked to reach this moment, how much effort she was putting in, but it really was draining—spending all those hours and hours, just to watch our little girl do her thing. And with the Super Bowl at least there's a full sixty minutes of game action. With Missy's swim, most of these events, there was just a minute or two of action, so if you separate yourself from the situation, and forget for a moment that it's your kid and that you're at the Olympics, it hardly seems like a fair trade.

One good example of how separated we were from Missy was kind of funny, although it's only funny now in retrospect. At the time, it was infuriating. It's a story Missy only learned later, but once she heard it she was all over it. You see, her old man was mugged. By a woman. In a wheelchair. Okay, so maybe *mugged* is too harsh a term. I was pickpocketed, really, but it felt like a mugging. Like a violation. The woman made off with my wallet, which had about $600 in it. Fortunately, my passport was back at our house, so that was one headache I didn't have to deal with, but I did have to spend hours and hours on the phone with the banks, canceling my credit cards. In the middle of all this great excitement, to have to deal with something like this, it was a real hassle. Normally, Missy would have given me a hard time about something like this. To have my wallet stolen—by a woman in a wheelchair, no less? She would've given it to me good. That's the kind of teasing relationship we had. She would've called me a loser or an old man, whatever. And we could have had some fun with it. But she didn't hear about it until much, much later. And at that point, I was pretty much over it.

It's funny how seeing your daughter win four gold medals at the Olympics can make you forget a small nuisance like being in another country and having your wallet stolen on the tube platform.

⌒

DAD: You know, there's an interesting story about how my sister-in-law, Cathy, took in Missy's 200-meter backstroke. As D.A. mentioned, her sister was there as the team doctor for the Canadian women's soccer team, so she was in an unusual position. Auntie C.J. really was Missy's biggest fan, outside of her proud parents. My brothers and sister made it to meets when they could, but C.J. made it to almost all of them when her schedule allowed. In this case it did and it didn't.

She was able to watch Missy's 100 back, with the soccer team and staff, which was a mixed blessing. She really wanted to be in the natatorium with us, or to be with her partner, Linda, who was back home. She knew the pressure of that race, going up against a fast international field, and she wanted to be there to support the family. But this was the next best thing.

The soccer venues were outside of London, in a variety of locations. Coventry, Manchester, Newcastle... there was really no way for C.J. to get back and forth, while still doing her job. Canada hadn't won a medal in a Summer Olympics team sport since the men's basketball team won the bronze in 1928, and Missy's performance became a kind of rallying point for the team. They all knew her as "Doc's niece," and there started to be this feeling around the team that if Doc's niece could win gold, then a medal was within reach for them, too. It's like Missy was the team mascot—she'd been "adopted" by the whole team.

For the run of the games, C.J. was able to catch all of Missy's swims on television, until Missy's 200 back. The soccer team kept winning and winning, against all expectations, and it worked out that they were due to play in a quarterfinals match against heavily favored England at seven o'clock in the evening, the same start time as the 200 back finals. C.J. took her job seriously, so during the game she wasn't about to take her eyes off the field, off her players. And yet at the same time she was desperate to know the results of the 200 back finals. So she worked out a system with one of the FIFA officials, a woman from Scotland named Jo Hutchison, who was also a big Missy fan. They arranged some kind of messaging system so that C.J. could look back at Jo, who was sitting right behind the bench in the stands. One finger for first place, two fingers for second place, and so on. And then there were a whole bunch of follow-up signals, like a thumbs-up for a world record, an okay sign for an Olympic record. So when Jo flashed one finger, C.J. knew Missy'd won the gold, and then when she flashed the thumbs-up, C.J. knew she'd set a world record, and she told us all later that she welled up with tears, thinking of all of us at the pool, thinking of her niece, thinking of what she was missing. But then, her attention was drawn back to the field, because the Canadian women were beating that strong England side and about to move on to the semifinals. It really was an amazing Olympic experience for C.J. as well, because the team went on to win the bronze medal, so it was just one excitement after another, even if she couldn't be with us at the Aquatics Centre.

⌒

MOM: Missy's final event was the 4x100 medley relay, and Team USA won the gold in a big way. They broke China's world record of 3:52.19 with a time of 3:52.05. Missy, Rebecca Soni, Dana Vollmer, and Allison Schmitt were thrilled. What a way to end the meet! Missy always said this was her most exciting event, and she was so happy to be part of such a special relay team. People refer to swimming as an individual sport, but Missy argues the point. Sure, it can be an individual sport, but the team aspect was what Missy had always loved about it. It all depends on how you approach it, and what you want out of it, and what

Missy wanted was that sense of camaraderie, and here she got to experience it on the biggest possible stage.

The next morning, Dick grabbed a taxi and headed over to the Olympic Village to sign Missy out. She was still just seventeen years old, and the responsibility of the USOC, so she couldn't just come and go like the other athletes, but now that she was free of her swimming responsibilities we all wanted to spend some time together. Originally, the plan had been for us to fly home immediately after the swimming events, but Missy asked if we could stay on. (We were so lucky our rental was extended—imagine having to book a second week of accommodations, right in the middle of the Olympics!) She wanted to walk in the closing ceremonies with her teammates, especially with Kara Lynn Joyce, who was like a big sister to Missy. Kara had moved to Denver eighteen months prior to the games, when she started training with Todd Schmitz and the Colorado Stars, and she and Missy really bonded. Their friendship was chronicled by the documentary filmmakers Christo Brock and Grant Barbeito, who would go on to produce a powerful documentary about their relationship, and the dedication required to make it to the Olympics. It was called *Touch the Wall*, and it really got to the heart of what it means to swim at the international level. Kara had worked so hard to make the team, and she and Missy pushed each other for months in practice, so it was like a special blessing for the two of them to be able to participate in the closing ceremonies together. Of course, we would do anything we could to make this happen for Missy, so I immediately changed our return flights and booked our house for another week.

Over the course of that next week, our house became like a sorority house. (Poor Dick!) Some of our family members stayed on for a few extra days, but we also housed quite a few swim team members. The way it worked, the USOC housed its swimmers only until their events were completed, so a few of these women had no place to stay, and Dick and I were only too happy to open our doors to them. Trouble was, the house was in a sketchy part of London, and now I felt responsible for everyone's safety. And now there was a lot of hardware in the house, with this group. All those gold medals, not to mention the silvers and bronzes! I told everyone to send their valuables home, because I couldn't vouch for the neighborhood. I even called in Larry Buendorf, chief security officer for the USOC, who turned out to be very helpful. He told us we needed to start getting used to a whole new level of fame with Missy. For the rest of the games, he wanted us to give him a schedule, let him know our comings and goings, so he could make sure there was always someone on his team who knew where we were. He told us we needed to be careful about stopping for pictures and autographs. He said if Missy stopped for even one person, it would quickly turn into a crowd. He even advised Missy to "dress down" in public—to wear a hat, or sunglasses, or maybe a hoodie—but then he acknowledged that she was so tall, and so recognizable, this probably wouldn't work.

One piece of advice I acted on right away was hiding Missy's medals. We wrapped them in a pile of blankets and stuffed them into the mouth of a non-working fireplace. Every time we came back to the house, there was a mad dash to the fireplace, to make sure the medals were all there. We made sure to count them every time.

Four golds.

One bronze.

Not a bad haul for our not-so-little girl.

My Hundredth-of-a-Second Moment

A lot can happen in a fraction of a second. A lot can not happen in a fraction of a second, too. And that's pretty much what happened and what didn't happen at the 2012 Olympics.

How's that for a cryptic opening paragraph? I can be a little overdramatic sometimes. Maybe I should back up and explain.

By almost every measure, the Games of the XXX Olympiad were a giant success for the US Olympic team, and for me personally. But by one all-important measure—one precise, hard-to-get-my-head-around sliver of time—it featured a personal victory disguised at first as a defeat, a distinction that was almost incalculable. You see, at the Olympics, every triumph, every failure, every hiccup, is magnified. It all means so much more, because it feels like everyone in the whole entire world is watching. Because, well, they are. Also, because you never know when you'll get another chance to compete on such a glorious stage. For a swimmer, the Olympics is like the Super Bowl, the World Series, the Stanley Cup. It's the pot of gold at the end of the rainbow. The ultimate event to cap what's essentially a four-year season. Oh, sure, we've got worlds, nationals, Pan Pacific Championships, but a gold medal at the Olympics is the big, big prize. And yet, for all the bells and whistles, for all the hype, the Olympics are exactly like every other meet on our calendar— a jam-packed week of tightly scheduled events that for the most part play out in the same pool. The difference is that it only comes around for most of us once or twice in our careers, so it's tough to treat it like any other swim meet.

And yet at the same time it is like any other swim meet. There might be a different order to the events, from meet to meet, but there's usually no change from Olympics to Olympics, from one worlds lineup to the next worlds lineup, so at each meet you have to sit down with your coach and figure out a schedule that makes sense. You look at the order of events and see how it fits with your strengths. Maybe you're a monster freestyle swimmer whose second-best event is butterfly, but because the fly is scheduled right before the free the coaching staff decides to scratch you from butterfly to make sure you're fresh for your main event. There are all these outside factors at play. In London the semifinal for the 200-meter freestyle was scheduled just fourteen minutes ahead of the 100-meter backstroke final, and this presented a potential problem—or at least a worry. If things went my way and I swam to expectations, best-case scenario on top of best-case scenario, it would be a tight, tricky turnaround, so this was definitely something to think about. Only it wasn't really something *I* was thinking about as I headed off to these games. I usually left it to Todd to figure this stuff out for me, while I tried to keep my focus on what I had to do in the pool. Seemed to me I had enough to worry about without worrying if my 200 free bumped up against my 100 back.

For the most part, I liked to swim on a need-to-know basis. Tell me when I'm up and I'll be good to go—that was my thing.

Of course, it's not enough to just psych yourself up and go for it. There's a lot to think about, a lot to anticipate, all these outside factors, so Todd sat me down the second day we were in London to walk me through the lineup and get my thoughts. My thing was to focus on my time in the pool. Todd's thing was to make sure I understood his thinking and he understood mine. At this stage in my career, since I was still just seventeen, he also involved my parents in a lot of these discussions. For this talk, though, it was just the two of us. We went to this little seating area they'd had set up in the Olympic Village and grabbed a couple of cups of coffee. We sat down on a bench. It was late in the afternoon, the sun was shining, there was lots of activity. To my great joy, there was laughter all around. Turns out the Olympic Village is a very happy place to be.

I didn't know it just yet, but this would play out to be a significant moment. To me, going in, it was just a cup of coffee with my coach. But to Todd, he had a whole script he meant to follow. He pulled out a piece of paper and across the top I could see he'd written the words *seven golds.* Actually, he wrote them in big letters: *SEVEN GOLDS.* He didn't point the words out to me, or hand me the piece of paper, but he knew I'd see them, and he knew those words would freak me out. He noticed me noticing, of course. That was the whole point. At first I was thrown. Seven gold medals! I'd never even allowed myself to think along those lines—it was an impossible dream. So, obviously, I was thrown. Seven golds! For generations of swimmers, that had been an unreachable standard, set by Mark Spitz at the 1972 Olympics in Munich. For my generation, Michael Phelps would rewrite that standard with eight gold medals at the 2008 games in Beijing. Either way, that wasn't at all what I wanted, wasn't at all what I was expecting.

He said, "What's the matter, Missy?"

Like he didn't already know.

I couldn't think how to answer, so I just kind of nodded in the direction of the piece of paper, expecting his eyes to follow mine . . . and they did.

"Oh," he said. "That."

"Yes," I said. "That. Seven? Where did that come from?"

He said, "Does it scare you, that number?"

I said, "No, it doesn't scare me. I just don't get it. That's not why we're here. That's not what we talked about."

"No," he said. "It's not. But I want you to think about that number. I don't want you to be intimidated by it. I don't want you to think of it as some unimaginable feat. This is not what I'm expecting of you. This is not what anyone's expecting of you. This is just a number, but it's a number you should feel good about."

"Okay," I said, trying to figure out where he was going with this. Truth was, I felt confident that I would have had a good chance to medal in any one of the seven events I'd qualified to enter—freestyle, backstroke, relays. And, if I was good enough to medal, maybe, just maybe, I was good enough to win, if everything fell my way. But I couldn't possibly compete in so many events and expect to do well in all of them. My body might break down. The schedule would work against me. Something had to give.

It was at this point that Todd told me about the turnaround time (or lack thereof!) I'd face with the 200 free and the 100 back. He laid it out for me. He said, "That gives you just fourteen minutes, Missy. To go from a semifinal in an event where you're just hoping to make it to the finals, to the finals in an event you're hoping to win. That's not a lot of time."

I could only agree with him. "No," I said. "It's not."

He said, "Can you swim the two hundred free and still take the gold in the one hundred back?"

I thought about it. A lot of times, I liked to leave it to Todd to sort through this stuff. But this was the Olympics, after all, so of course I weighed in—even though what came out wasn't the most emphatic decision. After a couple of beats, trying to get my head around the gravity of what he was suggesting, I was all-in. I said, "Yeah, I really think I can."

"You really think you can or you know you can?" Todd said, making sure. Remember, the 100-meter backstroke was key. I felt like I had a better chance of swimming well in the 100-meter backstroke than I did in the 200-meter free, but that didn't make the 200-meter free any less of a priority. Still, I truly felt I'd have a better chance to medal in the back. The 200-meter freestyle was of course important as well, but I knew it would take a lot for me to even medal.

"I know I can," I finally said. "Definitely."

And so it was decided, and when it came time for my semifinal heat in the 200-meter freestyle I went out and swam a picture-perfect race. Really, it was the most technically sound, most tactically sound race of my career. I managed to touch the wall with a time that put me in exactly eighth place going into the finals, meaning I found a way to put in the least amount of effort, to conserve the most amount of energy, in order to give myself a fighting chance in the 100-meter backstroke and to keep me in the pool for the 200-meter freestyle finals. I came out of that semifinal swim thinking I couldn't have written the script any better.

Now, the 200-meter backstroke was my race. Going into these Olympic Games, I'd told myself it was my race. But that's not what I told others. The line I'd always use when people asked me how I expected to do in London was that I hoped to swim well. Most of the time, that's where I'd leave it—not because I was trying to soft-pedal my hopes and dreams, or because I was worried about jinxing my chances, but because just making it to these Olympic Games was a blessing, a dream come true in itself. I truly believed that. However, I also believed in my ability, so I'd tell myself I expected to make it to the finals. Or maybe, if I was feeling it, that I hoped to earn a medal. But the truth was—deep down, in the secret corners of my heart of hearts—I was counting on the 200-meter back. I'd been working my whole life for the chance to swim for a gold medal, and this was my best chance. But then, alongside the 200-meter back, there was also the

100-meter back, and now it appeared within reach. In the 200-meter freestyle, I just wanted to make it to the finals. Yeah, this was the Olympics, but it was just another swim meet, and I needed to remind myself to continue doing the things that worked best for me. My US teammate Allison Schmitt was one of the best in the world at that distance, and the international field was incredible, so I knew I had my work cut out for me. I'd placed second to Schmitty at the Olympic trials in Omaha, but she was a full body length ahead of me. The rest of the field, at the top, was also unbelievable. But at the same time, I saw myself in the pool with all these great swimmers. I did. You have to let yourself think that way, right? You have to give yourself permission to be among the very best; otherwise, you'll always be on the outside looking in.

In other words, "Throw that dang signed teddy bear into the crowd with pride!"

Could I have gone at it any harder and shaved a second off my semifinal time for my 200-meter freestyle? Could I have given myself more of a cushion, maybe put myself in one of the middle lanes for the finals, in third or fourth position? Absolutely, but it would have cost me. Just what it would have cost me was hard to say. All week long, in my preliminary swims, the idea was to use my legs a little less, to kick a little less, to come off the walls with a little less power. A little here . . . a little there . . . that's how you conserve energy with all these back-to-back swims. I could have gone for it, but I would have felt it in my legs. I would have felt it in my recovery. And mostly, I would have felt it in terms of mental exhaustion.

Psychologically, you give yourself an edge when you hold

something back and get the same result. Even when you move about the Olympic Village a little more slowly than usual, when you're trying to conserve your energy, you get back a little something. You tell yourself you're ahead of the game. And you are. Just by thinking in this way, you are. You're putting all this positive energy into your body, building these great reserves of mighty mojo, so that when it's time for you to fly you can do just that . . . you can fly. It might sound like a lot of nonsense, like an extra effort to gain a fraction of a second shouldn't really change the equation in a meaningful way, but the mind-body connection is a powerful muscle. It all ties in. It really does.

I climbed out of the pool feeling strong and relieved. Feeling great about my semifinal swim in the 200 free. Feeling superconfident about the 100 back final, too. The fourteen minutes between races couldn't pass quickly enough, as far as I was concerned. There wasn't time for me to do a full warm-down so I jumped into the dive pool and did a quick three hundred meters, then hurried to the ready room to check in for the 100-meter backstroke final. Of course, Team USA had to make an appeal to officials at FINA, the international governing body of swimming, in order for this to happen, but we were good to go.

Happily, mercifully, the race couldn't have gone any better—I touched the wall at 58.33, a hair ahead of Emily Seebohm of Australia and Aya Terakawa of Japan. And in just that moment, it was looking like that eighth-place swim in the semifinals of the 200-meter freestyle had made all the difference in the world.

So far, so good, right? I'd won my first Olympic gold medal! But this isn't a story about the 100-meter backstroke. It's not a story about what it means to make it to the tippy-top of your sport. And it's not a story about finding that sweet spot between holding something back and putting it all out there, either. No, it's about all the stuff that can happen and not happen in that fraction of a second I wrote about in that cryptic opening paragraph. Remember? It's about the craziness that can find you in a moment, after you've spent a lifetime preparing for that moment. It's about the space between winning and losing—between working, working, working on the things you can control, and hoping, hoping, hoping that the things you can't control end up going as well as they possibly can. And it's about the little deals you make with yourself at different points in a long meet, and the lesson you take from it all in the end.

It worked out that the schedule leaned in my favor the day after the 100-meter backstroke final, the third day of competition for us swimmers. I had the morning off (my first session off since the start of the Olympics!), so I took the time to clear my head and switch my focus from merely surviving in that 200-meter freestyle semi to finding a way to thrive in the final.

I also took some time to geek out over Justin Bieber and Taylor Swift tweeting congratulations on gold the night before!

It helped that I had that extra time, because it's not so easy to change your approach in what's essentially the same race. Think how the same shift might apply in your own life. Like, say, you're applying to your dream college, and you're worried you won't even get in, but then once you've been accepted and you actually enroll you start thinking if you work hard enough you can become valedictorian. It's a big leap, right? That's kind of what was going on for me. I had a lot of confidence going into the final, because I'd been able to make it into the finals even though I'd been holding back, but now I needed a whole new mind-set. The other finalists were all swimming their own races, of course. They had their own busy race-week schedules to balance. It's possible Allison Schmitt had left a little something in the tank in the semifinals, that's how dominant she was in this event, but the rest of the girls had probably been swimming all-out. This was the Olympics, after all. Nobody's coasting or conserving their way through a semifinal round unless it's absolutely necessary, as it had been for me.

But now I was fresh and confident and thinking how much better off I'd have been if I was swimming in one of the center lanes instead of at the edges in the eighth lane. That half second's worth of extra effort I might have spent in my semifinal win might have put me in a better spot. But then, it might have cost me in the 100-meter back, so I was excited to be in the outside lane. As long as I was in the finals.

When there's a semifinal or final, lane four goes to the swimmer with the fastest time; lane five goes to the swimmer with the second-fastest qualifying time; the third-fastest qualifying time is assigned to lane three; and so on to the outside lanes, where the slowest qualifying time of the heat occupies lane eight. That gives those fastest qualifiers from the morning who are swimming in the middle of the pool an edge. Why? They get to see what the field is looking like on either side of them, and adjust their races accordingly. Yeah, everyone has to swim the same distance, but when you're in the middle you have a kind of home field advantage. When you're in the outside lane, it's like you're off in Siberia. You can still see what's going on, a little bit, but it's not the same as being sandwiched in among the three or four favorites, where you're right there in the thick of it, instead of being on the outside, pretty much on your own.

Those outside lanes can be such a disadvantage, there's even a phrase for those rare times when someone in lane one or lane eight touches the wall first and actually manages to win. They call it an "outside smoker," and it's an incredible thing to see. All of a sudden, you see this body whoosh by, four lanes over, and you think, *Wait, what is she doing? She's not supposed to be here!* But, of course, she is. She'd found a way to make it into that pool for that finals heat, and she's swimming for the same prize as those swimmers in the middle lanes.

So you never know, right? And I think it helped me, being all the way on the outside like that. It left me to swim my race, a race nobody thought I'd win. (Okay, maybe my mom thought I'd win, but she always thinks I can win.) It left me to focus and find my rhythm and not worry where I was in the field. I touched the wall at 1:55.82, a best time for me, by a big margin. I was thrilled, because in just that moment this was a great victory. This was me, putting everything into my swim, and getting everything out of it. I saw the time flash on the wall and right away I thought of what my father would always ask me after a meet. He'd say, "Did you do your best, Missy?" He never really cared if I won, only that I did my best. That was the barometer for him. And here I knew I could look him in the eyes and give him that answer. I could look at myself in the mirror and tell myself the same.

Over in the middle lanes, I could see Allison Schmitt celebrating her gold medal—an Olympic record, it turned out. I was so happy for her—I've never met anyone more deserving. Really, really. And then I could see Camille Muffat of France and Bronte Barratt of Australia celebrating their second- and third-place finishes, and I was so happy for them, too. Really, really. But then I looked up at the scoreboard and saw Bronte's time: 1:55.81. And in just that moment I went from feeling good about myself and being happy for these other swimmers to thinking I'd let a medal slip through my fingers. To thinking my best could have maybe been just a little bit better. One one-hundredth of a second! That's like no time at all—and yet it was all the time in the world, in the 200-meter freestyle. Because at these London games, at least, it meant the difference between fourth place and another Olympic medal.

What had happened to change my thinking? Perspective, I guess. Context. A bunch of *What if?* scenarios that had nothing to do with my reality. There I was, over the moon with my performance, and then—just like that!—I was despairing. Stuck thinking what might have been instead of what was. It's funny the way the same time, the same result, can mean two different things, depending on how you look at it, and here I came to realize I was looking at it in the wrong way. Falling one-hundredth of a second short of a bronze medal shouldn't take away the pride I'd felt just a couple of moments earlier. If anything, it should have made me even happier, to know I was that close to a medal.

Did I even have that extra fraction of a second within me to spend on this race? I don't think so. That's not how I swim. In a final, I put every ounce of energy and effort into every stroke, every kick, every turn. (Those are my "relentless" marching orders, remember?) I leave my heart and soul in the pool with every race. And here that effort paid off in a personal best that shattered my previous mark.

Eventually, I was able to look on this race as a great victory instead of as a shattering blow. It took time—for a couple of weeks, it went from shattering blow to a small pinprick of a disappointment, before I got really comfortable with the silver lining aspects of it. A change of perspective doesn't just happen overnight. Another medal would have been nice. You can always add to your collection! But I came to think the lesson that found me on the back of this swim was even more valuable than the bronze medal would have been. Because, hey, if someone can beat me by a hundredth of a second in an Olympic final, then on some other day, under some other set of circumstances, I can come back and beat her by the same small margin.

So now it fell to me to get back to work and find a way to take back that small sliver of time and make it my own.

SIX

HAVE A LITTLE FAITH

It's impossible to overstate the power and reach of the Olympics. It doesn't matter how much you prepare for it, you can't know how a successful showing on the world stage can turn your life inside out and upside down.

Things got a little wild after London, and not always *good* wild. We came home to a lot of madness and weirdness and wonderfulness. (Is that even a word, *wonderfulness*? I think it should be!) The madness and weirdness usually went hand in hand, like the time Mom caught someone going through our garbage. It wasn't the first time, and it wouldn't be the last, but that day was different. On that day, a woman came to our door at about eight o'clock in the morning with an old swim bag I'd thrown out the night before, asking if I could sign it.

A little out there, but not such a big deal, in a vacuum. Trouble was, there was no such vacuum. This was our new reality, at least for the first while.

The wonderfulness came about in all kinds of sweet, unexpected ways. There was the usual press of media interviews and appearances (so exhausting!), a lot of local parades (so amazing!), the goose-bumps thrill of walking into one of my favorite local restaurants and having everybody stand and applaud (so embarrassing!), the endless stream of little girls who'd drive by our house hoping to catch a glimpse of me and settling instead for a quickie photo of themselves standing on my front lawn (so humbling!). Oh, and the bags and bags of letters and pictures and trinkets that kept arriving on our doorstep, some of them addressed only to "Missy, USA." The postman actually told us that the only other "person" who received so much mail, addressed to just a first name, was Santa.

To this day, I'm amazed that all that stuff got to me—an affirming reminder of how our great big world can be made smaller and more accessible when we move about as our very best selves.

There were welcome-home events and parties and invitations to participate in fashion shoots and charity auctions and all kinds of exciting opportunities. One highlight: I had teeny-tiny speaking parts in *Pretty Little Liars*, one of my favorite shows, and *The Internship*, with Vince Vaughn and Owen Wilson, two of my favorite actors—so much fun! Another highlight: I was a guest on *The Tonight Show with Jay Leno*, and when I decided to take my dad along with me he was mostly excited about seeing Jay's fabulous car collection. So typical! It was all so, so special and awe-inspiring, to be on the receiving end of such abundant warmth and good cheer, and I tried to take everything in stride and return it all in kind, but I think my mom was a little terrified by the sudden surge of attention.

MOM: I'm sorry, but I was really worried about Missy's safety. She was always pretty grounded, always able to take care of herself, but things were different now. I started coaching her on how to be safe, what kinds of precautions to take, what to watch out for. She was such a trusting soul, I was afraid she'd get caught off guard. I'm sure most of the attention came from a good place, people just wanted to show their appreciation or admiration, and we were all so grateful for that. But you have to be careful. That's just the world we live in these days. Missy was driving by that point, so I wanted to be sure the car doors were locked before she pulled out of the garage, that type of thing. I even had a security person come to the house and check everything out, and one of the things I asked about was the doggy door we had leading out to the back for Ruger. He was a big, big dog, and this was a large opening, and still I worried that someone could crawl in, so we found a way to lock it. I was a little obsessive about it, and I'm afraid I was scaring the daylights out of poor Missy, but I didn't care. Nothing was more important than her safety, but she didn't like to think about any of that. What really had her worried was the way her friends were treating her at school and around town. Her good friends were terrific, very supportive, but of course there were other kids who maybe wanted to take a picture of her, or maybe treat her a little differently because they'd watched her on television. All of a sudden, they started paying attention to her. It's hard to suggest it was a burden, being on the receiving end of all that attention, because it was such a blessing. Be careful what you wish for, right? But I don't think we were prepared for the enormity of the Olympics, of Missy having gone to the Olympics and winning all those gold medals. It changed absolutely everything about our lives, and on balance those changes have been to the good. But early on, while we were still getting used to it, while it was at its most intense, it became a bit stressful, I think, all of that attention. It was nonstop. If she wanted to go to a football game at her own high school, we had to call ahead and let school officials know, so they could call in extra security. It was impossible for her just to get back to her routines.

I was going into my senior year in high school, and Mom's right—I wanted it to be as normal as possible. I wanted to be like every other girl in my class, just another "sister" in the sisterhood. My classmates and I had been through so much, and now here we were, approaching the finish line of this special time in our lives, and I wanted to see it through. One of the ways I chose to do this was to keep swimming for Regis. It seemed like such a given to me, a no-brainer, especially after talking it over with my teammates and coaches, but it set off a small storm of controversy. I would practice with the team as much as possible, and go to meets as much as possible, and basically just be a part of things as much as possible, which was basically what I'd been doing the previous three years, heading into the Olympics. I wouldn't have missed it for the world.

Looking back, we should have expected that this decision would get a lot of media attention. The headline was almost too obvious: OLYMPIC GOLD MEDALIST RETURNS TO COMPETE FOR ALL-GIRLS CATHOLIC HIGH SCHOOL SWIM TEAM. But it never occurred to me that people might think I should sit out the season. In truth, the only people I'd even thought to ask were the other girls on the team and my coaches, and they were all completely fine with it—they were great with it, actually. But a few parents from our opponents' schools, as well as some opposing coaches and athletes, seemed to have something to say about it. A lot of journalists and commentators had their own opinions, too. The bottom line was that people felt I'd already had my moment in the sun, and that by continuing to swim I was taking a similar moment away from these other kids. Another worry was that the attendance levels would spike at these meets, as they had the previous year, making it difficult for many parents to get tickets to watch their own children swim. I could absolutely understand the concern, because news crews would show up at these meets and point all those cameras at me, but I chose to put the burden for that one on the media, not me. It would have been so much easier, I think, if people didn't think I was trying to take something *away* from these other girls, from these other programs. I was just doing what I thought was right, in a way that honored the swimming program at Regis Jesuit and my wonderfully supportive teammates there.

We even received a package of homemade cookies at our front door just before Christmas, just as our season was getting under way, from a mother of one of the swimmers at a rival high school. Keep in mind, we'd known this family for years—the Colorado swimming community can be a tight-knit bunch, and I'd been on a club team with this woman's daughter. The cookies came with a card addressed to my mother that said Merry Christmas in a saccharine-sweet way and then read, "We hope you'll convince Missy NOT to swim with the team so that the other girls will have their chance to shine."

Those cookies went right in the garbage, of course.

In the end, I tuned out all the criticism and found a way to enjoy my senior season with my friends. Together, we swam our way to another state championship, which was a great way for us seniors to end our high school careers. I even managed to set state records in my off-events, like the 200 IM and the 50 free, but that wasn't the reason I was swimming. I wanted to be with my friends, to finish the journey we'd started together as freshmen. Nothing was more important. And to watch my best friends as captains, and to step to their roles as leaders, was amazing.

⌒

Why was it so important to me to finish out my high school career in this way?

Why was I so reluctant to give up my final high school season swimming with my friends, after I'd just competed on the biggest stage in sports, at the London Olympics?

What was I out to prove?

The answer was simple. I wasn't out to *prove* anything. It's just that I loved high school. I loved my friends. And I knew we'd all be headed off in different directions after graduation. This time in our lives was coming to an end and I wanted to hold on to it for as long as I could, in whatever ways I could.

You see, Regis was a godsend for me—literally.

Before high school, I'd never really thought about faith or religion. We didn't belong to a church. We celebrated Christmas and Easter, but not in any kind of spiritual way. God wasn't a part of my parents' lives, and so it followed that he wasn't a part of mine. And the thing of it is, I didn't even know that part of my life was missing, at least not on any kind of conscious level. It's hard to say you're missing something when you don't even know what that thing is, right?

As I hope I've made clear, my parents always encouraged me to be my own person, to fight for whatever I believed in, whatever mattered most. Here I had to think that once they signed me up to attend an all-girls Jesuit high school, they must have known God would be there waiting for me. On some level, they must have known. Oh, they knew I'd be taking theology classes, and going to mass, and learning more and more about Christ and Christianity, but even more than that they had to know that I might respond to all of this, in a fundamental way.

I did—thank God, I did—and in the process, I became my own person.

It happened almost immediately. Gradually, but immediately. There was just a different feeling that came over me, the moment I walked through the doors at Regis. It's like a light had found me, but it was only dim at first. I felt safe, comforted. I felt like I belonged. I have a specific memory of coming home from school on my very first day, and my mom asking me how things had gone, and me answering excitedly about a song I'd learned in our welcoming mass. It was the most uplifting thing, the most surprising thing.

The most blessed thing.

Of course, I didn't have the first idea what I was doing, what it all meant. Freshman year, I was just kind of figuring things out. It was a little intimidating, actually. Some of the girls in my class had come from a private, Catholic school background. Others had been raised Catholic and went to mass every week. They knew the language, the routines. They'd been taking these theology classes their whole lives—singing the hymns, participating in the service. It was second nature to them. For me, it was almost like I was taking a God-as-a-second-language course. I was wide-eyed and enthralled, taking it all in. I had so much to learn.

Those first few weeks in mass, I had no idea what to say. The priest would say something and the other girls would answer back. It was a beautiful call-and-response, and I couldn't really participate. I could only nod, and mouth what I thought were the right words. But—curiously, wonderfully—nobody ever made me feel like I didn't belong. I might have been on the outside looking in for the first while, but I was always made to feel welcome. These other girls knew how to go down and receive Communion. They knew how and when to cross themselves. Me, I didn't know anything, but I paid attention. I took notes. I figured it out, and before long it was a part of me.

Of course, I wasn't Catholic, so even if I'd known the rituals I would have missed out on Communion. I couldn't perform the sign of the cross. But it was all so beautiful to witness.

One of the great things about coming to God and religion in this way was that it was on my own terms. It wasn't an "inherited" sense of faith, passed down to me by osmosis or routine. It wasn't expected of me. No, it was genuine. It was truly something

I found for myself, and my parents couldn't have been happier for me. They were even happy to make room for it at home, to open up their lives to make room for what had opened up in my mind. It was important to me, so it was important to them.

At school, it was the most natural thing to pursue this new relationship with God. It wasn't forced on us. It was just there. We could build on it or set it aside. Our teachers and the priests left it to us to think things through for ourselves. We could live our lives in the name of God. Or not. It was up to us. They just taught us what it meant, to be in his light.

Like I said, it was a gradual awakening for me. I felt him right away, as soon as I walked through those doors on the first day of school, but it took a while for me to get comfortable. A lot of people have what they call an "I said yes" moment. Like, "I said yes to God." "I said yes to him being my savior." "I said yes to letting him into my life." But for me it wasn't like that. It was a relationship that grew over time, like any other relationship. When I meet someone new and explain to them how I came to God and faith, I tell them it was like meeting a stranger, and then becoming friends with him, and then becoming best friends with him, and the next thing you know you catch yourself thinking, *How on earth did I live my life without him?* The more time you spend together, the more you learn about each other. So there was no one moment where he appeared before me and I welcomed him into my life, into my heart. It was just a collection of experiences and classes and books and discussions, through which he revealed himself to me, and before I knew it he was an integral part of my daily life.

Instead of an "I said yes" moment, I had what I would call an "Oh, there he is!" moment. Sophomore year, one of the first masses of the year, we went through the entire service and at the other end I realized I'd hit all the right notes, said everything at the right time, moved about in all the right ways. Somehow, the service had become a part of me and I no longer felt like I was finding my way. From there, I just kept growing.

I wasn't alone on this journey, of course. I already had a lot of great friends at Regis from swimming. And as soon as school started, I had a whole bunch more. It was the kind of place where you were close with everyone. I started going to church with my closest friend Abby and her family. Sophomore and junior year, I joined them almost every week. If it worked out that the Cutlers were out of town, or couldn't go to church for some other reason, my mom would go with me. She didn't want me to go to church alone. We even managed to drag my dad a few times, for Christmas Eve services, even though he got annoyed with all the sitting and standing he had to do—typical Richard!

DAD: Missy was really committed to her faith, so of course D.A. and I did whatever we could to support her. But at the same time I couldn't change my stripes entirely. Missy knew who I was. She knew that wasn't me. I'd go to church to support her, but that was where it ended for me. We'd say grace with her at home, because it was important to her, but when it was my turn to say a few words I'd just say, "Grace." I couldn't help myself. I wasn't being disrespectful, and Missy knew I wasn't being disrespectful. I was just being me. If you must know, I admired Missy enormously, for opening herself up in just this way. I believe it took a tremendous amount of courage for her to sign on so wholeheartedly to God and religion, coming from a background like hers, a family like ours. I'd say we were a faith-based family, but our faith was always in doing the right thing, in pushing one another to be our best selves. But here Missy had embraced a whole new kind of faith, a faith in something much bigger. I wanted to honor that, but at the same time I had to honor the ways we'd always interacted as a family. I had to be true to who I was, because ultimately that was the great lesson I wanted to share with my daughter. Be yourself. Be true to yourself. Missy wouldn't have bought it if I'd shed my old skin and jumped in right alongside her. To me, that wouldn't have been respectful. She would have seen right through me. We'd always joked and teased with each other, so the way I looked at it was that this was just something new to joke and tease each other about. The few times I did go to church with her, Missy would catch me napping or complaining and jab me with an elbow. That was just her way of teasing me back, giving as good as she got. Somehow, D.A. and I found a way to stay true to who we were and still be there to support Missy as she went down this new path. It was so very exciting for her, and I was so enormously proud of her growth in this way, but I could only be myself.

With Mom, it wasn't even a question. She would go to church just to support me, keep me company. With Dad, it was more of an ask. In any other family, it would have been a big ask, but my father would do anything for me, so it was more of a small ask. Only, he couldn't change who he was, and I wouldn't have wanted him to. He could go through the motions, keep me company, but that was where it ended for him. My mother, too. They couldn't possibly have the same intense feelings that I was developing on my own, and that was okay. Absolutely, that was okay. In fact, it was kind of great, because going to church became my thing. Saying grace became my thing. My parents could see that there was this fire inside of me now, and it was beautiful, and they wanted to help me stoke that fire in whatever ways they could.

At this point, all these years later, I'm knee-deep into it, so I go to church by myself a lot of the time. I'm on solid ground, at long last—the prayers, the hymns, the rituals . . . they've become a part of me. But in the beginning, when I was trying all this on for the first time, it was super important for me to have the support of my parents, the support of my friends at school. Mom would even ask me back then if I remembered to say my prayers—like I needed her to remind me! But that was just my mom being a mom. She reminded me to eat a good breakfast, and to keep hydrated, and to put on sunscreen when I went outside. (We're talking SPF 100+, folks.) It was all part of her job, she thought, and I appreciated that she stayed on top of me in this way, even with something as private, as personal, as prayer.

I pray in my own way. Sometimes I kneel down at my bed before turning in. Sometimes I'm a little more casual about it. I'll just clasp my hands together and have at it—wherever I am, whenever the mood strikes. Before meets, I'll pray during the national anthem. During my warm-downs, too, no matter how things went in the pool. Win or lose, I take that time to pray, to give thanks.

Always, I think about Jesus the same way I think about my good, good friends. I'm not going to grow in my relationship with a friend if I only see her or talk to her for five minutes at the end of each day. I like to keep connected throughout the day, either on an as-needed basis, or just as a way to check in. If I'm in the car and I hear a sad story on the radio, I might just pull over and catch myself saying, "Hey, God, please keep these good people in your prayers. Let them know there are people thinking about them." Then I'll switch the station, find a song I like, turn up the volume, and drive on.

He's with me all the time, and so I talk to him all the time. I don't just reach out to him when I need his sure hand. No, I tell him everything. The good stuff, the bad stuff, the stuff in between. I'll even tell him about stupid, inconsequential stuff, like an amazing new sandwich I tried at Panera Bread, just to keep connected.

And do you know what? I hear back from him. I do. Not in the ways you see in movies or on television. I'm a firm believer in the notion that God speaks to us in a variety of ways, through our interactions with others, through the songs that find us on the radio, or the books we're reading, or the colors of a brilliant blue sky. If I'm praying about something in particular, or if I'm stressing about a decision, I'll catch myself in a conversation with one of my girlfriends, and all of a sudden it feels like she's speaking directly to my heart about what's troubling me. She might have no idea what's going on, deep down, but she'll offer up the perfect piece of advice, or just the right words of love or encouragement.

That's a God moment, and I thank him for putting this person in my life in just this way.

It used to startle me, to hear from him like this, but by now I've gotten used to it. By now, I expect it. He doesn't *always* get back to me, mind you, but I know the message is getting through. I know he'll get back to me in his own way, in his own time. Sometimes, it can take weeks and weeks—months and months, even. Whatever had me worried or depressed, it might slink into the background, or take care of itself on its own, but then he'll reveal himself to me in an answer and I'll get why things are happening the way they're happening. And those moments that go unanswered? I know they'll become clear to me in time.

When I meet someone new and tell them how I came to God in the halls of my high school, they often suggest that it was swimming that brought me to this place of faith and acceptance. After all, it was largely because of swimming that I'd chosen Regis when I graduated from middle school. But that's not how I see it. How I see it is I wasn't supposed to find God until that time in my life. This was how it was meant to be.

I heard a sermon once that said that if you deny God 233 times it only means that he will keep after you 234 times. That idea really resonated with me, because it was my own experience. Because God was in all the little details of my life all along, and it was only later that I was open to him. I wasn't raised with God in my life, but I came to him on my own. I hadn't been ready, but later I was good and ready, and when you come to God you need to be good and ready. I believe that, deeply. So it wasn't swimming that brought me to God—at least, not directly. I would have made my way to him eventually. When I was good and ready.

~

I wrote earlier that our state-championship win my sophomore year at Regis was what convinced me that I wanted to swim in college, and now that my time at Regis was coming to a close it meant I had to find a community of swimmers and like-minded souls where I could pursue my intercollegiate career.

In a lot of ways, the process of looking at colleges was a lot like looking at high schools. I wanted to be at a place where I could get a great education and the best possible training. I wanted to team up with a group of girls (or *women* . . . now that I was passing myself off as a young adult) who shared my passion for swimming and for life in general. And I wanted to find a coach who understood the "baggage" I'd be bringing to the program, which meant that I was determined to balance my short-course training for the college season with the long-course training I needed to do to continue to compete at the international level.

I wasn't the first national-team swimmer to compete at these NCAA distances, so coaches expected to work with their top swimmers to achieve this balance. Every coach who recruited me said all the right things, and I went pretty far along in the process before deciding on Cal Berkeley. We were visited by coaches from USC, Florida, Cal, Texas, and Georgia. We visited only Cal, Texas, and Georgia, and the moment I walked onto the Berkeley campus, I felt like I belonged—the same way I did when I stepped into the front hall at Regis.

Teri McKeever was a big reason for that. She'd been the head coach at Cal for more than twenty years, and she'd been the head coach for the US women's team at the London Olympics, so we had a happy history together. (She was also my group coach when I was fourteen at that Duel in the Pool in England.) Plus, I knew a lot of the girls (er ... *women*) who swam for Berkeley, and they all had terrific things to say about Teri. She'd put together a close-knit group of fun, talented, disciplined swimmers, and I wanted to be a part of that.

Mom and Dad pretty much left the decision up to me. We weighed all the pros and cons together. But, truthfully, there weren't a whole lot of cons on the Berkeley side of the ledger.

DAD: I was so enormously proud of the way Missy went about this process, but at the end of the day it came down to this gut feeling she had about the school. Her mother and I couldn't really argue with that, but at the same time I was torn. There were a lot of contrasts between Regis and Cal. Regis was small and nurturing and intimate, and a Catholic school to boot. And the Berkeley campus was sprawling, with an enormous student body—anything but nurturing and intimate—and when you read about some of the nonsense Berkeley students can get up to, it felt like more of a faithless environment than a faith-based one. But this was Missy's call. That's a hard thing for any parent to accept, but here there was a piece to it that's unique to parents of athletes like Missy. It's different from the typical college send-off experience, I think. Here we had this child who'd excelled at her sport and made it all the way to the Olympics, where she'd won four gold medals. She did this on her own, but she did it under our roof—on our watch, so to speak. And now we were entrusting her future, her career, to the care and feeding and training and decision making and imprint making of these strangers. Teri and her coaching staff, they seemed like good people. But there'd be all these people getting into Missy's head who she'd never been exposed to before. Professors, advisers, coaches, team psychologists, trainers, all with their own agendas. For the first time, D.A. and I would have no control, no input over what they were saying to our little girl, or how they were saying it, or how Missy was taking it all in and learning from it.

Clearly, Dad was freaking out a little bit. Mom, in her own way, was freaking out as well. She had a hard time with the concept of coed bathrooms! But sometimes if you want your parents to grow you just have to let them go, right?

My "Welcome to College" Moment

don't care how "ready" you are to go to college, or how much you're looking forward to it, the moment sneaks up on you. It catches you looking the other way—your parents, too, some-times. At least that's how it was in our house. In fact, the way my schedule worked out, I was all the way on the other side of the country when it came time to move into my dorm room at Cal; that's how unprepared we were to make the transition.

I was in New York with my dad at the US Open. I'd agreed to cohost this great event called Arthur Ashe Kids' Day, a fun, celebrity-packed program that celebrates the legacy of tennis legend and humanitarian Arthur Ashe. It's a concert, exhibition, and kids' party, all rolled into one. The event is always held on the Saturday before the start of the tournament, in late August, which was right around the time I was supposed to start school.

I don't think we even bothered to check the calendar when I agreed to participate, but it looked like such a blast and I wanted to be a part of it. Ariana Grande was performing, along with the Wanted, and there were appearances by a bunch of great tennis stars, like Serena Williams and Novak Djokovic. The stadium was packed with kids and families. Probably the most thrilling, most humbling moment was when Michelle Obama came on the stage and thanked me for the way I represented the United States in London.

Pinch me, people!

Starting school was probably the furthest thing from my mind that day at the Billie Jean King National Tennis Center in Flushing Meadows, New York, but one of the reasons I didn't have to think about it was because Mom was all over it. Literally, figuratively, and every which way you can imagine. Oh, I was thinking about it, too, in my own way, but I wasn't really paying any attention to the logistics. That was Mom's job. You see, while I was in New York with Dad and my uncle Doug, she was out in California, moving me into my dorm. Really. People look at me like I've got a screw loose when I tell them this story, but this was the only way we could make everything work, and Mom was happy to "take one for the team." It never even occurred to me that there was anything weird about it, or that other students and families didn't do the same thing. And it's not like I wasn't involved at all. We'd packed up all my clothes at home, and or-dered bedding and linens and other stuff I'd need from a local Bed Bath & Beyond in Berkeley, so the plan was for Mom to fly to California, collect our order from the store, and start setting up my room.

Move-in day was a bit of an ordeal, but not in the ways you might think. The manager of the swim team let Mom into the dorm, and he'd set it up so two of the seniors on the swim team were available to help unpack the car and haul my gear up to my room, so it's not like she had to deal with any heavy lifting. What she did have to deal with, though, was the wave of emotions that came over her as she did her thing. She was such a mess! The slightest thing could set her off—she told me later she was crying the entire time. My roommate, Kristen Vredeveld, hadn't moved in yet, so she couldn't really give me the deets, but a few people on my floor told me Mom was pretty weepy. She'd gotten a hotel room near campus, and my father and I were supposed to arrive that night on a late flight, spend the night with her in the hotel, and say our good-byes in the morning. While she was waiting for us, these really nice Cal alumni recognized her in the lobby, and when they approached Mom to say hello and tell her how excited they were that I was coming to Cal she just exploded into tears. It was such an emotional time for her, sending me off to school— just as it would have been a really emotional time for me, if I'd allowed myself to sit still and think about it. Who knows, maybe I was distracting myself from any kind of separation anxiety by keeping so busy.

The really hard part for Mom came the next day. She and Dad took me to my dorm room early, and gave Kristen a hug. We met some of the other students on my floor for the first time. They'd all moved in the day before, so they'd had a bit of a head start, but I hit the ground running. Everyone was super friendly, super welcoming, and most of us were in the same situation, living away from home for the first time, not really knowing anyone. I kind of wanted to kick my parents to the curb and get started on this next phase of my life, but then I found out there were some team meetings and other welcome-type sessions I had to attend, and that Teri wanted my parents to accompany me to one of them. This was unexpected. My parents had a flight to catch, so we huddled as a family and decided Dad would head home as scheduled and Mom would stick around another day to join me at this meeting. This was where the transition became harder still for my poor mom, because the meeting was with the chief of campus police and what he wanted to talk about caught us a little bit by surprise. The meeting went on and on. There were all kinds of safety issues the security people felt the need to discuss with me specifically, since I was a well-known athlete. They wanted to keep me from getting any unwanted attention.

So on its face, then, this was meant to be a useful, informative session, set up to help me feel more comfortable in this new environment, but as we listened to the chief's presentation, Mom started to freak out. To tell the truth, I started to freak out, too, but mostly for how it all must have sounded to her.

The chief of campus police said, "This isn't Denver anymore."

He said, "Things are a little different here. There's going to be a lot of people out to get you, so you have to watch your back."

Then he gave me his cell number and told me to call him if I ever needed anything, and at any time. He said, "If you ever get into trouble, be sure to call right away. I've seen students in tough situations and I'd want to help."

This last statement sent Mom over the top. Here she'd been having a hard enough time just letting go and sending me off to live on my own, and now she had to listen to this campus police chief talk about drug use and violent crime in and around Berkeley. He had her thinking about the vagrants and miscreants in the community surrounding our campus. And he put it out there as a given that all students drink and do drugs, and that I would be falling in line right behind them.

The guy was just doing his job and playing devil's advocate. He was giving me the lay of the land and letting me know I needed to make good choices and that the campus police were there to help me if I needed them, but Mom and I kept flashing each other these looks, like we were wondering if Berkeley was the best place for me after all.

At one point, I leaned in to Mom and whispered, "Why does he think I'm some wild party girl? Am I giving off that vibe?"

She squeezed my arm, and I got that she understood. This wasn't me. The person this police chief was describing, that would never be me. And the campus he was describing, that wasn't the Berkeley community I'd wanted to join. I could see that Mom was trying to play it cool, but underneath she was shaken by what she was hearing. Drugs? Vagrants? Arrests? People out to get me? She told me later that she wanted to grab me and head straight for the airport.

Really, I think it took every ounce of restraint in her mom genes to keep from saying, "You don't belong here, Miss. This is a terrible mistake. Why don't you come home on the plane with me and we'll figure this all out tomorrow?"

Of course, that wasn't about to happen. It was unsettling, to have to listen to this man's negative spin on what I could expect to find at Berkeley, even though we understood that the officer was just trying to send me a clear message. He wanted me to know that campus police had my back. That's all it was, really. But I think Mom and I both knew that the real reason we found it so alarming was because we were afraid to let go. Underneath all this necessary talk about security issues, there was the talk Mom and I should have been having, just the two of us, about how much we were going to miss each other.

Remember, it was my father who'd cut the umbilical cord when I was born. Now it was my mother's turn. And here was this campus police person making it sound like I was about to enter some den of iniquity, making this moment way harder than it needed to be, while underneath, deep down, Mom and I were too busy trying not to cry. She and my dad had been with me every step of the way, and I wasn't too worried about the two of them no longer being involved in my swimming life because I knew they'd find a way to make it to most of my meets. No, it was the day-to-day that was about to slip away from us—at least, that's what we both thought—so to have to listen to this security guy run through all these different worst-case scenarios . . . well, it seemed to me a little beside the point. A part of me wanted to stand up and tell him he didn't have to worry about me making good decisions, here on in.

My parents had already taken care of that.

SEVEN

HAVING MY BACK

In success, my parents have been an enormous source of support, encouragement, and great good cheer.

In struggle, they've been my salvation.

And in those moments *between* success and struggle . . . well, that's when they've really had the biggest influence on me, because that's where we live our lives.

The best way to illustrate the role they continue to play in my life—a role they will always play!—is to highlight a time when I was down so low it looked like I'd never see up again. I guess we should call that a *lowlight*, right? If you've followed my career, you'll know there was one giant hiccup on the way to my second Olympic Games. Actually, to refer to it in this way is to strip the incident of its power and its impact, but I've chosen to file it in my memory like it was no big deal. Of course, it was a *very* big deal at the time, and reducing it in this way is probably just a defense mechanism or evasive tactic. Who knows, maybe it's some kind

217

of motivational strategy. But the truth is, if I dwelled on the enormity of this "hiccup" I might never get out of bed in the morning, or step to the starting blocks with the kind of certainty and confidence I need to swim at my best, so in my head I've set it aside and moved on. And yet if I'm out to truly share some examples of how the strength of family helped me to work past an occasional difficulty, I suppose I have to spend some time on this giant hiccup, and to tell it like it was, not like I've chosen to remember it.

So here it goes. . . .

It was August 2014, my very first summer swimming with Teri, which meant it was my very first long-course season under her tutelage. We were still getting used to each other. In a lot of ways, it's a whole different sport, long course versus short course. I was used to working with Todd, but Teri had her own approach, and she'd been very successful with it, so I was open to whatever she threw at me.

Still, I was a little hesitant heading off to the Pan Pacific Championships in Queensland, Australia, that year because I wasn't really where I wanted to be. The Pan Pacific meet (or Pan Pacs) is a key marker for any swimmer on the international stage. It sits on our calendars like an exclamation point. It's held every four years, in the "even" year before the Summer Olympics, and it falls at the exact middle in our Olympic training cycle, so for a lot of us it signals the start to our final training push. It lets you know in no uncertain terms where you stand, what you're up against, and where you're falling short.

And, significantly, it's also our last chance to qualify for the FINA World Aquatics Championships (or worlds), to be held the following year in Kazan, Russia.

Teri had been named one of the head coaches for Pan Pacs, with Bob Bowman, so she would be my coach there, too.

One thing you should know, when I say I wasn't where I wanted to be it's not a knock on Australia. Gold Coast, Queensland, was beautiful. The Aussies were so welcoming, so friendly. But when you fly halfway around the world like that, it takes some getting used to. You can't help but feel a little out of your element—and here I was, far, far away from home, not exactly firing on all cylinders. Not just yet, anyway.

Now, I might have been far, far away from home, and a long, long way from my routines and my comfort zone, but my parents made sure that the essence of home was always close at hand. And that essence—always, always, always—was the two of them. They made this trip, as they made so many others, and even though I didn't get to see them all that much, it was a reassuring, reaffirming comfort to know they were there. When you switch things up and set off on a new path, it helps to hold on to the constants in your life—your touchstones, your anchors. Just having my parents around gave me a great competitive advantage, because I knew that in their eyes I could do no wrong. Whatever was going on in the pool, I could look up and pick them out in the crowd—Mom always had this special area where she'd like to sit, and she and Dad were such physical opposites, they were easy to spot. It's like my eyes were drawn to them, so I'd always look to them for support, validation, reassurance, whatever I might have needed at the time.

All I needed was a smile or a thumbs-up from one of these two and I was good to go.

Typically, when you travel such a long distance, you give yourself an extra day or two on arrival to get acclimated. For this trip, we had an even bigger cushion, because there were eight days of training camp before the meet actually started. I felt only so-so during the last two days of training camp. I wasn't really hitting my paces, wasn't really myself. But, physically, I felt fine. I couldn't have pinpointed anything "off" about my fitness. I might have been disappointed with how I was swimming, but I felt fine. But then I noticed during warm-ups that my lower back seemed super tight. It wasn't something to worry about so much as it was just something to notice. I thought, *Okay, that's interesting.* Truth is, I didn't really think about it at all, except to recognize the tightness and come up with a plan to ignore it. I figured I would just get on the table after my warm-up and let the massage therapists work on me. Whatever was going on, they'd figure it out and set me right, same way they'd always done.

Coincidentally enough, I'd been starting to feel pretty good in the water. A little closer to where I wanted to be. A little more comfortable. I'd had a couple of strong workouts, was finally hitting my paces, so I was excited about that, but then I went to do a backstroke start and that's when it happened! I pulled up into the start position and all of a sudden my back went into spasm—total meltdown spasm. I'd never experienced anything like it. The pain was excruciating, almost unbearable, but even more than that was the fear that came along with it. I was terrified that this was happening, too scared to even move out of that start position. Has that ever happened to you? Your body tells you it can't move, and you're so completely freaked out by this sudden intense pain you're afraid to even flinch because you think it'd make the pain even worse? I had no idea what to do.

There was about a four-foot gap between where I'd lifted myself and the surface of the water, so I had no idea how I was even going to get out of the pool. Plus, it's not like anybody else had even noticed, at this point. During warm-ups, there's so much activity in and around the pool, there's no one set of eyes on any one swimmer, so everyone was just off doing their thing.

Instinctively, I looked into the stands, to the area where my parents liked to sit. But, of course, the stands were mostly empty. It was just a workout session. Mom and Dad were back at their hotel. A different hotel from where we were staying, by the way, since Team USA likes to keep the athletes away from distracting influences like our fanatic parents and family members. I knew they weren't at the pool, but I sought them out anyway, as if by reflex, hoping against hope that they'd magically appear because I really, really needed to see them. I was frightened, and a reassuring look from them would have meant the world just then.

But I was on my own in this, at least for now.

Three or four coaches and trainers lifted me out of the pool and lay me down flat on the pool deck. I couldn't talk, because I was in a kind of trance. A state of shock, I guess. I was frozen.

One of my teammates, Leah Smith, was the first to come over to me. She said, "Miss, are you okay? What's going on?"

I had no idea how to answer, so I just burst into tears.

Teri was down toward the other end of the pool. There was a lot going on. She was about to start timing me when my back began to spasm, so she noticed this little bit of commotion around me and came rushing over. She grabbed two members of the medical staff on the way.

One of the big concerns, everybody told me later, was the media. Oh, they were all worried about what was going on with me, but underneath all that there was this separate worry. There were reporters and cameras all over the pool deck, so Teri understandably wanted to get me behind closed doors. She didn't want the press telling the world that I'd been injured before the medical staff even had a chance to figure out what was going on. Of course, it ended up coming out anyway. There was a Canadian news crew on the scene, and they captured the whole thing. (Let me tell you, that's a real fun video to watch—and here you can feel free to add just the right level of sarcasm in your head as you read.)

Somehow, they got me off the pool deck and into a more secluded area. I couldn't walk. I had my arms draped across the shoulders of a coach or trainer on either side of me, and it's like they were dragging me—I was deadweight. The trainers rushed a massage table over to me, but I couldn't even lie down on it. If you've ever had a back spasm, you'll know that there's no way to get comfortable. Your whole body is thrown into a painful clench. When you're in the middle of it, it's all you can do to keep from bawling, and I wasn't even doing such a good job of *that*.

Lying down hurt.

Sitting up hurt.

Standing hurt.

Finally, I was able to find the least uncomfortable position and lie down on the table so the trainers could work on me. I was on my belly, my face pressed into the little cutout they have at the top, in an absurd amount of pain. Oh my . . . I'm back in a desperate panic just writing about it, reliving those low, low moments.

The team doctor was on the scene at this point, and what seemed to me like a whole lot of people running all over the place. I was crying, crying, crying. And Teri—God bless her—she was crying, too. She was with me the entire time, holding my hand, telling me everything was going to be okay, when really, she had no idea if everything would be okay.

It was great that Teri was there with me. I couldn't have gotten through any of this without her. But, meanwhile, I was still looking around for my mom and dad. The little girl in me wanted my parents to swoop in and wave their magic mommy and daddy wands and make the pain go away. But that's not how it works, is it? And yet here I was, a college athlete, a national-team swimmer, an Olympian, and all I wanted was to curl up in my mom's lap and have her tell me everything was going to be okay. To have my dad crack a corny joke to distract me from the pain.

The doctor, Dr. Lynch, asked me a bunch of questions, trying to figure out what was going on, but I couldn't really answer him, I was in such agony. I do remember that he asked me to rate the pain on a scale of one to ten, the way they always do, and I answered without hesitation: "Ten!"

I have never in my life said any pain was a ten out of ten, and I never thought I would have to. Just hearing that word out of my mouth was terrifying, because I knew what it took to say it.

There was a wonderful massage therapist on hand named Beth, and she was working on me the whole time, trying to get me to relax. She told me later that it felt to her like there was a metal rod in my back. She'd never felt anything like it.

By this point, some of the other swimmers had picked up that something was going on with me, and a few of my friends came by to see how I was doing. Tyler Clary was a godsend—he didn't leave my side. And weeks later, Dana Vollmer told me that when she heard my answer to the "pain scale" question, she knew I was in bad shape, because for an athlete to rate the pain at a ten out of ten, that's really saying something. What it's saying is, "This is not good."

No, it's not.

No, it wasn't.

After a half hour or so, Beth had me feeling looser. The pain was a little more manageable—still super intense, but at least I could breathe. And think. They'd started doing some acupuncture on me, which offered some relief. And the doc was able to give me some pain meds, a muscle relaxer specifically, but only after checking with Global DRO (an online drug reference site that provides athletes with up-to-date information on the prohibited status of specific medications). There are certain approved medications you're allowed to take when you're "out of competition," and another group you're allowed to take when you're "in competition," and even though the Pan Pac meet hadn't officially started yet we were operating under the "in competition" restrictions, so Teri and the other coaches were careful to make sure I wasn't in violation.

When it looked like they could move me from the pool to the hotel, they stuffed me in an empty minivan with the seats laid down to make a big bed for me. We were about a half hour away from the hotel, so I was dreading the ride, but I couldn't stay in that training room forever. Teri sat with me in the trunk, holding my hand and comforting me the whole way. It felt like the drive took just about forever, and I think I cried the entire time.

Teri kept saying, "Don't even think about the next couple of days. Don't even think about swimming. We just need to focus on right now, on what we need to do to get you better."

Meanwhile, Teri had called my parents at their hotel and made arrangements for them to come and meet us where we were staying. I wished I could have been the one to make the call, because I knew if Mom could hear my voice she might not freak out so much, but I'm told they took the news okay and went immediately into rescue mode. That's how they operate in a crisis.

I ended up going to Teri's room, because she was on the ground floor, and the doctors and therapists came to check on me there. They gave me some more acupuncture, some more medication.

DAD: We didn't know what to think. Poor D.A. was about to burst, she was so upset, but at the same time she was scrambling to find out what she could about what had happened. She put on her doctor hat and started asking questions, but then we heard from someone that Missy was talking about swimming the next day. That's Missy for you. She's wracked with pain, all knotted up, her back in spasm, and she's thinking about getting back in the water. "Put me in, Coach." That was always her thing, but this was new territory for us, this kind of injury. It could have been the worst thing for her, to try to swim, but she let it be known that this was her plan. She started talking about swimming right away, we were told, as soon as the pain started to subside a little. I heard that and didn't know what to think. It was so aggravating. Here you have your child, who in your mind is still just a little girl, and she's so determined to push herself you worry she might do some damage to her spine, or put her in some kind of jeopardy for the rest of her life. And here you have these coaches and trainers, trying to help her. And we're not even on the scene yet, putting all of this together, feeling completely helpless, completely powerless to help our daughter. You want to believe these people have your daughter's best interests at heart, and they surely did, but at the time you just don't know. You don't know what to think.

MOM: We were getting all these different reports about what had happened. I spoke to one of the trainers, and I thought I had a pretty good idea what was going on, but I was still frantic. When your daughter is hurt, you just want to go with her, you just want to be with her. You need to see her with your own eyes, you need to hold her, and cry with her. So that had to be the longest half hour of my life, from the moment we got the call until we were able to get to Missy at the hotel. That's about how long it was, and it was the most frustrating feeling, knowing there was nothing I could do for her. Knowing she was in such tremendous pain. Oh my goodness, I was such a mess. Thank God Dick was with me, so we could support each other. He was just as upset as I was, of course, but he knew there were things we needed to be doing, questions we needed to be asking. So we did what we could to keep each other sane and whole until we could get to Missy's side.

Poor Mom burst into tears when she came into the room. On the ride over, my father had been telling her to keep it together, reminding her that the medical staff had things under control, pointing out to her that it would have worried me to see my mother looking so upset. She meant to put on a brave face, but she couldn't help herself. I was her baby girl, and it killed her to see me in such torment. And even though the muscles in my back had started to loosen up a bit, and the pain had started to feel manageable, I was still in agony. Everything is relative. Maybe I'd gone from a ten to a nine on that pain scale. It wasn't much, but it was something.

It was decided that my parents would stay with me that night. This was decided by my parents, naturally—but Teri and the rest of the coaching staff concurred. Most of the swimmers had roommates, and it wouldn't have been fair for me to put one of my teammates through that kind of ordeal right before a big competition, but it had worked out that I had a room to myself.

I don't think I could have gotten through that night without my parents. They had to help me shower, help me go to the bathroom, help me change. Basically, I needed them with me to be the constant reassuring presence they'd always been, only more so. I couldn't walk by myself, and every time I tried I had to keep asking myself if this was really happening to me, if I was really in *this much* pain. I'd never known pain like this, never even considered it, and I couldn't really understand it or recognize it. Does that make any sense? No, I guess it doesn't, but I kept having these little conversations with myself, trying to process what was happening to me. There'd be this voice inside my head saying, "Is this really happening?"

Saying, "There's no way I'm in this much pain right now."

Saying, "Can I really not walk by myself?"

In a lot of ways, it's like I was having this out-of-body experience, because I could see myself struggling, I could see my parents helping me in the shower, figuring out how to get me comfortable in bed. I could see my pain in their faces, if that makes sense. It's like I was watching a movie, but then I'd catch myself and check myself and realize it wasn't a movie; it was real. This was me, suffering. These were my parents, absolutely beside themselves with worry, and their own suffering, too.

My mom has this thing, when she's taking care of me—she switches into a state of triage, like she's back at the hospital. She puts on her doctor face and becomes almost clinical. Whenever I got sick as a kid, or had my little scrapes or bruises, she'd take care of me almost like I was any other patient. But that was all out the window in Queensland. Here she was so broken up, because she knew what this could mean, in terms of my swimming and my goals and dreams. There was the pain itself, which was bad enough, and then there was what the pain could mean, so she was trying to keep it together, to not let me see how worried or upset she really was. But let's just say she's not much of an actress, my mother. I could see right through her.

By some other miracle, I was able to walk the next morning. A little bit. I was able to think. A little bit. The surreal parts of this ordeal were starting to fall away, and I let my mind turn back to swimming. For the first time, the *idea* of swimming seemed possible. During the worst of it, I don't think I had a single swimming-related thought, other than the basic thought that I still wanted to compete in these championships. I tell that to people, and they think it's a line, but it's the God's honest truth. Yeah, I wanted to jump right back in the pool and see what I could do, but I didn't have a single thought about my future beyond that. There was no room in what was happening to think what it all might mean for our upcoming season at Cal, for worlds, for my career. No, it was just something to endure, to get past, and now that the very worst of it seemed to be behind me, my focus turned to the events on the next day's schedule, when the competition was due to begin.

I hadn't slept much that first night after my injury. I mostly lay in bed not moving, sandwiched between my mom and dad, trying to keep calm and focus on what lay in front of me. My parents kept checking on me, and whispering and tiptoeing so I wouldn't know they kept checking on me, but I knew. I was just too tired and too beaten down to say anything, so I mostly kept my eyes closed and tried to will away the pain. As I lay there, I kept hearing Teri's voice telling me to take it one moment at a time, and as soon as the sun came up and my parents started stirring I thought I'd try to get out of bed and see if I could walk. So I did— and, lo and behold, I could move about the room without any help. I thought, *So far, so good.* Then I thought I'd try to bend, and, lo and behold, it was impossible. Whatever metal rod Beth had felt when she was working on me in that back room off the pool was still there, in full force. So I thought, *Okay, so bending is out.* I ran through this whole checklist, did a whole inventory of what

I could do and what I couldn't do, and at the other end of it I thought it made sense to get back in the water.

This was my solution, the answer to all my problems. I could barely move, so I might as well swim. Genius, huh? But this was me, relentless, refusing to quit, even though my body was telling me to shut it down for the next while.

My poor mother thought I was nuts, but I wanted to see how this injury had left me, so Teri arranged for me to go to a private pool away from the craziness of the meet, away from the media. There was no one else there. Just me and Teri and one of the trainers. I only swam 1,000 meters, I didn't want to push it, but at least I was swimming. Really, I was moving about okay. Tentatively, but okay. I couldn't do any flip turns, and I certainly couldn't do any starts, so I had to do a barrel turn each time I hit the wall. There was no way I was getting into that tuck position. And it hurt. Like I said, I was okay, or at least, way closer to okay than I'd had any right to imagine the day before. But every stroke was painful. Actually, every stroke was *doubly* painful, because here again, there was the pain itself, and the accompanying worry about what that pain might mean. I repeat myself, I know, but those two things, bundled together, were pressing down on me like you wouldn't believe.

I wanted to know what was wrong with me. But at the same time, I *didn't* want to know.

People asked me later if I was worried that I might have done further damage to whatever was going on with my back by swimming so soon after I went into spasm, but I honestly didn't care. I got it in my head that this meet was all-important. I wasn't ready to give up on worlds. And I wasn't ready for my teammates to give up on me. That's the thing with me and the team aspect of swimming. I'd been looking forward to swimming in the relays, and I knew my team needed me. We needed each other, really. Of course, they needed me at full strength, and who even knew if I'd be able to help them at all in my present condition? But I had myself convinced that I owed it to the other girls to push myself, to see what I had. Honestly, if you'd asked me at the time if I would have risked more serious injury by swimming, I wouldn't have cared—that's how important it was to me to swim in this meet, to do my part. It wasn't smart, but this was how I was wired. This was me, wanting nothing more than to pick up my team and represent my country in the best way I knew how.

When I got out of the pool, I told Teri I wanted to swim my events the next day. She of course mentioned that the doctors still hadn't figured out what was going on with me, and that the smart thing would be to sit this one out, but I wasn't hearing any of that.

She said, "Are you sure, Miss? This is serious."

I said, "Yes, I'm sure. And I'm completely serious."

She said, "You have my full support either way. If you don't swim at all, I'll be behind you. If you swim every event, I'll be behind you."

I had no idea if I could even swim well enough to qualify for worlds or to help my team. Only that I had to try.

The way the Pan Pacs work is that Team USA can qualify only two American swimmers into an A final. Even if you post one of the top eight times in the preliminary heats, you've still got to be one of the top two Americans to make it to the finals, so that's what makes Pan Pacs one of the toughest meets on the schedule, but also one of the most exciting. And then, just to play it all out, you need to post one of the top two American times in order to qualify for worlds, which are held every two years.

Team USA has so many strong, talented swimmers, the very best in the world in a lot of events, that the Pan Pac mornings become a kind of intramural competition. We're going up against each other in those preliminary heats, trying to get into that A final, so I had all that going on as I was getting ready to push past the pain and try to swim. Because, of course, it wasn't enough *just* to swim. I had to be competitive. There had to be something on the line, and there was absolutely everything on the line, for *everyone* in the pool.

Was I at full strength? No. Was I pain-free? No. Would I be any better or stronger with one more day of rest, before my first morning swim in the 200-meter freestyle? Maybe. But one thing I knew for sure: I was able to suck it up and swim. Whatever pain I was feeling, it wasn't so bad that I couldn't tolerate it for the time it takes to swim a 200-meter race. I'd worked too hard, traveled too far, to let a back spasm keep me from competing all-out.

Let me tell you, getting up on those blocks for my 200-meter free and preparing to dive and knowing I would be in an incredible amount of pain for what I prayed to God would be under two minutes . . . oh man, it was the worst feeling imaginable. And yet it wasn't something I couldn't power past. I wasn't even concerned about going a best time. Just making it through the race would have been victory enough.

And do you know what? I did okay. Not great, but okay. Good enough to finish third among American swimmers in the 200-meter freestyle. The pain wasn't any worse than I'd imagined.

But it wasn't any better, either. It was what it was, and it put me in the B final, where my goal was to find a way to post a better time than one of the two American swimmers in the A final, Shannon Vreeland and Katie Ledecky.

DAD: I must admit, I don't think I ever felt more proud of my daughter than I did at that meet in Australia. To see the kind of pain she was in, to stay up all night with her and try to comfort her, and then to see this absolute resolve come over her when she decided to swim the next day. It was just incredible, like nothing I'd ever seen, and this goes back to my days playing college football. I'd been around athletes my entire life, but I certainly wasn't expecting to see this kind of grit, this kind of fortitude. And it's not that I would have ever doubted that Missy would show such fire in the face of such adversity, just that it had never come up. Until the Pan Pacs, I never had any reason to stop and think what she'd do in this kind of tough spot. It wasn't an issue. But now here it was, and this little girl was tested in this incredible way. My little girl. Only she wasn't so little anymore, was she? It was difficult to watch, because her mother and I knew what kind of pain she was in. Probably we were the only ones in that arena feeling that pain with her. But we were also the only ones who knew how deeply important it was to Missy to see this through. However it turned out, she had to see it through. And she did.

Well, to this day I don't know how I did it, but in the B final I put up a time of 1:56.04, which managed to hold up against Shannon Vreeland's time in the A final, so by yet another miracle I qualified for worlds the next year, and it was in that moment that I realized I could accomplish all my goals for this meet. My time in the B final set a Pan Pac meet record, breaking Schmitty's 2010 time of 1:56.10, but it would be the shortest-held record of my career, because Katie Ledecky swam an incredible 1:55.74 in the A final, just moments later.

But the record was the last thing on my mind, just then. All I cared about was that I'd qualified for worlds, and that my body was telling me I could swim at a competitive level for the rest of this meet. Make no mistake, it would be the most difficult meet of my life, but there it was, within reach. Whatever pain I would endure for the few minutes I was in the water each race, I could take it. Whatever doubts or worries were in my head, I could chase them away. And I knew in my heart that my parents were at the core of that certainty I now felt. Without them, dropping whatever was going on in their lives to travel all that way just to watch me swim in Australia; staying up all night with me and holding me and easing me through the worst of the pain after my back went out; believing in me wholeheartedly, no matter what. Without them, I wouldn't be in a position to swim, let alone post any kind of world-class time.

If somebody had told me two days earlier while I was bawling by the side of the pool that I would be back in the water, qualifying for worlds, I would have laughed at them through my tears. But here I was, doing just that—also through my tears, just to be clear, because I'd never known this kind of pain, mixed with this feeling of accomplishment. It was the strangest mix, I'll say that, but it left me feeling like I could accomplish just about anything.

It turned out *just about anything* was *just about everything*, as far as that meet was concerned. I ended up swimming all my events, something Teri had her doubts about, but not me. She said, "Missy, doing one event is one thing, but trying to do two events in one night, is that the smartest thing?"

I knew she wanted what was best (and safest!) for me.

I said, "It's not about being smart. It's about whether I can, and I think I can."

And I could. And I did. I qualified in my 100 and 200 back, my 100 and 200 free, and I was even able to swim the relays I wanted to swim. The relays were actually more emotionally draining than my individual swims. Why? Because I felt a responsibility to the other girls on the team. In an individual event, if I came up short, it was on me. It was a personal test. But in a relay, I had all these other girls counting on me. I was swimming for Team USA, so I had to perform at a certain level. Of course, the coaches wouldn't have let me swim the relays if they didn't think I was up to it, but knowing this didn't make it any less stressful.

I'd already hurt myself; the last thing I wanted to do was hurt my team.

At the end of this ordeal, I still had to fly home, and I was dreading the flight. It was one thing to take the half-hour drive stretched out on that seat-bed in the team minivan, back and forth from the pool to the hotel, but quite another to fit myself into an airplane seat for a twelve-hour flight. I had no choice, though, and as soon as I got back to Northern California there was a constant stream of doctor visits and MRIs and bone scans.

At first, nobody could tell me exactly what had happened in that Queensland pool. Eventually, though, the picture came clear: I had a minor bit of scoliosis, which we'd known about over the years, a slight curve from my L1 vertebra to my L5 vertebra, and what had happened was I'd started getting some serious bone buildup in and around my facets. Everything was inflamed, and when that happens the bone mass begins to press on the nerves, and that's what causes the spasms—a condition known as irritable facet syndrome.

Mom had her doctor hat on, so even though I had some of the best doctors in sports medicine weighing in on this, from Team USA and from Berkeley, she was riding point. She was back home in Colorado and she wasn't technically in charge of my care, but in reality, she was.

> **MOM:** The good news, really, was that there was no fracture. That's what had us all so worried. That, or a disk problem, or even a tumor. It wasn't anything that required surgery. But at the same time, the good news came with a bit of bad news, because there was no guarantee that the problem could be fixed. The bone buildup was there. It was a fact of Missy's life. The minor scoliosis was there, another fact of Missy's life. There was no guarantee that this flare-up, if that's what it was, wouldn't happen again. All we could do was work to get Missy stronger, and try to keep that inflammation from happening again. It was probably the best diagnosis we could have gotten, given what poor Missy was facing, but it came with its own

problems. It meant there'd always be this nagging worry, in the back of Missy's mind, that she'd clench up again. And she wasn't completely right for the longest time, after Pan Pacs. She was back to her full schedule, getting her strength back, but every week or so she'd have to cut her workouts short because her back was flaring up. This happened less and less, over time, and as I write this it hasn't happened in a good long while, but Dick and I worried that it would get inside Missy's head in some way. And when I say Dick and I worried, what I really mean is that I worried, because that's my job in this family. Dick wasn't like that, and thank goodness Missy seems to get this part of her personality from him, because it didn't seem like she was too worried, either. I'd try to talk to her about it, from time to time, because I knew it must be weighing on her, but she didn't want to hear it. Her focus was always someplace else. When she got back to school, her focus was on getting ready for her sophomore season. After that, it was getting ready for worlds. And soon it was easy to forget Australia ever happened.

Relax, Mom. I'm okay. And you and Dad are a big part of that. But I'll let you in on a little secret. You're not the only one who worries about me. I worry, too, but I do it in my own way. I deal with it by worrying about the things I can control. If my back flares up again, I'll deal with it. I'll work like crazy to make sure that doesn't happen—but if it happens, it happens.

One of the ways I worked like crazy when I got back to school was going to physical therapy, in addition to my regular workout routine. Two or three times a week, to start. There was no time to put a pin in what I was doing and concentrate entirely on what was going on with my back. I had classes and practices. There weren't enough hours in the day to do what I needed to do. Teri set it up so I could keep my workouts light, but I didn't want to lose any ground, so I pushed myself. Still, like my mother said, I'd get hit with a little twinge, some little hiccup, every week or two, so I wasn't completely in the clear.

Finally, I set aside a couple of weeks at the end of the year just to focus on my back with my trainer, Ann Caslin, and my physical therapist, Kristy Illg. We called it the "Twelve Days of Rehab," and we went at it, hard. I was still swimming, here and there, but it wasn't too, too intense. I ramped up my physical therapy to every other day, and I took full advantage of the break in the academic calendar to rest during the day, between workouts. Whatever was going on with me, I wanted to get ahead of it—so far ahead of it that I could at last put it behind me. In February 2015, six months after my injury, I received cortisone shots in my back (after confirming that the treatment was approved by the World Anti-Doping Agency!), and that's when I at last felt like I had some control over what was happening. The inflammation was gone. The bad days fell away. And I was able to get back in the pool and do my thing. As my routines became routine once more I could look on my one-word rallying cry in a whole new way. *Relentless*—it was written on my soul.

My 1:39 Moment

Never underestimate the power of goals. Setting them, chasing them, breaking them . . . I love it when there's a carrot for me to grab at, a place for me to put my focus, my energy. I think I got that from both sides at home. My dad was always on me to challenge myself, and my mom was always on me to do my best, so of course it followed that as I got more accomplished as a swimmer the challenges kept getting bigger, and I kept telling myself my best could be just a little bit better.

Coming back from Australia, trying to fight my way to full strength, I set a lot of incremental goals. Trouble was, it was taking a long time to get back to where I felt I needed to be. My back was okay, not great, so the usual goals didn't really apply. As swimmers, we live by our times. Our best times define us and push us further still. But when your body's beaten up and you're scrambling just to reach a certain level of fitness, those times either lose their meaning or they remain frustratingly out of reach.

And yet . . . and yet . . . there was one time I held out in front of me like a lifeline. A carrot. Three little numbers that came to mean more than anything.

Here's the *back*story (pun very much intended!): I continued to swim after Pan Pacs, but I also continued to struggle. Somehow, I'd managed to push past the pain in Queensland and find a way to swim at a high level, but looking back I think I got through that meet on a rush of adrenaline and an iron will. Plus, I hadn't really lost any fitness by the time the competition started. Once the initial flare-up eased and I learned I could tolerate the pain, I was good to go, but now that I was addressing the injury and working to prevent a reoccurrence, I was out of my routine. Here I was, several months later, and I still wasn't myself—I was getting better, stronger every day, but I was not where I was before the injury. I was in the pool, building my strength, building my confidence, but there was a lot of ground to cover. A lot of the rehab work I was doing kept me out of the pool when my teammates were swimming, so I wasn't exactly "game ready." I was pain-free for longer and longer stretches, but I hadn't really had a chance to put it all together and swim to my ability.

This was a problem, as far as the national championships were concerned. For a college swimmer, this is the biggest meet on the calendar. But unlike other championship meets, it comes around in March, which is way early on the swimming schedule. I'd managed to compete during our regular season, and to make a contribution, but the NCAAs were a whole other level. It's tough enough just to qualify, and I'd managed to swim well enough to make it, along with fifteen other swimmers from Cal. (That's a big number, by the way, from one team. Roll on, you Bears!) Now I'd be swimming against the best of the best, and I wouldn't have to worry about swimming any of the off-events I sometimes needed to swim to help the team, but the calendar didn't leave me with a lot of time to prepare. I could see where I was, and where I needed to be, so I started to get a little nervous after our season was under way, and I remember going to my physical therapist, Kristy, one day and telling her how worried I was about my training.

She said, "Why are you worried?"

I said, "Because I need to go a 1:39 in my two hundred free in just a few months, and I'm not really training for that right now." That was my target number, because my thing wasn't just to win—I wanted to set a new standard.

She said, "Oh, but you are. You're training for a 1:39 right now."

I said, "Umm . . . how? I'm barely in the pool."

She said, "If you don't get ahead of this, Missy, you won't be in a position to go a 1:39. You need to get strong."

Kristy was right, of course. And I was right, too—right to worry, at least.

Those three little numbers I talked about earlier? Here they were, lined up like they had something to tell me: 1:39.

In my day, which really wasn't all that long ago—just last year, as I write this!—the national championships were held over a three-day period. Now they do it as a four-day meet, which makes a big difference. (Gee, thanks, NCAA!) When it was just three days, when you were swimming a compressed schedule, there were some back-to-back swims. I wasn't sure how my back would hold up under such an intense schedule. The 200-meter freestyle was to be held on the second day, and I got it in my head that this was the most important race of my collegiate season. It wasn't just me who built the race up in this way. If everyone swam to form, I'd go up against Simone Manuel, a freshman at Stanford who also swam for the national team. I'd known Simone for a couple of years, but this was the first year we were college rivals. And if you know anything about college rivalries, you'll know that the one between Cal and Stanford runs pretty deep. Simone had kicked my butt in this event at our dual meet earlier this season, at home, just before I got my first cortisone shot to alleviate some of the lingering tightness in my back. Then I managed to hold her off in the Pac-12s, despite a big kick—her signature move—where she would hang back and then move in for the kill at the very end. I wanted to lead from the beginning. That was the way I told myself I had to swim against Simone—any other swimmer, I could chase her down with a big final push, but Simone had such tremendous closing speed I wanted to put her behind me as soon as possible, by as big a distance as possible. I wound up beating her by just a couple hundredths of a second. So in the minds of a lot of people who followed college swimming, this was shaping up as the big matchup of the NCAAs.

It was a big race for me, too, but not just because of the supposed rivalry with Simone Manuel. The year before, I'd won the 200-meter free at the NCAAs with a 1:40.30, setting an American record. That's why that 1:39 mark was such a big deal. My obsession with 1:39 started in 2014, months before my back injury, months before I knew Simone would be swimming for Stanford.

One thing had nothing to do with the other. I wanted to come back the following year and win with a 1:39; that's all. Those three numbers meant everything to me, just then. No American swimmer had cracked that threshold.

I didn't care if I came back and touched the wall in 1:39.99. I would have been happy—thrilled, actually. Again, that time was in my head before I hurt my back, and it started to loom larger still while I was rehabbing. Those three numbers grew in significance as I fought my way back to whole. They were more than just numbers to me. They became a powerful symbol, a lure. I set it up in my head that if I hit those numbers I'd be able to race at my best again.

But there's a downside to attaching too much significance to any one goal. That's another great lesson I took in from my parents. Remember, Dad had been a competitive athlete, and he understood the value in taking a slow and steady approach. Too much, too soon wasn't the way to build or sustain a career, so what I got from him was the benefit of the long, hard climb. And from Mom I got that the weight of a disappointment should never be so great that it could break you. She'd been through so much, at such a young age, and yet no one setback could ever really set her back. The idea was to hold your disappointments to a manageable level. To learn from them. To make it so they couldn't beat you.

I didn't want to fall short at the NCAAs and come away thinking I was done—because, clearly, that wouldn't have been the case. It would have just meant I still had some hard work to do. But I wasn't planning on missing my mark. Every day when I woke up for my early workouts, when I went to physical therapy, when I did my strength training . . . I closed my eyes and saw those three numbers.

1:39.

It's like they were lit by neon. If I felt sluggish, didn't want to get out of bed, didn't think I had it in me to power through another workout, I could just close my eyes and look at that neon sign.

1:39.

If I was just sick and tired of the grind, not seeing any real progress, not feeling like I could fight my way to the other side . . . same thing. Those three numbers kept me sane, kept me going.

The night before the 200 free, I was really nervous. And, somehow, really calm. I took this as a good sign, because when I was teetering between nervous and calm, that's when I was at my best. It told me I was excited to swim but also confident. I was nervous but not anxious. There's a difference. With nerves, you can find a way to set them aside. Anxiety is a whole other mess.

That night, I kept thinking about those three numbers. And about Simone Manuel. She was in my head, because she was amazing at this distance. It's like the race was built for the way she swims. I knew she was going to hold something back and then find a way to surge over that last hundred, so I told myself I couldn't hold anything back, coming off the blocks. I knew she'd be coming for me, gunning for me, but it would be a mistake to leave anything in the tank the first half of the race. The way to win was to push—basically to put my first hundred up against her second hundred.

May the best hundred win, I told myself.

Typically, I don't spend a lot of time worrying about a specific opponent. The idea is to swim my race. But this race was different. I'd built it up in such a way that it represented more than this one race. It stood before me like a validation. And as I stepped to the blocks I was overcome by this powerful feeling. I don't want to say I felt invincible, but it was a little like that. Has that ever happened to you? You work so hard to get to a certain place, you're pointed so long in that one direction, you're dialed in in such a way, that you know you can't be denied? It wasn't something I could have put into words, wasn't even something I was thinking on any conscious level. It was just there. And there I was, too—good and ready.

The moment I hit the water, it was all over in my mind. Nothing against Simone, who is a tremendous swimmer, but as I swam I was myself again. Everything kicked in. The pain and uncertainty of the past months were washed away. I was in London again. I was on top of the world, on top of my game.

I touched the wall at 1:39.10. I shattered my record by more than a second, beat my number by almost a full second. That might not seem like a lot if you don't swim, but to a swimmer, that's an eternity, and I didn't have to look at the clock to know I'd hit my mark. In my bones, I knew, but when I finally looked up and saw that I'd beat my number, I went a little crazy, especially for me. I feel bad about it now, looking back, because I don't like to celebrate in such an obvious way. I'll do a little dance in my heart if I win a big race, I'll burst into a smile, but I don't want to show up the other swimmers. I'm mindful of the fact that a good result for me doesn't always mean a good result for them, so I try to be a little more reserved. But on that day, at that moment, it all came pouring out of me. The frustration, the doubts, the pain . . . they were gone, in that instant, and in their place was this sweet rush of pure joy. It meant so much more than just winning a national title, although that was certainly a part of it. It meant so much more than the twenty points I'd just earned for my team, although that was an even bigger part of it.

What it meant, really, was that I was back. So I fist-pumped my little heart out.

"That which does not kill us makes us stronger." That's a line from the German philosopher Friedrich Nietzsche, and you'll see it on posters in locker rooms all across the country. It even showed up in a Kelly Clarkson song, kinda sorta. And here the same thought found me in that pool, whooping it up in this uncharacteristic way.

1:39.10 . . . I did it.

EIGHT

HOME, AGAIN

Sometimes you need to change things up.

Trouble is, change can be hard. I know, I know. That's not exactly a "stop the presses" statement. You won't find it on a poster above my bed or printed on the band of my goggles. But it wasn't so obvious to me when I was faced with another huge decision. Remember those big decisions I'd made when I was thirteen and fourteen years old? To go to Regis Jesuit instead of my feeder school, Arapahoe High School, and to keep training with Todd Schmitz and the Colorado Stars when half my friends were bolting to swim with Nick Frasersmith's new club? Well, those two decisions had worked out to glorious good, but I was just a kid back then, and now I was facing the biggest decision of my newly acquired adult life.

Once again, I had the full support of my parents—but, once again, they left it to me to call the shots. After they had given me a ton of things to think about, of course.

What was new this time around was that I also had the full support of my faith, which as I shared earlier had kicked in when I started high school. It had only deepened in the years since, and once I got to Berkeley it took on a whole new complexion. One of the great reasons for that was a student group called Athletes in Action (AIA), which you'll find on several campuses. And I started going to a wonderful church called Reality San Francisco, where there was a hip, animated pastor and the services were just amazing, so I was on good solid ground here, knowing full well that God and my parents had my *back* on this. (Forgive, please, the corny play on words—but you've been reading for a while by this point, so you know I just can't help myself!)

The dilemma was this: as I was recuperating from my injury and struggling to get back to form for my sophomore season at Cal, in early 2015, I was realizing more and more that I'd hit a kind of brick wall in my training. But then, maybe it's a little harsh to put it just this way. It's more like I'd come to a fork in the road. I could either go one way, into unknown territory, or another, onto familiar ground. This wasn't me being critical of anyone or anything—this was just me taking a harsh look at where I was and where I was headed. This was me knowing my strengths, my weaknesses, my comfort zone.

This was me coming at long last to the realization that, just as there is more than one way to make a family, there is more than one way to go to school and still somehow train for the Olympics.

Before I get into the nuts and bolts of this decision, I want to pause for a bit and reflect on my time at Berkeley, because it really was a wonderful, transformative, foundational experience. I've got to admit, I was a little worried about how I'd fit in as a young woman of faith in such a liberal, anything-goes type of environment, but there was a place for me in Athletes in Action. I joined almost as soon as I arrived on campus, and I had some teammates for company: Caroline Piehl, Taylor Nanfria, and Caitlin Leverenz. It helped that I'd known Caroline from Stars, and that I'd met Taylor on my recruiting trip (and that she was my "big sister" on the team), and that I'd swum with Caitlin on the national team a few times, but here we were charting this new territory together. AIA was such a good, good group, made up of athletes from all different sports, from all different walks of life, knitted together by our love of God and our commitment to live a life in his glory. We'd get together once a week for Bible study, worship, and just to hang. A lot of times, there'd be guest speakers, with really relatable messages for young athletes, and opportunities to volunteer in our community. On Sundays, we'd go as a group to Reality San Francisco, which was a pretty non-denominational church where everyone was made to feel welcome.

That feeling of welcome extended to the rest of my team as well. I wrote earlier about the immediate warmth and feeling of belonging that found me when I first walked through the doors at Regis, and there was a similar welcome that found me on the Cal campus. Right away, I was struck by the unique culture and chemistry of our team. I'd seen flash-glimpses of this when I visited the school, and of course I'd come to know a lot of the swimmers over the years and they'd all shared their experiences with me as I was making my decision to go to school there, but the Cal culture is not something you can really understand until you're in the middle of it. Mostly, it has to do with the points of connection Teri McKeever instilled in our team, along with our wonderful assistant coach, Kristen Cunnane.

Teri's big thing was "accountability"—it was in the air and all around. We were all made to be accountable to one another, to ourselves, to our coaches, and to the university. We were expected to show up every day for practice—twenty minutes early, on "Teri Time!"—and to give our absolute best, at every single workout. The positive, purposeful attitude that came out of this was amazing. I'd never been in such a team-oriented environment, and I loved it. Straight out of the gate, I loved it. For the first time in my swimming life, I was surrounded by a group of teammates who had exactly the same goals as I did. And it was just one goal, really—to win a national championship.

Now, I'd had a taste of this kind of esprit de corps in high school, but other than my freshman year I'd never had the full, all-in experience at Regis. Here at Cal, though, we were stocked with world-class talent, and we were thrown together 24-7 in pursuit of this shared goal. Up and down our roster, there were young women who could count themselves among the very best in the world in their events, so the ways we pushed each other, the ways we held each other accountable, they were all tied up in a deep respect for our abilities as a group, and our commitment to compete at the very highest level.

As for Teri herself . . . I'd had an incredible experience working with her. She taught me so much about being a leader, about being a strong, independent woman, about fighting through adversity and pain and disappointment. I probably learned more from Teri *away* from the pool than I did in the water, because her focus was so keenly oriented on the development of our character.

And so, for all these reasons, and so many more besides, I considered my decision to leave the swimming program at Cal very,

very seriously. But I tried to set my personal feelings aside and focus on a kind of bigger picture. And now, following those back spasms in Australia, I was starting to think there'd be some sort of recurrence, as I moved toward the end of the four-year Olympic cycle. Mostly, the tug and pull between long-course and short-course training hadn't allowed me to focus fully on the work I'd need to do to (hopefully!) defend my gold medals at the Rio Olympics, or (also hopefully!) to collect a few more. Of course, once we got through the NCAAs sophomore year, I'd cease short-course training, but the tentative plan had been to stay on at Berkeley and continue to train with Teri McKeever. In this way, I'd keep those all-important connections to Cal, and to my great friends on the team, and to the other coaches and trainers who'd been such a blessing in my life.

But once I got hurt I started to feel a different kind of tug and pull. Namely, the tug and pull to go home. When I looked honestly at myself and the progress I'd made in the nearly two years I'd been at Cal, I realized I wasn't firing on all cylinders the way I'd been when I was swimming with Todd. When I was swimming at altitude, which, believe me, makes a *huge* difference in terms of fitness and stamina and all those good things. When I was sleeping at home, in my own bed, away from the academic, social, and cultural distractions of being away at college.

So there I was, at this fork in the road.

I thought about it, prayed about it, stressed about it. A lot. Teri had been so dear to me during those agonizing moments in Queensland. Really, I don't think I could have gotten through that ordeal without her. And she'd been so supportive of me and so helpful, going all the way back to London. She was the main reason I'd decided to swim for Cal, and I was so glad I did. The swimming community at Cal was like my family, and Teri was a big part of that, a big reason for that. But as I looked to the year ahead, and all the new distractions that would come my way once I finally "turned pro" and could no longer swim in NCAA meets, I found myself leaning more and more to home, where I believed I would be in the best position to tune out all those distractions and fight my way back to whole.

DAD: I had some concerns about Cal and Teri and swimming at the collegiate level. But I knew in a lot of ways that Missy was thriving at Berkeley, so I held my tongue. I'd sometimes question why Missy wasn't swimming backstroke, for example. Sure, there were a lot of strong backstrokers on the team, and it made sense to let them swim those events if they were good enough to win and to save Missy for a long-distance event, like the 500 or 1,000. It was all about putting your swimmers where you could score the most points as a team. That would have been the case wherever Missy went to school. I understood that. D.A. understood that. And Missy was fine with it; she really was. She was always about doing what was best for the team, but as her parents we could see that what was best for the team wasn't always what was best for Missy. Her muscles hadn't really been trained for these events, and in some respects she was sacrificing some of the training she should have been doing in order to keep swimming at a world-class level. I believed that a lot of what Missy was being asked to do really wasn't in her best interests, but she never questioned it. In fact, she loved it. She was team-first, all the way. And I don't set this out as a criticism of Teri McKeever, not at all. It's just that Teri's agenda, as head coach of Cal swimming, was to win meets and keep that top three ranking and get to a national championship. And as I just said, the same situation would have presented itself at any collegiate program. Missy's agenda was somewhat different. And as long as I'm on it, why is it that the NCAA is stubbornly sticking to these arcane distances? In the United States, the leader of the world, why are we still on the linear system and not on the metric system? We've been deeply involved in this sport for nearly fifteen years, and I've yet to hear a logical explanation for this. Why do we take our elite swimmers and put them back into 25-yard competition in college when the rest of the world puts its Olympic hopefuls in 25-meter and 50-meter pools year-round, to make them better month by month? It just blows my mind, that this is how it is. Short-course swimming and long-course swimming are really two completely different sports, like racquetball and squash. Okay, so both of them have racquets, and both of them are played in a contained area, but that's where the comparisons end. Only in swimming, long course versus short course, yards versus meters, our top college swimmers are somehow expected to compete in both arenas. The mechanics are completely different— shorter course, more turns, more underwaters. It's

apples and oranges. Nothing against Teri, but I felt
Missy needed to take a different approach. And yet I
didn't really say anything, because our philosophy was
to let Missy come to this decision by herself, if she
came to it at all. She needed to own it. She needed to
come to the realization that she'd gone to Berkeley
after becoming the first woman in history to win six
gold medals in a single world championships, and that
she hadn't been close to that level of dominance since.
So was I surprised to hear that Missy was thinking of
moving home and picking up where she'd left off with
Todd Schmitz? Not at all. Was I greatly relieved? Oh,
absolutely.

I hadn't counted on the ways my decision to go back home to
Colorado to train with Todd would impact those around me. There
was this whole ripple effect. Of course, I knew Teri wouldn't be
happy about it. She'd known all along that I would only compete for
Cal for two years before turning pro, but the expectation was that
I would stay on in Berkeley and train with her as part of her postgraduate program, which is what they've set up for the swimmers
who are no longer competing at the intercollegiate level but continuing to train with Teri and her staff and making full use of the
Cal facilities. That was my expectation, too. And now here I was,
midway through the final season of my NCAA "career," getting
ready to pull the plug on those expectations and go home
immediately following the spring semester of my sophomore year,
just in time to prepare for the 2015 world championships. Why?
Because my heart was telling me to go back home and continue

what I'd started with Todd that very first day I showed up to swim for the Colorado Stars when I was seven years old. The very first day *he* showed up on the same pool deck to begin his career as a coach. I also wanted to return to my fantastic dry-land trainer, Loren Landow, who had prepared me so well for London and Barcelona.

This is probably a good spot to shine a light on Loren, who deserves all the love and props I can send his way. He's been working with me since I was a sassy fourteen-year-old (and somehow managed to retain enough sanity to continue training the sassy fifteen- to twenty-one-year-old as well). I was one of the first swimmers he'd ever trained, if not the very first, and until I met Loren I'd worked with trainers who had zero interest in anything outside the weight room. Loren was cut a little differently, and we connected right away. He took the time to ask how I was feeling after every workout. Before we'd even start in, he'd want to know what I was working on in practice with Todd. Then he would moderate what I was doing, based on what was going on in the pool. For the first time, it felt to me like I was lifting weights with a purpose. Before Loren, I was lifting blindly, but he made sure to explain to me how what we were doing in the gym would directly benefit what I was doing in the pool. It was all tied in.

He's been such an incredible influence in my life—a real game changer. And one of my biggest cheerleaders. He's the same way with all the athletes he trains—professional football players, hockey players, baseball players . . . even mixed martial artists. I can't imagine how he has the time to devote the same care and attention to guys like Tim Tebow, Peter Forsberg, and Troy Tulowitzki as he does to me . . . but he does. He's constantly texting back and forth with Todd, comparing notes, telling him to go easy on my kick sets because he'd worked my legs particularly hard, or something like that.

So Loren was a big part of my thinking, too, as I was *weighing* (alert the pun police!) the pros and cons of continuing my training in Berkeley or returning home to Colorado. The other huge piece to this dilemma was my roommate, Kristen Vredeveld. Teri must have sensed something in us, because she put us together ahead of our freshman year, and we clicked immediately. I'm a firm believer in fate, and I know in my heart that God has a plan for us, and here I believe he put this young woman in my life to be my best friend, someone I can lean on, someone to support me in these difficult moments. At the same time, though, I had to believe that God (and Teri!) put *me* in Kristen's life for the flip side of the very same reasons, so obviously I was torn about how the decision to head home would impact our friendship. My decision was all about what *I* needed, and not at all about what Kristen needed, and that just wasn't fair—and so, in a lot of ways, the person I was *most* nervous to talk to about all this was Kristen, even though I knew she'd be the one person who would totally understand. She meant the world to me, and I hated the thought of being separated from her. The last thing I wanted was for her to feel like I was leaving her behind, or that I was choosing someone or something else over her. It was an irrational worry, because Kristen's not like that, and the situation wasn't like that, but I worried just the same. We'd met on our recruiting trip, and we'd been like sisters ever since, and even though we'd been together less than two years at this point I couldn't imagine waking up every day and going about my routines without seeing her reassuring smile, or drawing on her strength—or, even, sharing in her tears (and by "her" tears I really mean mine, because I was most definitely the bigger crier).

She was a part of me—a part I was terrified to be without.

Oh my goodness . . . I was so torn. For a while, it felt to me like I was the first person in the history of college athletics to find herself at these particular crossroads, but it was hardly unusual for a swimmer to change her training environment heading into an Olympic year. In fact, it's quite common: Allison Schmitt, Cierra Runge, Simone Manuel, Katie Ledecky, Abbey Weitzeil . . . and those are just a few from this Olympic cycle alone! A lot of our top swimmers sit out or defer a year in order to prepare for an Olympic run. What I had in mind was nothing new.

I kept coming back to the fact that I wasn't where I needed to be in terms of my fitness and training. We were headed into an Olympic year. I didn't have the luxury of hanging back and crossing my fingers and hoping things would turn out okay, and my gut and my head and my heart kept telling me I was meant to be back in Colorado, sleeping in my own bed, surrounded by the love and support of family, and swimming once again with the coach who'd helped me to climb to the upper reaches of my sport, and doing my dry-land workouts with the trainer who'd helped to put me in the best shape of my life.

I'd talked to a few people privately about this, before I went to Teri. People close to the team and the sport, who knew the dynamics of that environment. I wanted to make sure I handled it in the right way, showing Teri the respect she deserved but at the same time letting her know that I had thought this through. Probably the worst thing I could have done was put it out there that this was something I was just kicking around, like I wanted Teri's opinion, or needed to run something by her before making a decision. No, the thing to do was tell it to her straight, like ripping off a Band-Aid, but there was no good way to deliver the news. It was pretty much like, *How can I make this situation the least horrible it could be?* Because I knew it would be horrible. There was no avoiding it. And there was no avoiding the adverse effects my decision would have on my teammates, which was the worst feeling of all.

Whatever we're doing, whatever goals we're pursuing, we tend to take a narrow view. We look at the world from our own perspective—that's just human nature, right? In my house, growing up, my parents made an extra effort to get me to see how my actions might impact others. When I got back from London and let it be known I was planning to swim senior year for my high school team, they pushed me to think how my role on the team would be viewed by others. That's why I wasn't totally surprised when those Christmas cookies arrived on our front door with that weirdly creepy note. We'd sat down and looked at it, every which way. There was a positive to it, and a negative, and it fell to me to consider both sides and find the right middle. My parents couldn't help me with that. My friends couldn't help me with that. They could take turns pointing out how it might come across, my continuing to compete for Regis after swimming for the US Olympic team in London. But, end of the day, it was on me.

Only, here at Berkeley, January of my sophomore year, the right middle wasn't in the least bit apparent. What made sense for the team, for the program, didn't necessarily make sense for me. And what was *right* for me wasn't necessarily *right* for my coach, or for my teammates. This was that more-than-one-way-to-make-a-family, more-than-one-way-to-make-a-swimmer argument, on full display. It didn't really occur to me that Teri would hear my news as some kind of slap in the face. Yeah, absolutely, I expected her to be surprised, saddened, maybe even disappointed. I was feeling some of those same emotions myself. We'd been through a lot together, and had been looking ahead to a whole lot more.

In many ways, it was Teri herself who'd empowered me to think along these lines in the first place. Remember, her focus was to develop us not only as swimmers but as strong, independent women, able to make tough decisions and think for ourselves. It was one of her great strengths as a coach, and I'd taken that message very much to heart. And here I was, thinking for myself that this was the approach I needed to take.

My plan was to meet with Teri personally. I'd worked the whole conversation through in my head, rehearsed it every which way. But then I sent her a note and told her I wanted to meet with her to talk about my training plans for the coming year, and she hit me right back and said she was free in five minutes and to give her a call. It's like the conversation had a momentum all its own. I didn't know what to do, so I called, thinking we could set a time to meet, but when she answered I got right into it. I just put it out there, and what came back . . . well, it was more than I expected. You see, Teri and I were looking at this decision from two very different perspectives. Me, I was thinking of my own career. I cared deeply about my teammates, make no mistake, but I was also determined to return to that Olympic stage and continue what I'd started at the London games. Teri was of course thinking what this move would mean to her program. Absolutely, my leaving would send a signal to my teammates, to the swimming community. It might make it harder for Teri to recruit, because now she'd have to explain to prospective swimmers why I'd left the program. It might make it harder for us to coalesce as a team, because my teammates would know I had a foot out the door. It might jeopardize Teri's chances to serve as a coach for the Olympic team, because a lot of times those invitations go to coaches of the high-profile swimmers who are going to the games.

Mostly, it suggested that I wasn't happy at Cal, when, really, that couldn't have been further from the truth. I was super close with Teri, and the girls on the team, and I wouldn't have done anything to hurt them. We were a family. I was connected at the hip with my best friend and roommate, Kristen, and with my core group at AIA—those relationships meant the world to me. But at the same time my focus was on upping my game, and finding a way to improve my times, get back to that level of peak performance I'd had going into London. I really thought it was better for me to swim with Todd, to swim at altitude, to train with Loren, to live at home, where I could keep my distractions to a minimum.

MOM: Missy wasn't expecting to have this conversation with Teri on the phone. We talked about it, and we were all in agreement. This was something Missy needed to discuss with her coach face-to-face, away from the team. But that's not exactly how it happened, and I know Missy was broken up about it. There's so much that gets lost over the telephone, especially when you're delivering a difficult piece of news. The emotions are lost, or bent out of shape. You can't really get a good read on the other person. And Missy just felt awful about it, the way it happened. She called home that night, and she was so upset. With Missy, she was always good about taking responsibility for her own decisions. When she was a little girl, and she'd have to talk to a coach or a teacher, Dick and I encouraged her to do so on her own. She didn't need her parents to advocate for her. But when she told me how the conversation went with Teri, I wished I could have been in the room with her, holding her hand, letting her know that things would work out in the end. It might have been difficult in the moment, but she needed to hear that it was going to be okay.

Meanwhile, we were still in the middle of our season. No one on the team had any idea what was going on—not yet. I'd told my roommate, Kristen, because I knew there was no way I was getting through this alone, and one other coach on the team, because I wanted to get some advice on how to approach Teri, but other than that it was business as usual. I showed up for practice the next morning not knowing what to expect. I gave Teri a wide berth, and she seemed to do the same with me. It's like neither one of us wanted to confront or engage with the other. One of the things we'd talked about in that endless phone conversation the day before had been how and when to let the team know, and together we'd agreed that there was no reason to say anything until after the NCAAs. Neither one of us wanted to put our team chemistry at risk. That would have broken me, more than anything else.

But people pick up on things. In a team setting, a family-type environment like the one Teri had built, you develop a kind of radar. The group dynamic is palpable, knowable. You spend so much time together, it's like you're wired in the same ways. You can sense when things are a little *off*, a little different. And here some of the captains picked up on that. They saw it in my body language, in the subtle change to how I responded to reporters when I was giving interviews. Someone asked what I was doing after the NCAAs and I said I wasn't thinking about that now—an innocent answer to an innocent question. But my teammates heard that and their ears perked up. Typically, I'd take a question like that and say, "I'm just gonna keep on doing what I'm doing." But this one little shift got them thinking, and out of that they got to talking, and out of *that* . . . well, it wasn't too hard for everyone to start to think something was going on. We were a team-first sort of group, so this wasn't really an issue, except, of course, for me, because I was so concerned about doing or saying anything to upset the program in any way.

A lot of girls took my decision to mean I was abandoning the team, but that was the absolute last thing I wanted to do. I'd always been a team-first kind of athlete. All you had to do was look at all the off-events I'd been swimming for the team to know that this wasn't me. But there's no denying that a collegiate swimming environment isn't necessarily the best place for an athlete hoping to swim in the Olympics, especially leading into an Olympic year. Of course, many other swimmers had done well in this situation, but I didn't think it was right for me this time around. There are completely different agendas at play. At a school like Cal, when you get into the championship season, you start to taper in the beginning of February. You come back for the Pac-12s, and then you taper again for the national championships. It's a whole different schedule, a whole different approach. It works out to about two months of training in the six months leading up to Olympic trials that are completely skewed toward the college team. That's great for the team, but it's not always so great for the individual athlete. And Teri, to her credit, was well aware of this. To counter it, her plan that year was to send her postgraduate swimmers to the South Pacific for a month to work with one of our stroke coaches, to keep pushing them. That might have been a great solution for a lot of swimmers, but I didn't think it would be so great for me. I felt uncomfortable going to a whole new environment for an entire month, four months out from Olympic trials, doing a new kind of training. There was too much at stake, I thought. And it's not like we were going across town—it was halfway across the world, so I worried about my body clock and all these other variables. (Plus, it's not like my *last* trip to that part of the world had gone all that well!) The more I thought about it, the more firm I was in my thinking. I needed to be home, in my childhood bedroom, eating my familiar foods, reaching back for the familiar routines that had taken me all the way to the London games.

Meanwhile, we still had the balance of our season in front of us. I've kind of foreshadowed this part of the story in the "moment" leading up to this chapter, so I'll cut right to it: the NCAAs that year was the best short-course meet I ever swam in my life. I couldn't have asked for a better way to end my collegiate career. I went best times in all of my events, in some cases by *seconds*! I was over the moon with how I did, but none of that would have mattered if my teammates weren't right there with me, swimming their own best times, putting together the best short-course meets of their careers. We ended up winning the whole thing (Go Bears!), and for a few moments in there, while we were celebrating our national championship (Go Bears!), I could forget the tension and uncertainty that had followed me around the pool since I'd told Teri I was leaving. We could come together and celebrate what we'd all accomplished (once more, because you can never have enough, Go Bears!), and in the middle of all that hugging and whooping it up find a way to acknowledge that we'd been good for each other and for the program.

(In case I haven't made myself clear how I felt about all this ... one last *Go Bears!*)

> **DAD:** It wouldn't be right for Missy to boast about her accomplishments in the pages of her own book, but I don't think anyone could fault her dear old dad for singing her praises. Out of that season, she was received the Honda Cup as the nation's top female college athlete, and she was up against the top athletes in every sport— basketball, volleyball, gymnastics, soccer. She'd helped to lead her team to a national championship, and coming out of that horrific injury in Australia this was all the more impressive. If you'd have asked me on the morning after that long first night in Queensland, when her mother and I stayed up with Missy in her hotel room, if there was any way she could have come back and finished her season on such a tremendous high note, I would have looked at you like you had a screw loose. She was in such excruciating pain that night, I

caught myself thinking her career might be over. I wasn't even worried about her career, frankly. I just wanted to help her manage the pain, she was in such agony. But somehow Missy was able to power past this injury and will herself back to fighting shape and find a way to help her teammates to a national title. That's something, don't you think? She still wasn't where she needed to be, in terms of regaining the form and the strength to compete for another Olympic medal, but she'd made some great progress. And now that she was coming home, now that she'd be reunited with her long-time coach, now that her mother would be cooking for her and catering to her every need, we all felt it was time for Missy's star to shine, shine, shine once again.

Gee, thanks, Dad. I'm glad *you* were so sure things would work out. Me? It took some time, together with a lot of prayerful reflection. And some second-guessing. I've got to be honest here, I was in a hard place when I came back home. Physically, I still wasn't where I wanted to be, coming off my back injury. Emotionally, I was shaken, torn. It's tough to go from a club environment to a college environment and then back to a club environment, and I don't mean to suggest that I'm not grateful for the teammates I have now on the Colorado Stars—they're a blast to swim with, and we raise one another's games every time we get into the pool. But it's not the same as having the emotional support of twenty-five of your closest friends, every single day. It's not the same as having a national championship in your sights, a shared goal you can work toward together, all season long. It's not the same as living, breathing, eating, with your teammates with this great sense of common purpose, the way it can be when you're in the bubble of a college sports season.

In the beginning, it's not like my days were all that different. Some of my closest friends from high school were home from college over the summer, so there were happy distractions all around as I resumed my training schedule with Todd. There were other taking-care-of-business-type distractions, too. Choosing an agent (shout-out to Mark Ervin, who within months had already become a huge part of our family, and the amazing team he's put together at William Morris Endeavor–IMG!); meeting with sponsors (so proud to represent my great new friends at Speedo, GoPro, Visa, United Airlines, Wheaties, and Minute Maid!); and helping to promote causes and programs that held great meaning for me (honored to be an ambassador for the Laureus Sport for Good Foundation and USA Swimming Foundation!).

But by August 2015, most everyone I knew was drifting back to college, and there was just me and my parents and my new routines with Todd and the Colorado Stars. Intellectually, I knew this would be a dramatic change, and I could kind of see it coming. Only, I didn't *really* see it coming. One day I looked up and saw that all my good friends from home were back at school, moving on with their lives. And all my good friends at Cal were back in Berkeley, moving on with their lives. I was moving on with mine, of course, doing what I needed to do to prepare for Rio, and yet I couldn't shake the feeling like I was stuck in place. It snuck up on me, this feeling, and it took a few weeks for me to get into my new routines, and to accept that my Cal Bears teammates were going on with their routines without me.

MOM: I don't want to get too far away from the business aspect of Missy's career, because her father and I were so enormously impressed with the way she conducted herself during this transition period. She was a full participant in our search for an agent. In fact, I think it's fair to say she even took the lead in this search. She was so busy with her academics and swimming, and there were a dozen agents in contact with us. There were a lot of balls in the air, so Missy asked us to take the first round of meetings and help her bring the list down to four. Missy was as involved as any of us. It was a huge decision! And it was her decision to make. We could only give her our opinion, but it came down to Missy in the end. That's how it should be, yes? This was her life, her career, so Dick and I took the same approach we took when she started swimming. We took that all-important step back and let Missy do her thing. She kept saying her goal wasn't just to find an agent to help her with this phase of her career. She was looking for an agent for life. And she knew she found it with Mark Ervin. Right away, she knew. In Mark, she saw someone who shared her values, who would help her align with sponsors who also shared these same values. And Dick and I could only agree, because Mark was really the perfect person for her. He saw what Missy saw, what we all saw. That there was great value in staying true to who you are and what you believe in. As a professional, Missy could only be herself. She couldn't stand behind a product or a cause she didn't wholeheartedly believe in. She wouldn't be who she was, and Mark understood this. He understood that Missy needed to be in the pool, working hard to achieve her dreams, and building on her success as a swimmer to inspire others to achieve their dreams, too. Sponsorship deals, endorsements, other opportunities, either they'd come to Missy on the back of that ideal, or they wouldn't, and Missy was okay with that. We were all okay with that.

All of a sudden, it's like swimming was a *job*. This makes sense, I guess, when you talk about what it means to turn professional, but I wasn't expecting to feel this way. And it's not like swimming was ever a chore . . . oh, no, I love it too much for it to ever be any kind of a burden or a grind! It's just that when you strip away the fun and the friendships and all the team-building elements that attach to the sport, it can be a lonely pursuit. And the loneliness takes some getting used to. It does. Again, I love my Colorado Stars teammates to the moon and back, but we go our separate ways after practice, move about in our own orbits. We're at a different stage in our lives, a different place in our lives, and while on the one hand I was totally ready to embrace those differences, it wasn't so easy to check in with my friends at school and see that life at Cal was going on without me. We talked all the time, and kept plugged in to each other through social media, but it felt to me like I was missing out, big-time. And I was—absolutely, I was. It's like all my friends were living my college dreams without me, while I was mostly treading water.

But I was also moving forward, big-time. I was back at home, living with the most amazing parents on the planet (sorry, I'm a little biased!), devoting myself completely to the hopes and dreams I'd set out for myself when I was a little girl.

This new world of mine would just take some getting used to; that's all.

Our Moment of Trial

MOM: As far as Dick and I could tell, the runup to the 2016 Summer Olympics in Rio was going pretty much as planned, but as we look back there were signs of trouble. We tend to take a sunny view in our house, so we told ourselves things were going swimmingly—forgive me, but I'm afraid Missy's love of puns is contagious. Of course, that sunny view was almost always rooted in reality, and here we could see that Missy was working hard, laser-focused, in the best shape of her swimming life. Missy hoped to qualify in four individual events—the 100-meter and 200-meter freestyle and the 100-meter and 200-meter backstroke. There was every reason to look forward to another strong Olympic showing. But then we got to Omaha.

Missy knew something wasn't right before we did, but she wasn't letting on. Not just yet. It worked out that her room was next to ours at the Hilton, but that didn't guarantee we would see her at all during the meet. We were used to that by now. She would eat with the athletes every day, or with her coaches. That was just as well. We had a ton of family with us—C.J., Linda, Doug, Deb, Harry and Harry's brother, my "uncle" Roy. We all got together for dinner at our hotel on Sunday night, just before the start of the meet, while Missy was off doing her thing with the other swimmers.

When we did see Missy, though, it was business as usual. She seemed excited, confident, eager to get the meet started, and for her first swim that Monday morning, there was no reason to think she was "off" in any way—no reason that I could see, at least. She's since told me she was stressing out, not happy with her times, off her game, but in the middle of competition she just tried to breathe deep and power through. And her father and I, we fell into our familiar routines. We got to the pool early so I could sit with my sister and watch the warm-ups. We visited with friends and family. We hoped like crazy for a happy result.

Missy came in fifth in her 100-meter back prelims, which was nothing unusual. Remember, her whole strategy, for years and years, was to hold a little something back in those preliminary swims, putting in just enough effort to advance to the next round. The idea was to make it to the semifinals with a little something in reserve, and then on to the finals with another little something in reserve. But now, in hindsight, I can see that she was cutting it a little close. In the semifinals that first night, she came in seventh, which put her in one of the outside lanes for the finals the next day—not exactly where she wanted to be.

Still, I didn't really think anything of it, until she called later that night and asked me to come to her room. She just wanted me to hold her while she cried. It had been a long time since I'd seen her so vulnerable, so unsure of herself. It broke my heart—and took me completely by surprise. For a long time, we didn't speak. I could only hold her, and try to comfort her, and try not to break down in tears myself. After a while, she looked at me and asked, "What happens if I don't make it, Mama?"

Oh my goodness, that was just about the last thing I expected to hear from this strong, self-assured young woman. But she was shaken. And now, so was I. Clearly, this wasn't the time for me to hesitate as a parent, or to join Missy in her uncertainty, so I fought back my own tears and told my daughter what I knew to be true, what I thought she needed to hear. I said that I knew she would be disappointed if she didn't make the Olympic team, but that there was nothing she could ever do to disappoint her father or me. I told her she was already a winner, as an Olympian and a woman. I also said that if missing out on the Olympics this time around was the worst thing to happen in her life, she'd be very fortunate. I offered to spend the night, but she said that she needed to get up in the morning feeling like it was a new day. So I hugged her, told her I loved her, and told her how proud I was of her.

I went back to our room next door with a heavy, heavy heart. I knew how devastated Missy must have been feeling. Dick could see straightaway that something was wrong, so I filled him in, best I could. We both knew how devastated Missy must have been feeling. How alone. She had wanted to have the opportunity to defend her Olympic title, and she had worked so hard to get to this point. It was all close enough to touch, right there, within reach, but to her it felt so far away, and now we were separated by this one thin wall in the Hilton, unable to comfort each other, support each other, lift each other, the way we always had.

I don't think I slept much that night—I probably didn't sleep at all. I kept thinking of Missy, what she was going through. I was most upset by a reference she made to the Bible. A lot of times, she'll tuck what she's feeling into a story or a psalm, and I'll have to scramble to catch her meaning. This time, she'd said that she felt like Job, one story from the Bible I knew pretty well, but I let Missy tell it to me all over again. I listened to her hurt, her confusion. She told me how Job was dedicated to God but that Satan had challenged God and made a kind of bet with him to prove that Job's devotion wasn't genuine, and that Job wouldn't love the Lord so much if God took away his many blessings. As a result, Job's family was killed and Job became very ill. He was put through every imaginable hardship, every conceivable struggle, and yet through it all he remained faithful to the Lord.

It was the ultimate test of faith, and here it felt to Missy like she was going through her own trial. Missy's faith was so important to her and had helped her persevere through so much, and as she retold this story, I worried that she would start questioning that faith. No, her struggles weren't life and death, like Job's. The people she loved would continue to love her, be there for her. But her hopes and dreams were now more and more out of reach.

Meanwhile, whatever faith I had was definitely being questioned. I was so proud of the woman Missy had become, was becoming still. I had seen the way she had dedicated her life to doing good. I had witnessed how she had used her swimming success as a platform to reach out to others in need and become a good role model. So as I tossed and turned that night, I found myself praying, in my own way. Wondering. Questioning the Lord about why he was allowing my little girl to struggle in this way. My little girl who had put everything she had into her training, put her life on hold to make it back into an Olympic pool. I didn't understand it. And it just about killed me that she was right next door and I couldn't hold her in my arms.

Missy started her 200 free with prelims on Tuesday morning and tied for seventh with a 1:58.61. In the semis that night she moved to fourth with a 1:57.33. She had a lane in the finals for Wednesday night, and Dick and I were overjoyed. We could only assume that Missy was thrilled, too. That whatever doubts she'd been feeling the night before were now behind her. We didn't know it at the time, but Missy was still stressing down on the pool deck. She still wasn't where she wanted to be, wasn't swimming like she'd hoped for, like she'd trained for. Twenty minutes after the 200 free, she swam in the finals of the 100 back. I'm sure she was hoping to be an outside smoker, but it was not to be. She was eighth at the final turn and finished in seventh place. The defending gold medalist in this event, and she didn't even qualify. Didn't even come close. Her disappointment was mine, ours. But she was not defeated. She congratulated the top two finishers, now rookie Olympians.

I could see the disappointment in her expression and just wanted to hug her. I got an opportunity that night when she asked me to come back to her room. This time, she wanted me to stay over. She worried she wouldn't be able to sleep. I didn't tell her I hadn't slept a wink the night before. I just held her until she finally drifted off after several hours of tossing and turning.

On this second night, I did manage to sleep, but only fitfully. Mostly, I lay there next to Missy and tried to imagine what she was facing, what she was thinking, looking ahead to these Olympic Games, knowing that she now had all these people counting on her, pulling for her. It wasn't her new sponsors she was worried about, I don't think. It wasn't NBC, or any of the media people who'd been covering her all these years. It wasn't her friends or family. She was always very good about compartmentalizing all of that, and shutting out all these other distractions. And it wasn't even her teammates, because in a setting like this, Olympic trials, every swimmer is out for herself. The whole teammate thing comes later. In that moment, it's just about going best times and winning a spot on the team.

No, I had to think it was her little fans she didn't want to disappoint. I'm sure there was a part of her that didn't want to let down all those other people. That's just who Missy is. But letting down her fans . . . that was a whole other level of worry. All these little kids, thousands of them, back home in Colorado—all around the country, even. (All around the world!) Missy never set out to be a role model, but the way she lived her life, the way she carried herself, the way she competed . . . it was natural that all these girls (and boys, but mostly girls) started looking up to her. I had to think this was what had Missy so worried during trials. To worry what it would mean if she didn't make the team. Not because of what it would cost her, but because of what it would cost them.

It was enough to make me cry. And I did. I lay there, watching Missy sleep, thinking, *My little girl*, knotted up inside over the thought that she couldn't be a role model to these kids. And I couldn't help thinking, *She's just a kid herself.*

NINE

RIO

'll let you in on a little secret: this book-writing business is like a long-distance swim. A *really* long-distance swim. You set out with a plan for the race, but you can't always know how things will go.

As this book was taking full and final shape, we thought the thing to do was leave room for a final chapter about the Games of the XXXI Olympiad, in Rio. The Olympics seemed to offer a natural endpoint, although if you've read through to this point you know my goal isn't to recount my triumphs in the water. That, to me, would be really, really boring—probably to you, too. Clearly, this is not a typical athlete's memoir. It's more about the pieces we've put in place as a family that have allowed me to pursue my career as a swimmer and to look ahead to life beyond the pool. Still, we felt it was important to put a ribbon on our story with an update from Rio, since for the last four years these games have been our focus. *My* focus. It made sense to want to let readers know how it all went down.

Never in a million years did I think it would go *down*—I mean, *really, really, down.*

Now, in the goes-without-saying-but-I'll-say-it-anyway! department, I was hoping for a great Olympic meet. We'd set things up so I'd have a good shot to build on the success that found me in London in 2012. That's why I came home from school, spent a year training with my longtime coach Todd Schmitz and my trainer Loren Landow, put the rest of my life on pause so I could devote my full attention to these games and work myself into the best shape of my life. But as you now know, Rio didn't exactly go as planned. (How's that for the understatement of the year?) Oh, I fought my way onto the team, qualified in three events, but if I'm being completely honest (and again, the thing about this book-writing business is that it forces you to be completely honest!), this just wasn't my Olympic year. Not even close, it would seem.

I could tell at trials. Everyone could tell, looking back, but when I was down there in that pool, struggling to find my rhythm, my *mojo*, I could tell most of all. I was having panic attacks for the first time in my life. Loren, my trainer, would sit with me and talk me through these uncertainties, and help me to meditate. I don't think I would have gotten through that week in Omaha without his help. Without those meditations, my throat would close, I couldn't breathe, and I'd start to shake uncontrollably. I couldn't explain it, couldn't understand it . . . but there it was. And all I could think was, *What is happening? This isn't me.* This isn't me.

Thank God my parents were there in the same hotel, right next door. I'd call my mother to come give me a hug, or to come for a sleepover . . . anything to quiet the raging uncertainty inside my head.

I hated that the sport I'd loved so much, that had given me so much, was making me feel the way I was feeling during trials. So unsure of myself. So off my game. So *unlike* . . . me. Diving in for the 100 back that first morning, I knew. I was able to swim into the semifinals, but something was off, wrong, weird. I couldn't put my finger on it then, and here I am, almost two months later as I write this, still trying to sort through what was going on. Go ahead and look at those trial results and you'll see that I battled my way into the finals, but I knew I didn't have it in me to qualify in that event. Remember, all along, I've talked about how the thing to do is put out *just enough* to make it to the semifinals, *just enough* to make it to the next round. It's all about conserving energy for the finals, that's the key, especially when you're swimming multiple events. But here I put everything I had into that semifinal swim and could manage only the seventh-best time. It might have been enough to put me in the pool for the finals, but it wouldn't get me to Rio, not in the 100 back. I didn't feel like I had control of my body, if that makes any sense. My stroke, my timing . . . it was all just a little beyond my grasp. I couldn't get my body to do the things it was trained to do, and it wasn't because I was tired or distracted or injured. It's just that there was no *there* there. I was able to get to the finals on muscle memory and straight athletic ability, but there was no way I could swim myself onto the team, not against these great competitors.

I guess you could say I was done before the finals even

started—and before I could even get my head around the idea of *not* qualifying in an event I'd won four years earlier, I had to worry about swimming the 200-meter freestyle.

I wish I could remember where my mind went during those low, low moments, but I do know this: there's not a thing I would have done differently. Not a thing I *could* have done differently. All I could do, really, was fight through whatever doubts I was facing and keep swimming. And that doesn't just mean how I handled the unfamiliar pressures during trials—and, later on, during the Olympics. No, I'm also referring to the buildup to the games. I did everything I possibly could. I worked harder than I'd ever worked before. I found a way to balance the responsibilities that came with going pro, and working with great sponsors, with the demands of training—getting up at four o'clock in the morning if that's what it took to get the work in. I made all these great gains in the weight room, added extra yoga classes, new strength-training routines, physical therapy sessions to keep myself right and whole. I was even seeing a nutritionist, and cooking and preparing my own meals, taking extra care to put only the healthiest foods into my body.

It was a yearlong grind.

> DAD: Right here, Missy's hit on one of the missing ingredients in her approach, this time out. It's in the language she uses to refer to her training. She calls it a grind, and if you know anything about Missy, if you look back and try to understand the successes she's had in the pool, it comes back to the joy she felt that first time she hit the water. This was a child who

always had so much fun at practice, so much fun with her teammates. Even in London, she swam with such ease. Didn't have a care in the world. She was so loose, so comfortable, and she was out there having fun, breaking records. But this time out, she just couldn't get in rhythm. She'd left all her friends behind at Cal, did everything right to put herself into position to compete. On paper, she made all the right moves. But looking back, I think there was a missing ingredient. I don't think we left any room for joy in her swimming. It became a job, and it was a job she was good at, but she wasn't swimming with abandon. She wasn't loose, like she'd always been. And when I talked to her after Rio, and heard in her voice how genuinely excited she was to get back to Berkeley, to the friends she'd left behind, the life she'd left behind . . . that's when I knew. Technically, she'd had it all covered. Her mother and I, we thought she was making the right decision, coming home to train. We supported her, completely. We were convinced she had the best possible coaching, the best possible conditioning. She ate right, lived right, all of that. But there wasn't a whole lot of fun in her life, coming home each night, living with these two old folks. The pure joy of living, that's what was missing.

That semifinal swim in the 100 back . . . that's when I knew for sure that this wasn't something I could set right—not right away. I couldn't snap my fingers and *will it so*. My time was good enough to move on . . . but nowhere near enough to move *on*! So I flipped a switch and started thinking of my 200 free. Then that was all I could think about. One race at a time, that was my mind-set, and here it worked out that I had to essentially give up on that 100 back final in order to go full throttle in the 200 free. There's always a trade-off, only so much effort to go around. I took a quick inventory of what I had in reserve, where I was in the field, where I stood to gain the most. Truth be told, that 200 free semifinal at trials was actually the first race where I kind of felt like me again—the first time since the Minnesota pro series the previous November where I was happy with my swim. All those months, I'd kept telling myself I would be ready when I needed to be ready, but my times weren't getting any better and I wasn't getting any closer to ready, and now here I was, up against it.

I actually came out of the pool feeling positive about the finals. I was smiling a whole lot more, shaking a whole lot less. But then, thirteen minutes later, I was back in the pool, facing down a tough, tough field in the 100-meter back, and I could almost feel this fresh bit of confidence leak from my pores as I got into position. Sure enough, my start felt pretty good, but when I turned at the fifty I could see the whole field ahead of me—a sight I hadn't seen in a finals event in longer than I could remember. All I could do at that point was try to finish with everything I had.

There wasn't even time to cry, not right away. During warm-down, absolutely. But you have a long way to go before warm-down. First you have to finish the race and face the consequences. You get up, you congratulate your teammates. You're thrilled for the swimmers who made the team—really and truly. You're heartbroken for the ones who didn't—also, really and truly. You talk to the media, try to come up with an original way to say how disappointed you are, how you're still hoping to swim your way onto the team. And then you try to keep it together beneath the stares of all these well-meaning people who keep looking at you like you're . . . broken. Like there's been a death in the family.

Then, and only then, can you get back in the water in the warm-down pool and bawl your eyes out and get down to some world-class croggling.

⌒

Next day, I had the final in the 200 free, so I had to let go of that disappointment in the 100 back, and at that point I would have given every drop of sweat and blood I could muster to make it on the team. That was all I was thinking about, just then, because the idea of *not* making the team was unacceptable. There was no room for that outcome in my thinking, even though I'd left plenty of room for that outcome in the way I was swimming. And by some miracle, there was enough heart and soul and fight in me to power on the jets after that final turn in the 200. To this day, I have no idea how I got my hand to the wall ahead of all those other swimmers, finishing in second place. The last twenty-five meters, I was swimming out of my mind, like I was in a frenzy, and the devastation I'd felt the night before, the distress . . . it all came out in my performance. And it all came out to the good.

(Good enough, anyway.)

All along, you're taught to think in terms of finishing first or second to secure a spot on the Olympic team, but when there's a relay involved there are also spots for the third- and fourth-place finishers in a finals heat (and sometimes even the fifth- and sixth-place finishers earn invites). Normally, it's all about touching the wall first, but I was so far beyond *normally* by this point that all I wanted was to punch my ticket for Rio, to get there by any means necessary, and here it meant that by finishing second in the finals, I'd qualified in two events—the 200-meter freestyle and the 4x200-meter freestyle relay.

I was overjoyed—but at the same time, I was terrified, because it felt to me like I didn't deserve to be going to Rio. Like I'd been overmatched in Omaha and would only be more overmatched at the Olympics. It had taken every ounce of grit and guile I had over that final fifty just to qualify. I didn't see how I stood a chance against the very best in the world—not with the way I'd been shaken at the trials. Not with the way I'd been swimming.

It turned out that I managed to qualify in the 200 back as well—I guess because I let out such a huge sigh of relief I could finally breathe, and relax. But it also turned out that I was right to worry, because by the time I got to Rio I was so emotionally drained and unsure of myself I couldn't possibly swim to my ability.

Again, you could make the case that I was done before the games were even under way—I didn't even make it to the finals in my two individual events, and there's no need to revisit those letdowns here. (Too soon!) There was, however, the matter of our 4x200-meter relay team, which was the heavy favorite to win the gold medal, and because of my second-fastest time at trials I was virtually assured a spot in the relay final. At least, that's how it normally goes, but as I've already mentioned, *normally* went out the window in Omaha. You see, I wasn't the only one in Rio who was concerned about the way I was swimming. My parents were concerned, of course. My teammates could see I was struggling.

But my coaches were perhaps most worried of all because it fell to them to put together a winning lineup for this relay, which in turn had me worried because I didn't want to get in the way.

The night before the relays I sat down with Greg Meehan, one of our assistant coaches, to discuss the different roles I might play on the team. Greg is the head coach for the Stanford men's and women's team, and I was assigned to his "team" while in Rio. Todd was there at the games as well, but he wasn't part of the Olympic coaching staff, so Greg was the one who took care of me. Throughout the games, he was a tremendous source of support and encouragement. That day, he laid out the situation from the coaches' perspective. He told me that my second-place spot at trials put me in a special position that the coaching staff meant to honor, but that there were no guarantees. Technically, it gave me a spot in the finals, but ultimately it was up to the coaches to determine the lineup. He said I could swim the qualifying relay in the morning and see what happens. Or, I could sit out the morning and save my strength for the finals, with the possibility that four swimmers go faster than my individual times and I'd be out for the finals, too.

To me, it was a no-brainer. I had to compete. I wasn't thinking about a medal. I was just thinking how devastated I'd be walking away from this meet without even swimming in a single relay, when I'd been used to swimming in all three.

I told Greg I wanted to swim in the morning, but that I'd leave it up to the coaches. I said, "If I'm on a morning relay, if I'm on a finals relay, if I'm not on any relay at all, I'll support your decision. I want what is best for this team, whether or not that includes me."

These weren't empty words. They were heartfelt. I would have been crushed, of course, but I would have stood with my teammates and stepped aside as they made their way to the pool, because it wasn't about feelings at this point. It was about putting the team in the best position to win a gold medal. I believed this with all my heart—even though my heart was breaking a little bit, just by saying it.

I did swim that morning and managed to post the second-fastest split on the team. I didn't feel good about my time, but I felt good about my split—meaning, I did what my team needed me to do. We had the lead, and I stayed in the lead, and we got the team seeded first for the finals. Job done. As I was warming down, Frank Busch, our head coach, came over to the pool to talk to me. To his great credit, he came over straightaway and got right to it. He congratulated me on my swim, told me I'd done exactly what I needed to do, but said that he was going to go another way in the finals. He walked me through his thinking, which at this point was mine as well—unfortunately. He told me that Allison Schmitt earned her spot with flying colors, after leading us off with an amazing time of 1:55.95—the fastest split from *any* of the morning heats. He told me he was also going with Katie Ledecky—a given, since she was currently the best in the world at this event—and Leah Smith, a top collegiate freestyler who'd been part of the gold-medal US team in this event at the 2015 worlds, was also a clear-cut choice. That still left one spot, and I did the quick math in my head and thought for a moment it might fall to me, but he told me he'd decided to tap Maya Dirado, who was having the meet of her life, swimming absolutely incredibly. Maya didn't even swim in this event at trials, and yet she'd already medaled in the 200 and 400 IM, so she was a strong freestyle swimmer. Frank Busch told me he wished things were different, but that this was the lineup he and his coaches thought gave us the best chance to win. Basically, he said all the right things. But they weren't the things I wanted to hear.

And I said all the right things in response. I thanked him for the opportunity to swim on the team, and then I continued with my warm-down, getting ready for the 200 back the next day, already praying for each of the girls on that relay, knowing that they were going to make me and the entire country very proud. Later, Maya Dirado sought me out after she'd been told of the coaches' decision to give me a massive hug. She looked me straight in the eye and told me she was going to make *me* proud. I held her tight and looked right back at her and told her I had absolutely no doubt that she would—she already had!

> **MOM:** Missy sent me a text as soon as she was done with her warm-down. She wasn't the only one counting out those spots. Schmitty, Katie, and Leah, that's what we were all thinking, those three were a lock, but I had it in my head that the fourth spot might go to Missy, because of her second-place finish at trials and her second-fastest split in that morning's preliminary heat. I wasn't even thinking about Maya, although I probably should have been, because she was doing so well. But Missy's text just said that she wouldn't be swimming in the finals and that she was fine with it, so it's not like we had the whole day to sit and worry about what the coaches would do. Instead, I could

only sit and worry about how Missy was handling all of this. And I could only imagine that the other girls from that morning swim, Cierra Runge and Melanie Margalis, were texting their own mothers, telling them they wouldn't be on the finals team, either, carrying their own disappointments. The agonizing piece for us, though, was that we couldn't be there for Missy in any way. We were so separated from her during the games, there was just this little text exchange, when really the moment was so much bigger than that. It needed a hug or a cuddle or a good cry, but I guess this wasn't the time for a hug or a cuddle or a good cry because Missy still had some work to do, getting ready for the 200 back. Dick and I, we had to be strong for her, so she could be strong.

The timing for a lot of these finals was ridiculous. They were going off at eleven at night, sometimes midnight, sometimes even later. It gets to you, all those late nights, because the entire team is expected to be at the pool, cheering on their teammates. The only exception is if you were scheduled for a preliminary swim the next morning. In that case, the coaches wanted you back in the village, getting a good night's sleep.

A lot of nights, I'd duck outside our building in the village, where they had a two-lane twenty-five-meter pool. That was something they didn't have in London, but it made a huge difference, just having this pool right there. It was the best! We would go and do our main swims in the morning, usually as a team, but if we wanted to hop in the water around eight or nine o'clock at night, to make sure our body was used to being awake and swimming at that hour, we didn't have to get on a bus and trek across town to get the work in. We could just step outside and do a couple hundred meters and go straight back to our room. Early on, before my meet started to go *really* south, it was so much fun being in that pool, in that spectacular setting with my teammates, surrounded by these huge buildings in this beautiful city. But then there were some nights, like the night of the relay finals, when I was out there swimming by myself. Those moments, alone in the pool, all lit up against the dark sky, were so magical, so peaceful. I don't think I felt any more connected to the sport during these Rio games than I did in those lonely moments in the pool, alone with my thoughts, alone in the water. Just me in my element, getting ready for my 200 back.

Meanwhile, the relay finals went off as expected. The United States won, with Katie Ledecky swimming the anchor leg, which meant that despite my struggles at these games I'd earned another gold medal. The way it works in relays is that if you swim in the prelims and not in the finals, you still get a medal, but you don't get to stand on the podium. Of course, it's the four swimmers in the pool at the end who get all the glory, they're the ones people remember, but the medals go to the entire team. And all those times when it was me on the podium, I felt strongly that my teammates who swam in the morning were just as deserving of the honor—and I still felt that way now that the situation was flipped, even though it was a new experience for me to be watching my teammates stand on the podium receiving their medals while I sat in my room by myself, watching it all on television. A gold medal is a gold medal, and I'm very proud of this one, but it has a different story attached to it, a different set of feelings.

Anyway, a part of me was so relieved to be done with my freestyle events, and I allowed myself to think, *Okay, I guess I'm a backstroker at this meet, here on in.* Only that didn't work out for me, either, because I failed to make it to the finals. That was hard, and so disappointing. To put in all that work to make it to these Olympics, to qualify by the grace of God in three events, and to fall short of the finals in all three. But the hardest thing I had to do in Rio was climb into my seat in the athlete stands for the finals of the 200 back, an event I'd won in London, with a world-record time. An event that was going on without me.

I sat next to Cierra Runge, who was my roommate in Rio. We'd been at Cal together for a year, and we were incredibly close. We'd been on that morning relay team in the 4x200 free, and left to watch those finals from a distance, so we were struggling with a lot of the same emotions, the feeling of being on the outside looking in. And as the swimmers stepped to the blocks I turned to Cierra and said, "Can I just hold your hand during the race?"

She said, "Of course. Whatever you need."

So I held her hand, and for the next two-plus minutes I didn't feel so all alone, and together we cheered our heads off for Maya Dirado down there in the pool as she shocked the swimming world with a come-from-behind win over Katinka Hosszú of Hungary. It was such a thrilling win, and I couldn't have been happier for Maya, who really was having the meet of her life. Seeing the pure joy in her eyes, the emotion of what she had just accomplished (and having it happen to just about the best person you'll ever meet!), it almost helped me remember why I used to love the sport that was currently wreaking so much havoc in my life.

At one point, in the middle of all that cheering, I noticed that I was crying. Just a couple of tears, but I couldn't tell if they were tears of joy for Maya and the rest of my teammates, who were really having an insane Olympics, or tears of sadness or regret for the Olympics that might have been . . . for me.

The great takeaway of those tears was that they pushed me to make a decision. I could either kick myself and wallow in self-pity, or I could find a way to grow from this Olympic experience, and to stand as a different kind of role model in defeat. It's one thing to inspire all these little girls by winning a bunch of medals. That's easy. But it's another thing entirely to be an inspiration when things aren't exactly going your way. I thought about this a lot, as the Rio games approached. I thought about how I'd been moving about the planet with all these great expectations—expectations I'd placed on myself, mostly, but ones that were also shared by the media, by my sponsors, by my fans. (By the publisher of this book, even!) Goodness, I had only to look at my mug smiling back at me, billboard-size, as I walked through the airport past a United Airlines terminal to see that I'd been cast as one of the faces of these Olympic games, and even now I wanted to live up to that image, at least as much as I could. Unfortunately, I hadn't been able to live up to it as an athlete, but it was still on me to do so as a person, so that's what I was determined to do. I realized that if I wasn't able to be the athlete I was projected to be, all I had left was to be the person I was projected to be, so I wiped away those tears and vowed to do just that. I would stand in support of my teammates. I would be gracious in defeat. I would answer every question thrown at me by reporters. I would make time for my fans, my sponsors. I would still be that person on those billboards, still be the face of these games, only I'd be coming at it from a different place.

Everyone knows what it's like to fail—and here I'd failed in front of billions of people. I'd let my teammates down. I'd let my country down. I'd let myself down, most of all. And yet through it all I kept reminding myself that everyone knows what it's like to work hard for something and not get it. The real opportunity here was in showing the world what failure can look like, in a positive way. What it can mean to work hard for something and not get it and still look ahead to the next goal.

To be an *inspiration in disappointment*—the phrase just kind of lit up in front of me. That would be my thing, coming out of these games. It wasn't exactly the thing I'd set out for, but it was the thing at hand, and I would carry it proudly going forward.

As my time in Brazil came to an end, I was still trying to figure out what had gone wrong for me. I was praying and praying, but God wasn't with me just yet. That didn't keep me from searching for some kind of sign from him, and I finally found one on the plane, coming home from Rio.

All during the games, I had felt so deserted by God, so empty. I would go to pray at night and I just couldn't find the words, so I would sit there in his presence and be like, *God, I have nothing to say to you right now, but I'm here and I'm devastated and I'm still bringing this to you.*

I was desperate for a sign, a message . . . *something*. I didn't want an explanation. I didn't want an excuse. I just wanted to know that he was there, so I kept praying, praying, praying, the whole time not really saying anything, and still I was looking, looking, looking to feel his presence.

I was alone in this, mostly. I could talk to my parents about the disappointment of the games, but only on a surface level. I could talk to my best friend Kristen, and maybe a couple of my teammates. I could talk to the two psychologists working with the swim team in Rio. But there was no way to fill the hole I was feeling in my relationship with God—nobody to talk to other than him.

I was still feeling this emptiness when it came time to leave Rio, and I remember thinking maybe I'd have better luck finding some kind of peace or closure away from the excitement and anxiety of the games. I was on a flight with my parents, in the middle seat between them, which meant I'd have *two* shoulders to lean on, one on either side. But United bumped me up, which was a great surprise, and I jumped at it for the extra legroom. My plan was to stretch out and sleep, but when I sat down I was joined by a youngish-looking man, probably in his late thirties, early forties. We smiled at each other, said a brief hello, but as we were getting ready to take off, several people came up to me, asking for an autograph or a picture. Flight attendants, pilots, some passengers as they were making their way to their seats. I didn't mind it at all. Honestly, I was a little surprised (and excited!) that people even wanted my autograph at all, after the Olympics I'd had. I figured the commotion would die down as soon as the cabin doors were closed and we pulled from the gate, so I just smiled my way through it all.

Finally, the cabin quiet, my new seatmate turned to me and said, "I'm such an idiot. Clearly, you're famous. People know you, but I have no idea who you are. I'm so sorry."

This, to me, was the definition of *no biggie*. Really, I'm just about the last person to care about not being recognized—in fact, it's always a good and welcome thing, for the way it allows you to meet someone on equal footing. So I told this man not to worry, there was nothing to apologize for. Then I told him I was a swimmer. That's all, just a swimmer.

Still, he had no idea who I was, but since we were coming from Rio and he'd just been to the games, he was able to figure out that I must have just competed, but he didn't follow swimming at all. He had no idea of my story, no idea what I'd been through that week. He'd only been in Rio to meet up with his girlfriend, who was working there during the Olympics, but they weren't connected to the athletes in any way and had only taken in a few events.

For this man and his girlfriend, Rio was mostly about the scene. For me and my parents, it was something else entirely.

Again, he apologized for not knowing who I was.

Again, I told him it was fine. Really.

I asked him what he did for a living and he told me he was a cancer doctor. It was not at all the answer I was expecting. I said, "Wow, that's absolutely incredible. Congratulations."

Well, this was not at all the response *he* was expecting, and he thanked me for it. He said, "When I tell people what I do, they usually look at me with really sad eyes and tell me how sorry they are for me."

I could see that, I guess. But I didn't want this guy to think I wasn't sympathetic to his daily struggle, so I said, "Don't get me wrong. I can't imagine what you go through. The strength you must have, to do what you do for so many people. It's just incredible."

Then I went on to tell him that one of my favorite things to do was to visit the oncology ward at the hospital and spend some time with the kids there, and that led to a whole conversation that had nothing at all to do with swimming or the Olympics or the dispiriting week I'd just had in Rio. It felt so good to be outside myself, to be outside my head, even just for those few moments. "I hope you don't mind me asking," I said at one point, "and please tell me if it's too personal, but as an oncologist, as a person who deals with life-and-death situations every single day, are you a man of faith?"

I'm sorry, but I just had to ask.

And my new friend, to his great credit, was only too happy to answer. He said, "I'm not religious, but I'm a believer."

He said he considered himself a Christian, and he went on to speak movingly about God and Christ, redemption and salvation. Clearly, he'd spent some time thinking these things through, and he was so, so generous in sharing his thinking.

I said, "Oh my gosh, that's so awesome that you have that kind of foundation to rely on while you're going through what you go through."

Then he turned the question on me: "Are you a woman of faith?"

I told him that I considered myself a devout Christian, and that I'd been struggling that week for some sort of sign from God, some way to know that I was not alone, which of course prompted this man to ask me how things had gone for me at the Olympics. I mean, he had absolutely no idea who I was, no idea how the games had gone for me—it was just an innocent question from this total stranger. And I opened up to him, in a big-time way. I told him how devastated I was—how *flattened*, really. I told him about the year I'd taken off to train, about leaving all my friends at Cal and coming home to live in my parents' basement, about all these expectations I'd carried with me to Rio. I told him how I'd been grasping for a certain something I couldn't quite get my hands on, how there'd been nothing in my experience, as an athlete or as a person, that could have prepared me for such a letdown. And this man listened. We ended up talking for the next hour or so, sharing our most deeply personal and spiritual thoughts, and I started to feel like God was speaking to me through this man. It sounds crazy, I know, but this was my thinking. I'd been longing to hear from him, in some way, and here he was, speaking to me through this kindhearted oncologist who'd had no idea who I was before he sat down next to me. It was the most remarkable thing. This man was talking to me about our value on this earth, about how we are so much more than our accomplishments, about how difficult it is to be everything to everyone at all times. Together, we touched on all these subjects, all these thoughts and feelings I hadn't been able to put into words, hadn't been able to hear from anyone else since I found myself struggling at trials, and now it felt to me for the first time like I could put *these* trials behind me. At long last.

About an hour into our soul-searching, my doctor friend looked me in the eyes and said, "I am so happy for you."

I knew right away what he meant, and I started crying.

He said, "I am so happy you are going through such a challenging time, because that means God is going to do incredible things in your life, and he is working through you right now, in ways you cannot yet know."

It was such a beautiful, empowering thought, exactly what I needed to hear, and what I took it to mean was that God was so prevalent in my life at that moment, working so much within me and through me, and that he had been there all along. I was so grateful, that this man was giving voice to what I'd been aching to hear. And I said as much. I told the doctor that I'd never felt like God had spoken so directly to me through another human being. I told him it was such a gift, him sitting down next to me.

We talked awhile longer. The doctor told me how lucky he thought I was because when I fall short it doesn't come at a real cost. "When I fail, people die," he said. "Even when I do everything right, sometimes people die. But you have a different blessing. When you fail, you carry it on your heart."

There I was, on this ten-hour plane ride from Rio, with Jesus at my side. That's what it felt like to me, sharing such a meaningful conversation with this man. It was so uplifting! So calming! After that first hour, I felt so relaxed, so at peace with myself, that I fell asleep. It was the best sleep I'd had since we left training camp, and I only woke up when we touched down in Houston, where we scrambled to gather our things and make our connecting flights—him, to Dallas; me and my parents, to Denver.

My parents caught up to me from the back of the plane, and I could tell that my mother was eager to take my pulse, see how I was doing.

"How was your flight, sweetie?" she said.

At just that moment, I couldn't think how to tell her about this doctor, about the meaningful conversation we'd shared, about the revelation I'd felt, seeing my Olympic experience from his reassuring perspective. The best I could come up was "Good."

And it was.

⌒

A footnote . . . (actually, a *side* note, as you'll see . . .)

One of the first things I did after my disappointing showing at trials was make an appointment to heal. That sounds a little strange, I know, but let me explain. For the longest time, after London, I believed the Olympic rings I'd gotten tattooed to my hip would be the only body art I'd ever wear. For swimmers, those rings are like a rite of passage—I went to get mine done at a shop near my house with Kara Lynn Joyce, in a moment chronicled in the documentary we made, *Touch the Wall*, and at the time I told everyone the tattoo would be my one and only.

But something changed in me this past year, as I trained for these Rio games. I started thinking about what it means for me to feel at home, to be at peace with myself, and what it means to feel God's eternal love above all else. More and more, I came to realize that this thought was embodied in the majesty of the Rocky Mountains, right in my own backyard. There's a powerful verse—Isaiah 54:10—that I've always looked to for strength: "'Though the mountains be shaken and the hills be removed, yet my unfailing love for you will not be shaken nor my covenant of

peace be removed,' says the Lord, who has compassion on you."
Those words are a reminder that even though the earth may
shake and the mountains may crumble, we will continue to
stand. They take me back to knowing that the power that lifted
Jesus Christ from the dead resides within me, and to feeling like
that power resides in these great mountains that have enveloped
me my entire life. These earthly concerns are fleeting, after all,
and even though the mountains in our life might crumble, even
though our hopes might be dashed and our dreams forced to
fade, God's love will sustain us.

So that was the idea I'd been carrying around in my head for
the longest time, and alongside that there was also this: when I
came back to Colorado after my first two years at Cal, I started
to think about what it meant to be home. You have to realize, I
am so, so in love with Colorado. Always have been, always will
be. I've had the best life here, the best childhood, the best parents, the best neighborhood . . . everything was just so perfect.
But what I was slow to appreciate was that Berkeley had very
quickly become my home as well, and as I struggled through trials I found myself longing to get back there, and to live there with
the same intention and love and sense of place that I carried in
Colorado. One way to help with that, I thought, was to get a tattoo of a Rocky Mountain vista, so that my "home" could follow
me, everywhere I go.

In this way, the idea for a second tattoo came together, so I
made an appointment at White Lotus Custom Tattoo—the same
place I'd gotten my first tattoo—for right after the Olympics. I
didn't tell anyone, because I wanted to make sure I was doing it
for myself, and when the games didn't go my way it became

something to look forward to. A place to channel my energy. The image of those mountains, and the passage from Isaiah they called to mind, told me I was not alone, at a time in my life when I felt so desperately alone. It goes back to what I was feeling as I was finding my way in the pool, searching for some sort of sign from God that he was with me on this journey.

I sat with the tattoo artist for an hour, designing the piece. Because, hey, I wanted it to look sweet. I mean, that's the whole point, right? And let me tell you, I feel like a rebel now, moving about the planet with the Rockies at my side . . . literally! (Huge shout-out to Daniel, the amazing artist who helped me to realize my vision!) You can't see the tattoo in a practice suit, but if I'm goofing around on the beach in a two-piece, relaxing, on vacation, laying out, there it will be for all the world to see, and that leaves me feeling pretty great, because one of the empowering takeaways from these Olympic Games is that I'm so much stronger than I ever thought I was capable of being.

These mountains remind me that wherever I go, as long as I live with intention and purpose, I am home—and that, even in struggle, God is with me, always.

R elentless spirit . . .

　　The words mean something different to me now as I sign off. The *relentless* half of the phrase—the steady, foot-on-the-gas, eyes-on-the-horizon pursuit of a goal—that's very much in place. The *spirit* part, too—because my faith has only deepened after the ways I struggled in Rio, the ways I'm struggling still.

But as I began this book, my focus was on the push, on powering forward, and not on me as a person, and so as I look ahead to the chapters still to be written in my life, I mean to put my spirit first. This, I suspect, will be a challenge for me, because I have tended to put others first. That's how I've always liked it, how I've tried to live my life. I'm happiest when I know I'm making the people around me happy. But I can't do the kind of job I want to do in the pool if I make others my main priority. I can only turn inward, and look to make myself whole. To lift my spirit to where I can be a different kind of light for others.

I'm determined to rediscover the joy of swimming that helped me to win all those medals in London, putting up times that still stand as world records, Olympic records. I don't feel that joy right now, but I know it's in me. Deep down. Somewhere. I need only to tap back into it, embrace it, make it once again my own.

Oh, I'll still write the word on my wrist. I'll wear my *relentless* ring, my *relentless* goggles, but now I've got other messages to go along with it. Now I look to the mantra bracelets I've taken to wearing this Olympic summer. Do you know about mantra bracelets? They're the best! I was given my first by a little girl who also trains with Loren Landow. She was probably eight or nine years old, told me she swam for the Aces, another Colorado club. She approached me after one of my workouts, headed into trials, and gave me a little bag with an incredibly sweet note. Inside was a gold mantra bracelet with the following message: "She believed she could, so she did."

The words struck me. I wore that bracelet all the time, and as soon as I got back from Rio I bought myself two more—one in silver, one in bronze—to complete the set.

The silver: "Enjoy the journey."

The bronze: "Be true, be you, and be kind."

The first represents my mind-set going into trials. *She believed she could, so she did.* The others represent this new approach, because my belief in myself was now shaken, and I knew I needed the time to build myself back up again.

Relentless . . . that's still who I am, how I am, at bottom. Steady and persistent. A hard-charger, to the core. All-out, all the time. But now my *spirit* is very much in play, very much front and center, and I look to my wrist each day and remind myself to enjoy the journey, to be true to myself, good to myself.

To trust in me, above all.

ACKNOWLEDGMENTS

I stand on the very broad shoulders of my teammates, my coaches, my trainers, my teachers, my mentors, my ministers, my friends, my family . . . my parents. I am who I am because of them, and I make sure to let them know how special they are to me, at every opportunity. But here I want to give a shout-out to the people who came into my life to help us with this book project—people I don't always get a chance to thank in such a meaningful way. So here goes . . .

To Mark Ervin and his team at WME-IMG—to have an agent who believes in me as a person just as much as he believes in me as an athlete is something so unique and rare in this world. I knew from the moment we met that you were an even better human being than you were an agent, which is saying so much because you're the best agent who ever lived. Thank you for taking this wonderful idea for a book about family, faith, and focus and making it a reality.

ACKNOWLEDGMENTS

To Jay Mandel, Mark's colleague at WME-IMG—thank you for shepherding our story to publication, and for finding the very best publisher to honor our story. You were a strong advocate for our family and made sure to protect the private aspects of our tale until we were ready to share them with readers.

To Karen Linhart, my beautiful publicist—I truly don't know what I would do without you. You know my own schedule better than I do and find a way to make sure I'm always getting what I need. Let's also not forget what a fashion icon you are in my life. Work it.

To Jill Schwartzman and all the publishing professionals at Dutton who helped design, edit, and promote this book—I'm so, so grateful for the care you've taken with our words and the support you've given us on this great journey. The book we've written is not exactly the book we imagined together when we started out in this process, and you were with us every step of the way, cheering us on and offering your guidance, experience, and support. In the end, you gifted us with a book that can hopefully light the way for other families with children determined to pursue their own dreams.

To Daniel Paisner, aka Danny Phantom, aka Danny P, aka our fabulous and wonderful coauthor—you are disarmingly handsome, inside and out. We cannot thank you enough for taking our story, our values, and our love for one another and putting it into such elegant and purposeful prose. It is quite an accomplishment to spend as much time with our family as you did and not lose your mind. It was an honor for each one of us to get to work with such an accomplished and talented writer and person.